Small-Block CHEVY PERFORMANCE 1955–1996

JOHN BAECHTEL

S·A DESIGN

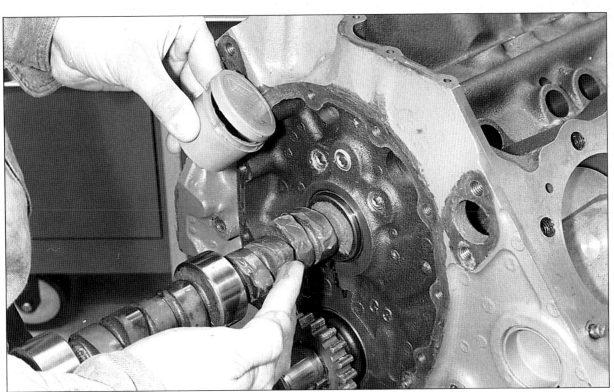

CarTech®

Edited by: Travis Thompson

ISBN-13 978-1-932494-15-0
ISBN-10 1-932494-15-4

Printed in China

Title Page:
Even if you aren't new to building small-block Chevys, this book contains all kinds of tips to make sure your engine goes together right the first time. Flat-tappet cams should be liberally coated with cam lube during installation. This heavy-duty lube helps the cam lobes survive those first critical moments during initial startup.

Back Cover:
Lower: Small-block Chevy engines were available in nearly every performance Chevrolet car and truck built from 1955 to 1996. If you're looking to find out the differences between a later-model LT1 and your original engine, this book has the answers. (Photo courtesy Bill Burt)

Upper: Selecting the right carb, intake, and fuel system can make or break your performance project. Selecting the right parts to work together will help you reach your high-performance goals.

CarTech®

39966 Grand Avenue
North Branch, MN 55056, USA
Telephone (651) 277-1200 • (800) 551-4754 • Fax: (651) 277-1203
www.cartechbooks.com

OVERSEAS DISTRIBUTION BY:

Brooklands Books Ltd.
P.O. Box 146, Cobham, Surrey, KT11 1LG, England
Telephone 01932 865051 • Fax 01932 868803
www.brooklands-books.com

Brooklands Books Australia
3/37-39 Green Street, Banksmeadow, NSW 2019, Australia
Telephone 2 9695 7055 • Fax 2 9695 7355

CONTENTS

INTRODUCTION

In earlier versions of this book, we discussed the original design elements of the small-block Chevy V-8 and charted its evolution from 1955 through 1981. In this volume, we'll expand that knowledge base and examine the engineering changes made to the small-block since 1982. The 1980s and 1990s bore witness to technical changes in the small-block, primarily designed to reduce maintenance, control oil leakage, and increase efficiency, fuel economy, and emission control through the introduction of electronic fuel injection and electronic engine management.

Chevrolet's original success formula was basic: build the simplest engine possible. Make it the cheapest, most efficient powerplant available, and it will prevail. Project engineer Harry Barr and production engineer E.H. Kelley devoted their considerable

talents—under the guidance of Zora Arkus-Duntov and Chevrolet's chief engineer, Ed Cole—to achieving this goal. Their efforts produced elegant components such as stud-mounted rocker arms, interchangeable cylinder heads, full internal oiling, and a one-piece intake manifold that also served as a valley cover. The large-bore, short-stroke combination provided an engine that could run fast reliably and still lug a family sedan along with ease. Time has brought numerous changes and improvements to the

small-block Chevy, but the basic design has proved extraordinarily resilient. In fact, prior to the early 1980s, refinements were pretty much limited to increases in displacement and whatever strengthening was deemed necessary to withstand increased power output.

Much of the engine's success stems from initial efforts to make it easy to produce. Its compact size and light weight were crucial to the concept. Through extensive research into new thin-wall casting techniques, GM

Chevy thunder first rumbled in 1955 when 265-ci small-blocks turned mild-mannered Chevrolet sedans into street terrors and racetrack winners. Small-block-powered '55 Chevys have since become one of the all-time classic cars.

Small-Block Chevrolet Basic Specifications

Engine	Bore (inches)	Stroke (inches)	Cylinder Volume (cubic inches)	Rod Length (inches)	Compression Height (inches)
265 ci	3.750	3.000	33.134	5.703	1.800
283 ci	3.876	3.000	35.398	5.703	1.800
302 ci	4.001	3.000	37.718	5.703	1.800
307 ci	3.876	3.250	38.347	5.703	1.675
327 ci	4.001	3.250	40.861	5.703	1.675
350 ci	4.001	3.484	43.803	5.703	1.560
400 ci	4.126	3.750	50.139	5.565	1.560
262 ci	3.671	3.100	32.811	5.703	1.750
305 ci	3.750	3.484	38.479	5.703	1.560
267 ci	3.500	3.484	33.520	5.703	1.560

Displacement Formula: CID = bore x bore x stroke x .7854 x 8 (cylinders)

engineers produced a cylinder block casting that used fewer casting cores than any other V-8 engine. Fewer cores meant less chance for core shifting and resulting component misalignment. Through nearly 50 years of successful operation, the engine's physical size remained unchanged, but displacement grew nearly 30 percent, and the racers made the engine produce more power than anyone ever thought possible.

The small-block Chevy grew from its original 265 cubic inches as more and more demands were made of it. Greater vehicle weight, power steering, air conditioning, and other accessories prompted increases to 283, 327, 350, and even 400 cubic inches. When various sport configurations and midsize models joined the fleet, they typically received small-block engines sized to augment their requirements. In the 1990s, the 300-hp LT1 Corvette engine featured notable changes such as reverse-flow cooling, a distributorless gear-driven ignition system, electronic engine management, and stunning performance.

All small-block Chevys through 1996 incorporate the legendary parts interchangeability that has become the hallmark of Chevy's performance equation. 1980s-style small-block engines incorporated more design changes to cut costs and boost fuel economy. Extra thin-wall cylinder castings and lightened cylinder heads have proven less durable, and

The 265-ci small-block was revolutionary in its approach to making power. Its light weight, compact size, and independently mounted valvetrain marked it for glory almost as soon as the first parts were cast.

should be avoided for serious racing applications. But that doesn't mean that there are not good pieces available for performance enthusiasts. All the necessary heavy-duty components, adapters, and hardware are available to interchange early and late small-block pieces for maximum performance and durability.

While automakers have designed and introduced numerous new powerplants to meet the unique challenges of the 1980s and 1990s, Chevrolet continued to produce small-block V-8s in record numbers. The small-block will certainly never lack support from the high-performance and racing community that it has served so well. Virtually all types of circle-track racing in this country are dominated by small-block Chevys. Championship drag racing owes its existence to the small-block Chevy. The record books are so well covered that it is unlikely that any other engine will ever dominate the sport as completely. Small-blocks continue to perform strongly in all

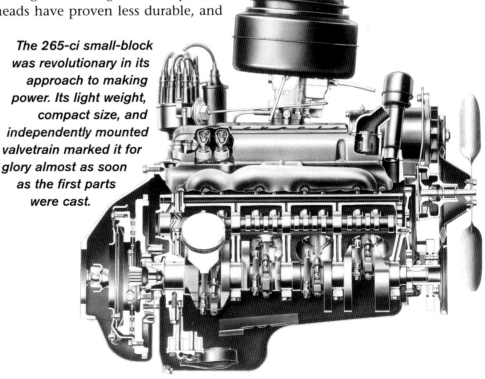

types of racing, including road racing, off-road racing, boat racing, and land speed record trials at Bonneville. Only Indy's brickyard has eluded the little Chevy's dominance.

Legions of supporters roam the streets behind small-block engines of every conceivable size and power level. Modern Corvettes and V-8 Camaros are powered by highly refined, technologically superior LS1, LS2, LS6, and LS7 small-blocks that are every bit as sophisticated as any new high-tech engine available. As long as there are automobiles, there will be small-block Chevys to power them. As long as one single crank and cylinder block still exist, small-block thunder will echo. And if the day ever comes that the last small-block Chevy is started for the last time, it will probably be a modified one.

This book covers the changes to the small-block Chevy over the years. It clearly defines the differences in small-block lineage and suggests the most reliable performance modifications available for early and late-model engines. You could build a more powerful or cheaper small-block than those presented here, but this information is documented and certified by literally thousands of racers, backyard mechanics, and factory sources. It will enable you to build a powerful, reliable small-block and allow you to join what may be the largest fraternity in the world: the fraternal order of the small-block Chevy.

Displacement Basics

The small-block Chevy has been produced in more than a dozen different displacements, but the amazing degree of versatility built into the line has provided enthusiasts with the raw material to build small-blocks of virtually any displacement. Fortunately, Chevrolet engineers saw to it that each successive refinement incorporated the best features of its predecessor. As displacement

Small-Block Chevrolet General Specifications

Configuration	90° ohv V-8 with cast-iron block and heads
Cylinders (front to back)	Left bank (driver's side) 1,3,5,7; Right bank 2,4,6,8
Bore Spacing	4.40 inches
Firing Order	1-8-4-3-6-5-7-2
Crankshaft	5 main bearings, thrust on #5 (rear)
Connecting Rods	Forged steel, 5.700-inch centers; 5.565-inch centers (400 ci rod)
Pistons	Forged and cast aluminum, slipper skirt
Lubrication	Full pressure oiling
Bore	3.500 to 4.126 inches
Stroke	3.00 to 3.75 inches
Displacement	262 ci to 400 ci
Compression Ratio	8.00:1 to 11.0:1
Carburetion	2-bbl, 4-bbl; 2 x 4-bbl and Rochester Fuel Injection
Power	162 hp to 375 hp
Torque	257 ft/lbs to 410 ft/lbs
Weight	550 lbs

increased, power and torque improved and highly stressed components were strengthened to maintain reliability. Many of these changes resulted in stronger parts that could be used to beef up earlier engines. By combining pieces from various members of the small-block family, a strong running small-block can be assembled in nearly any desirable displacement range.

Regardless of your engine's ultimate purpose, suitable performance components are readily available. The real trick is to identify your real needs and select the pieces that will best serve them. You can accomplish this by thoroughly familiarizing yourself with the small-block's evolution. Factory offerings are numerous to begin with, and there is virtually no end to the combinations you can derive from them. But first you have to know the players, so let's take a look at the lineup and see what kind of depth the Chevrolet team is fielding.

The 265

Aside from an ill-fated attempt at an early V-8 in 1917, the 265 was the first production OHV (overhead valve) V-8 engine to grace a Chevrolet engine compartment. Three different versions of the 265 were offered at its debut for 1955, including a 4-bbl engine that pumped out 180 horsepower at 4,600 rpm. Engines built during that first year lacked provisions for an oil filter, and any application other than a meticulous restoration effort should avoid these blocks. Like all small-blocks, the 265 was "over square," with a 3.75-inch bore and a 3.00-inch stroke. The compression ratios were 8:1 across the board the first year, but the single 4-barrel and twin 4-barrel engines offered in 1956 received a compression boost to 9.25:1. In 1957, only one 265 was offered—the 162-horsepower 2-barrel version.

The 265-ci engines oiled the lifter galleries from a metering slot ground on the rear camshaft-bearing journal. Therefore, if you install a cam without the slot, no oil will flow to the lifters and rocker arms. The best block to use when building a 265-ci engine is the 1957 version. It was used in both trucks and passen-

King of the drag race small-block, Bill "Grumpy" Jenkins' technical prowess has been widely acclaimed. He was a dominant force in early Pro/Stock racing with ground-pounding small-block combinations that shamed big-block and small-block racers of every brand preference.

ger cars and features a thicker deck surface for optimum strength and sealing capacity. These blocks were also modified to provide full pressure oiling, avoiding the oiling problems associated with earlier blocks. All 265 blocks lack provisions for side engine mounts; they can only be mounted from the front of the block.

Most recently, there was a 265-ci LT1 engine produced for use as the base powerplant in the 1993 Impala. This engine features all the high-tech LT1 innovations in a 265-ci package designed to honor the heritage of the first small-block Chevy.

The 283

When the 283 arrived in 1957, it featured an annular groove around the rear cam-bearing bore, which provided full-pressure oiling to the

lifter galleries. Early 283 blocks were actually overbored versions of the good 265 blocks, and although they had the thicker decks, they still had relatively thin cylinder walls. In 1958, Chevy introduced a new block with thicker walls. It featured side engine mounts, but it's usually considered less desirable than the 1959 and later blocks because it still used a rope-type seal on the rear main bearing. Until 1962, all 283 blocks were cast with a flat area around the base of each cylinder. When the longer-stroke 327-ci engine was introduced, this area was relieved to clear the larger counterweights of the 327 crank. Most 283s received the same treatment, which produced the possibility of building stroker motors with factory parts. You can drop in a 327 crank and revised pistons to increase the 283's displacement to 307 cubic inches. All 283s featured a bore of 3.875 inches (0.125-inch larger than the 265) with the standard 3.00-inch stroke. The 3.25-inch stroke of the 327 crank bumped displacement to 307 ci.

The 283 was such a good base engine that it remained in service until 1968, when it was replaced by a factory-built 307. Today, 283s can be built into strong and reliable street engines or screaming drag race engines. Incredible 287-ci (.030-inch

Zora Arkus-Duntov is one of many famous proponents of the small-block Chevy engine. His contributions to the development of the Corvette and the small-block engine are legendary.

overbore) engines still power many modified drag cars, and most of them produce well over 500 horsepower.

The best possible block for a 283-based engine is the 1964–1967 Chevy II block. These blocks featured thicker main bearing webs and cylinder walls, but they have become quite rare. They are easily identified by the large "62" cast on the side of the

The Corvette's small-block heritage is long and strong—and powerful small-blocks still lead the charge in C-5 and C-6 Corvettes. These Corvettes feature LS1, LS2, LS6, and LS7 engines based on Chevrolet's new Gen III small-block architecture.

Z28 Camaros have ridden the crest of small-block power to a virtually unchallenged position in the hearts of Chevy street enthusiasts. In 1993 the all-new LT1-powered Z28 fully restored the Z28's performance heritage. Its 275-hp LT1 gave the production Z28 150-mph capability. Subsequent LS1-powered cars are capable of exceeding 160 mph in production trim.

block, and the oil filter pad is recessed into a counterbore approximately 2.5 inches above the oil pan rails. The second best choice is the 1968-and-later 307 block, which has many of the stiffening features found in later four-inch bore blocks. Never use a block earlier than the 1959 piece, as all 1959-and-later blocks have neoprene rear main seal and side engine mounts. These blocks can be identified by the casting number "3756519."

The 327

The 327 was the first of the four-inch-bore small-blocks. This was the engine that first put real thunder in Chevrolet performance. It was introduced in 1962 and by 1966, it had been offered in several high-performance variations, including a 350-horsepower hydraulic-cam version, the 365-horsepower solid-lifter version, and the 375-horsepower fuel-injected version. The 327 became an immediate threat on the street and at the track, and it remains a capable performer today. These engines brought about the use of highly regarded big-valve cylinder heads and some surprisingly healthy camshaft and induction system combinations.

Performance was the byword, and 327s led the assault.

In 1968, the 327 was updated with larger bearing journals (the same as used in the then-new 350). It was discontinued in 1970, but it will always be regarded as one of Chevrolet's finest performance offerings. From 1962 to 1967, the 327 used the same bearing journal diameters as all other small-blocks. Main bearing journals were 2.30 inches in diameter and rod bearing journals were 2.00 inches. In 1968, the main bearing journals were enlarged to 2.45 inches in diameter and the rod bearing journals were increased to 2.10 inches. The 327 was never produced with four-bolt main bearing caps, but current four-bolt main blocks can be used to build 327-based engines. All two-bolt 327 blocks will provide reliable service as street engines and those that are not bored more than 0.030-inch over work quite well in race applications. To build a four-bolt main 327 or 327 derivative, use any of Chevrolet's four-bolt main blocks. These are large-journal blocks, but a small-journal crank can still be used with unique "thick" bearings made for this application by TRW. Large journal 327 cranks are rare because they were only manufactured for one year.

The 302

The factory 302 was a racing engine in the tradition of the high-horsepower 327. It featured a four-inch bore and a three-inch stroke and was designed to place the Z28 Camaro neatly into the 305-inch (5.0-liter) displacement limit for the popular SCCA Trans-Am racing series. It used a forged three-inch stroke crank, 11:1 forged pistons, big-valve heads, solid-lifter cam, aluminum intake manifold, and Holley 4-bbl carburetor. The 1967 version used a small-journal crank in a two-bolt main block, but it was updated to big journals and four-bolt mains for 1968–1969. All 302s were fitted with the famous Duntov "30-30" camshaft (PN3849346) first used in 1964–1965 Corvette fuel-injected engines. A Chevrolet service cam (PN3927140) was used in engines actually competing in the Trans-Am series. Street engines were rated at 290 hp with 290 ft-lbs of torque at 4,200 rpm. Race engines were good for around 450 horsepower when fitted with the factory-optional dual 4-barrel cross-ram manifold and Holley carbs. Currently, a 302 can be built from any standard bore, four-inch block by using a three-inch stroke crank. They are high-revving, powerful engines, but many everyday street performance enthusiasts prefer the greater torque and flexibility from a modified 327 or 350.

The 350

In 1967, the four-inch bore block used in the 327 was treated to a stroke increase that brought about the 350-ci engine still in service today. The new 3.48-inch stroke turned the small-block into a smooth, torque-rich performer suitable for a variety of applications. Only the 295-horsepower version was available for the 1967–1968, but in 1969, a 350-horsepower version was offered. In 1970,

Chevy really got serious with 360- and 370-horsepower offerings.

The ultimate 350-ci factory offering was, of course, the 370-horsepower LT1. Like earlier fuel-injected engines and the 290-horsepower 302s, the LT1 sported some serious high-performance hardware. Forged pistons, big-valve heads, and a new camshaft profile were all part of the equation. The LT1's performance upheld the high standards set by its race-bred ancestors.

Higher-tech versions of the 350 arrived in the mid-1980s with the briefly popular Crossfire Injection and the Tuned Port Injection (TPI) L98. These engines also received the one-piece rear main seal and corresponding crankshaft in 1986. In 1990, the all-new LT1 brought the small-block to the next performance plateau with high-tech engine management and numerous improvements, including reverse coolant flow and a gear driven camshaft and water pump.

The 307

The 307 was a convenient way to extend the useful life of the venerable 283. The 283 block was factory-equipped with a 327 crank to obtain a longer stroke and more torque, which was required for hauling around intermediate sedans equipped with air conditioning and other options. The long-stroke 283-based 307 did the job and still delivered good fuel economy.

The 307 provided admirable service in late Chevrolet and other GM cars and can be successfully modified for performance use. However, the 307 is not a very popular performance engine, largely because it was not offered in a high-performance factory version. The 307's size is confusing to many enthusiasts, and considerable money has been spent to needlessly convert a 307 to "more desirable" displacements. If you have a good 307 block and crank, you can use them for a street engine with considerable success. Admittedly, a racer who must build a specific displacement engine to suit class-racing restrictions may prefer a specific bore and stroke combination to achieve some small advantage. But this is expensive, often requiring special parts. For a strong street engine, practicality and economy considerations demand that you

A twin-turbocharged 368-ci small-block built by Mike LeFevers of Mitech Engineering powered the first full-bodied sedan to run over 300 mph at Bonneville. Joe Kugel piloted the sleek Pontiac Firebird to a 300.787-mph average to steal the thunder from a handful of big-block-powered cars attempting to break the 300-mph barrier. The LeFevers-boosted small-block helped Kugel punch a 1,400-hp hole in the air to capture a longstanding milestone in land speed record racing.

Proven Performance Engine Assemblies

GM 330-hp 350 HO

One of the best low-buck engine choices is GM's 330-hp 350-ci crate engine. Designed for street use in 1975 and earlier cars or trucks, the 330-hp 350 can also be used in any year off-road vehicle. Its 9.1:1 compression ratio delivers strong performance and it can physically replace any small-block engine from the 265 to the 400. Durability is the name of the game with its four-bolt-main block, nodular-iron crankshaft, PM steel connecting rods, and cast-aluminum pistons. Top that off with a pair of 64-cc Vortec cast-iron cylinder heads and a dual-pattern camshaft reminiscent of the 1965 to 1967 Corvette 327 cam. With chrome valve covers and timing cover, this engine will look great in your street rod, muscle car, or race car. You must supply your own intake manifold, distributor, flywheel, balancer, water pump, and exhaust manifolds. The engine is part number 12486041. It requires a counterweighted flywheel PN 10105832, 14088646,

14088650, 14088765, or 12554824, and the following balancers: PN 6272221 (6.75-inch) or PN 12555879 (8-inch), are recommended. You'll also need a six-bolt intake manifold designed to work with the Vortec heads. If you want take out the guessing work, the 350 HO Deluxe (PN 12496968) includes a carburetor, distributor, water pump, torsional damper, and automatic transmission flexplate.

Here is the 330-hp, 350-ci HO engine as it looks when you open the crate. Just add accessories, an intake system, exhaust manifolds or headers, and fire it up. It comes dressed with chrome timing cover and valve covers.

use whatever reasonable components are available. Don't worry about exotic combinations—use what you can get cheaply or what you already have.

The 307 was manufactured from 1968 to 1973 and there are plenty of them around. Remember that the blocks can also be used to build smaller engines by returning to the three-inch-stroke crank. All 307s used small journal crankshafts except for a rare number of large journal 1968 models.

The 400

Recognizing the increasing need for even more low-speed torque, Chevrolet updated the small-block again in 1970. By refining the internal structure of the engine, Chevy managed to achieve 400 ci from the same basic casting. Some serious changes were required to reach this displacement and still maintain reliability. The bore was enlarged to 4.126 inches, but to maintain the same bore space (4.44 inches), the cylinder bores had to be joined, or siamesed. The area between the bores is approximately 0.275 inch thick, giving the block considerable strength. These are still thin-wall castings, however, and many engine builders prefer not to bore them at all. The 3.75-inch stroke also required some changes. In order to fit everything inside the same external package, the connecting rod was shortened to 5.565 inches center-to-center. Main bearing

size was increased to 2.65 inches to further improve reliability.

The 400-ci engine was produced with four-bolt and two-bolt blocks. In 1970, most 400 blocks had three core holes on each side of the block, but many of the later-model two-bolt versions had the usual two holes per side. The 400 small-block was built through the end of the 1980 model year, so check the cylinder block casting number chart included in this chapter to see what kind you're looking at. The 400 blocks also have six steam holes drilled in each deck surface. Corresponding holes are drilled in the cylinder heads to prevent steam pockets from forming in the cooling system. If you install a cylinder head other than an original 400 head, it will have to have the holes drilled by using a head gasket for a template. Externally, the 400 is the same as other small-blocks, and all performance equipment will fit.

The 262

The 262-ci engine was introduced in 1974 and only lasted until mid-1976. With a bore of 3.671 inches and a 3.10-inch stroke, it is the smallest small-block ever produced. These blocks can be safely bored .030 inch over. They will accept minor performance bolt-ons, but are not really up to par for serious performance use.

The 305

In 1976, Chevy offered another new small-block. The 305 combined the long-stroke crank from a 350 with a 3.736-inch bore. Many shops are building mildly modified 305s that

Until recently, the most powerful production small-block ever offered was the awesome 375-hp, 327-ci, first offered in the '65 Corvette. It was a fuel-injected engine featuring 11:1 forged pistons, solid-lifter cam, and big-valve cylinder heads.

produce more torque and power while still delivering good fuel economy. They respond favorably to traditional modifications, and they can figure easily in any number of performance plans. In 1985, the 305 was equipped with tuned port injection (TPI) on high-performance models. These TPI engines can serve as the basis for

strong running street engines. Throttle body injection is the standard late-model induction system for the 305. The best choice is a fuel-injected engine produced after 1984, most of which had a higher 9.5:1 compression ratio. Also keep in mind the one-piece rear main seal incorporated on 1986-and-later engines.

The small-block was treated to exotic hardware almost immediately after its introduction. It had 4-barrel carburetion the first year, twin 4-barrels the second year, and factory fuel injection the third year. Fuel-injected engines were only offered in Corvettes and selected special-order cars and were discontinued in 1966. Twenty years later they replaced carbureted engines entirely.

Small-blocks became the most popular engine swap material in the history of the automobile. Here, a healthy small-block nestles snugly into the confines of a mid-1970s Vega engine compartment.

The 267

The least known addition to the small-block line is the 267. This engine also uses the 350 crank, but it has a very small bore, at 3.500 inches. The small size doesn't make it a favorable candidate for much performance work. However, car owners can fit the engine with most small-block performance parts. No serious performance work should be attempted with this engine.

The LS1

Chevrolet's 5.7-liter LS1 and subsequent LS6, LS2, and truck engine derivatives are based on new Gen III architecture. The 5.7-liter engines are actually 346 cubic inches in displacement. Additionally, there are 4.8-liter, 5.3-liter, and 6.0-liter engines built from the same design. These engines, while still technically small-

Virtually every type of Chevrolet has received the hot-rodded small-block treatment. This 327-ci-powered Chevy II has received a standard complement of bolt-on performance goodies: aluminum intake manifold, Holley carburetor, and headers, and God-knows-what lurks within.

block Chevys, are different from the engines discussed in this book, and are covered in depth in CarTech's *How to Build High-Performance Chevy LS1/LS6 V-8s* by Will Handzel.

The small-block Chevy is clearly a team player. Virtually every piece in the engine is well designed or can be replaced with one that is up to the job. Matching these components to your specific requirements is the key to extracting the type of performance you want from your engine. Although there are a lot of specific details, the basics of small-block interchangeability can be summed up in a nutshell. Essentially there are four primary stroke lengths, three different bearing journal sizes, two rod lengths, three basic bore sizes, and two types of cylinder heads. There are four fundamental steps to small-block evolution, and they all involve changes in stroke length.

Discounting the rare 265 engine, the first major player is the 283-ci engine. The 283 had a three-inch stroke, so most three-inch cranks are commonly referred to as 283 cranks. The 302 cranks have the same stroke, but they are all based on the original 283 configuration (with the exception of the 1969 large main-journal 302 crank, commonly called the 302 crank). The second is the 327 crank, which has a 3.25-inch stroke. All 3.25-inch cranks are referred to as 327 cranks. The next step up is the 350 crank, which has a 3.48-inch stroke. They are common only to 350s and are referred to as 350 cranks. The 400 crank has the longest stroke, at 3.75 inches, and it is common to 400-ci motors only.

All 283 cranks have the same size bearing journals (again, note the exception of the large-journal 302, three-inch crank), but 327 cranks have either large or small journals depending on their date of manufacture. The 400 crank has even larger

main journals, creating a special set of problems.

All 305 and 350 engines produced since 1986 use a one-piece rear main seal and a crankshaft with a large round mating flange. The 1986 and later blocks can use earlier cranks with a special adapter available from Chevrolet, but early blocks do not readily accept the 1986 and later crankshaft.

All small-blocks use 5.7-inch connecting rods, except the 400, which uses a shorter 5.565-inch rod. For a long time, the short rod was not recognized as a performance component. Over the years, considerable testing has shown that power and torque differences between the two rod lengths are pretty small. The most notable advantage is found with longer rods, which place less loading on the cylinder walls due to less rod angularity.

Common small-block bore sizes are 3⅞-inch, 4-inch, and 4⅛-inch. Producing an engine with suitable displacement, torque, power, and RPM operating range can usually be accomplished with some combination of these bore and stroke sizes. When it comes to cylinder heads,

The second most powerful engine was the late 370-hp LT1 offered in the Corvette and Z28 in the early 1970s. Besides a healthy short block and cylinder head combination, induction was handled via a factory high-rise aluminum manifold and an 800-cfm Holley carburetor.

Fast-Burn 385

The Fast-Burn 385 is a bolt-in replacement for any 265 through 400 small-block engine. It's based on the ZZ4 HO short block and a set of GM's new Fast Burn cylinder heads. The HO engine incorporates the latest in high-performance components, including lightweight aluminum cylinder heads, low-friction hydraulic roller tappets, and hypereutectic (high silicon) aluminum pistons. All ZZ4 engine assemblies are fire tested and final balanced at the factory to ensure quality. They feature a new low-profile dual-plane intake manifold PN 10185063 for increased hood clearance without power loss. The manifold has a dual-pattern flange that accommodates both standard-flange Holley and spread-bore Quadrajet carburetors and it incorporates all accessory brackets, exhaust gas recirculation (EGR) ports and integral hot air choke. (Block-off plates are installed on the EGR and choke stove on HO 350s.)

Special features of the HO engine included lightweight valvespring retainers that have half the mass of the previous design, valvestem seals on the exhaust valves for enhanced oil control, and aluminum heads that are built with radiused valve seat inserts. The HO engine's stamped steel rocker covers have PCV valve and oil filler holes on both covers. The engine is equipped with a torsional damper, a cast-iron water pump (standard rotation, long style), a 12¾-inch, 153-tooth automatic transmission flexplate, and a dipstick. It does not include spark plug wires, pulleys, starter motor, oil filter, oil filter adapter, fuel pump, exhaust manifolds, or accessories.

The Fast Burn 385 is an ideal choice for hot rods and street machines with its ZZ4 short block and Fast Burn cylinder heads. It makes 385 hp, using forged-steel crank and connecting rods.

you either choose one of two high-performance valve sizes or use the smaller standard-valve heads for economy and smooth performance.

There are a few simple rules to follow when combining these components. Knowing which crank to use in which block with which rod length and with which cylinder heads separates knowledgeable small-block builders from the tinkerers. There are numerous reasons for combining any of these parts, and we'll discuss the why and wherefore in subsequent chapters on individual components—beginning with a complete discussion of cylinder blocks, their selection, preparation, and application.

The 350-ci LT1 engine offered in the Corvette. It's a high-tech revision featuring reverse-flow cooling, gear-driven water pump, electronic fuel injection, and full electronic engine management for optimum performance.

The King Kong small-block is the 400-ci version introduced in 1970. The early 400-ci motors had four-bolt mains, 265 hp, and enough torque to pull down small buildings. It has since become a popular choice for building performance street engines.

BLOCKS

Any good-running small-block Chevy begins with the cylinder block. It's the foundation from which all important engine functions initiate. Cylinder block selection and preparation has a substantial influence on an engine's performance potential. Block selection is primarily dependent on the final application and desired displacement. While nonperformance applications can succeed with just about anything, high-performance engines should make use of selected cylinder blocks offering increased strength and reliability. For our purposes, we will only be discussing blocks that lend themselves to high-performance applications.

Block Basics

Standard factory cylinder blocks have, for the most part, been available with three basic bore sizes and three main bearing sizes. For convenience they can be referred to as 283 blocks (3⅞-inch bore, 2.3-inch mains); 302, 327, and 350 blocks (4-inch bore, 2.3-inch or 2.45-inch mains); and 400 blocks (4⅛-inch bore, 2.65-inch mains). Some of these blocks may be purchased from performance centers or located at

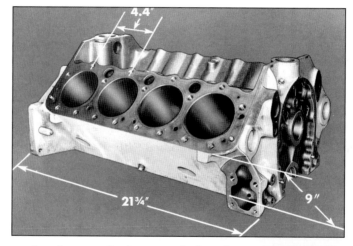

The light weight and compact size of the small-block Chevy has contributed greatly to its enduring popularity. External dimensions and bore centers have remained unchanged since 1955.

engine shops and salvage yards, but the core supply of blocks—other than 350 and 305 blocks—is rapidly dwindling. Mail order aftermarket blocks have also become very popular.

Chevrolet Bow Tie cylinder blocks are built in the same basic configuration for all current high-performance applications. These blocks feature revised coolant passages and further improved rigidity, thanks to beefier main webs, siamesed bores, and greater overall metal content. They weigh up to 15 pounds more than a standard small-block casting.

Standard four-bolt replacement blocks are currently available as PN 10066034 (two-piece rear seal) or

10105123 (one-piece rear seal). They feature the thicker, fully machined main webs, but are cast with the standard alloy. Large-bore 4⅛-inch blocks are also available, as shown in the

Engine ID numbers are stamped on a machined pad in front of the right (passenger-side) deck surface (see arrow). They typically feature an alphanumeric code indicating the year and application of the engine. Some codes have been reused, making a factory service manual essential for accurate identification.

Replacement blocks do not have ID codes. Many enthusiasts prefer to select blocks according to the casting number (arrow). This number is located on the flywheel housing, directly behind the left (driver-side) deck surface.

cylinder block selection chart at the end of this chapter.

An important thing to remember with any of these new blocks is that they are "green" or unused castings, which may experience dimensional changes unless they are heat-treated or subjected to considerable "run-in" prior to final assembly. Production engines are subjected to repeated heating and cooling and normal operating stress during their service life, causing the blocks to take a permanent set that cannot be duplicated in a green block. Once a casting has set or stabilized, dimensional changes are minimized, and the engine can make consistent power.

For certain racing or vintage buildups, used blocks will be required. For example, since all new factory blocks incorporate large-journal main bearings, if you need small crank saddles for a specific application, locating a suitable used block may be the only option.

Block Selection

The process of identifying and selecting the best possible seasoned block is often time consuming, but the results can be worth the effort. Casting numbers and engine identification numbers are used to identify blocks, but the accuracy of these numbers is often questionable. A Chevrolet source informed us that casting numbers only reflect general usage and that engine identification numbers are often more specific. Engine IDs use a letter and number code to indicate the year, engine size, and type of transmission. Combined with the casting number, they will usually provide an accurate indication of the block origin. Many racers check only the last three digits of the casting number, because they feel that certain castings are especially desirable.

Searching for a specific casting number is one way of selecting a block, but successful engines have been built from virtually every casting number around. It is more important to select a block that possesses all the correct physical characteristics. When you know what to look for, you can make an intelligent choice based on your actual requirements.

Inspecting a Used Block

Once you've selected a likely candidate, give it a preliminary inspection. If the block is dirty you won't be able to locate cracks, but you can still check certain features. See if the cam bore is centered on the front cam bore boss and if the lifter bores are centered on each individual lifter boss. If they are centered, there is probably only a little core shift and the block will probably have good cylinder walls. If the block looks good thus far, it's worth having it hot-tanked for further inspection. Be sure to select a shop with a tank that uses rotating jets or a rotating table, instead of a simple vat. It takes agitation to clean out all the debris, and soaking in a vat just isn't good enough.

After the block is thoroughly cleaned, carefully examine the deck surfaces for cracks and any deep gouges or scratches that can't be removed with normal decking. Check the main bearing webs for signs of cracks or previous damage. The main bearing caps should fit snugly into the main cap guide slot. They should exhibit no evidence of side play, and the parting lines should match smoothly when the caps are torqued in place. Examine the bottom of each cap for scouring, an indication that the cap has been moving around during operation. Also, examine the outside of the block for possible freeze cracks. Throughout this examination, you should keep in mind the ultimate application of the engine. For a high-

---

Basic Cylinder Block Specifications

Stock Block Specifications

Bore Diameter (inches)	Engine (cid)	Main Bearing Cap Design	Year
3.500*	267	Two-bolt	1979-'81
3.671*	262	Two-bolt	1975
3.736*	305	Two-bolt	1976-'94
3.875*	307	Two-bolt	1968-'73
4.001 (2.30-in. main saddles)	327	Two-bolt	1968-'69
	350	Two-bolt	1968-'88
4.001 (2.45-in. main saddles)	302	Four-bolt	1968-'69
	265	Two-bolt	1994
	350	Four-bolt	1968-'94
4.126 (2.65-in. main saddles)	400	Four-bolt	1970-'72
	400	Two-bolt	1973-'80

Available in two-bolt main bearing cap design only.

Standard factory blocks have been produced with six different bore sizes. However, most performance applications can be grouped in three bore sizes and three main-bearing sizes. They can be referred to as 283 blocks, which have 3⅞-inch bores and 2.3-inch mains; 302, 327, and 350 blocks, which have 4-inch bores and 2.45-inch mains; and 400 blocks, which feature 4⅛-inch bores and 2.65-inch mains.

Some of these blocks are available from performance stores, engine shops, and salvage yards, but the core supply of blocks other than 305 and 350 blocks is shrinking fast. The best alternatives are the Chevrolet Bow Tie blocks built in the same configuration.

Parts and Specs

Items	Quantity
Block (bare, cleaned, and prepped)	1
Front main bearing cap*	1
Number-2 main bearing cap	1
Number-3 main bearing cap	1
Number-4 main bearing cap	1
Rear main bearing cap	1
Main bearing bolts for small journal 2-bolt blocks—7/16 14NC x 3	10
Main bearing bolts for large journal 2-bolt blocks—7/16 14NC x 3-1/4	10
Main bearing bolts for 4-bolt blocks, long—7/16 14NC x 3-3/8	10
Main bearing bolts for 4-bolt blocks, short—7/16 14NC x 2	6
Freeze plugs—1-5/8-inch diameter	8**
Cam bearing plug—2-3/32-inch diameter	1
Oil gallery plugs—1/2-inch diameter	3

* All main bearing caps are marked at the factory, but they are often difficult to see. Remark them before removing them from the block.
** 400 ci 4-bolt blocks require ten 1-5/8 inch diameter freeze plugs.

---

horsepower package, everything should be right on, but a moderate performance engine in a street car is not going to suffer appreciably if the block exhibits a minor amount of core shift. Make your selection intelligently and don't pay for something you don't need. The final step is to have the block pressure tested and inspected for cracks. If it passes this test, you're ready to get serious with it.

Getting serious means more cleaning, deburring, more cleaning, block prepping, and more cleaning to get the block as near perfect as possible. If the block wasn't completely stripped of hardware for the first cleaning, do it now. Everything that can be unbolted, knocked out, or pulled out must be removed. It should be mentioned here that an engine stand is an absolute prerequisite to proper block preparation and engine assembly. It makes every part of the engine easily accessible and the cost (generally about $75) is not prohibitive. There's no point in trying to keep everything clean if you're rolling the engine around on the garage floor.

Block Preparation

These guidelines apply to both new and used cylinder blocks. As I mentioned earlier, new blocks are "green" and may experience some amount of dimensional shifting until they take a set. Fortunately, modern

The 400-ci block has a number of unique identifying traits. The notches at the bottom of each cylinder bore provide connecting rod clearance in the long stroke engine. Older blocks with four-bolt mains usually have three freeze plugs on either side while two-bolt blocks have the more conventional two plugs-per-side. Because of the increased 2.65-inch main bearing diameter, 400 main caps are unique; the bolt spacing is also wider than on a standard main cap. In order to maintain the standard 4.40-inch bore spacing with the 4.125-inch bores, the water-jacket surfaces of the cylinder walls had to be joined together (siamesed). The area between the cylinder walls is solid metal, which does not allow coolant to flow completely around each cylinder. Two small holes between each cylinder bore on the deck surface are necessary to provide a relief for steam pockets inside the water jacket.

technology has brought new methods of stress relieving blocks and other components so that the dimensional stability of new components remains consistent. Blocks can be vibrated at specific frequencies on a special table designed to ease stress slowly out of the part. Dimensional stability doesn't usually present a problem for basic engine applications, but racing power-plants often benefit from these high-tech, stress-relieving processes.

Start cylinder block preparation by completely deburring the casting. You don't have to get carried away here, but you should break all the sharp edges and radius all the corners. Remove casting flash that might break away under stress and smooth over areas where potential stress cracks might develop. Deburring can be done with a small drill motor and some sanding drums or even small files if you're really on a budget. Larger sections of flashing will require using small grinding stones. A high-speed grinder makes the job really easy. Work carefully and be sure not to gouge any machined surfaces. Small files are excellent for deburring the edges of main bearing webs and other short, straight edges. Be sure to tackle every remote part of the block including the distributor pocket, camshaft cavity, timing cover cavity, and lifter gallery. It takes some time to properly deburr a block so don't get impatient. The only place you can skip is the edge of the deck surfaces, since they will be rendered sharp again during the decking procedure.

Now you should spend some time running a tap or a thread chaser through each threaded hole in the

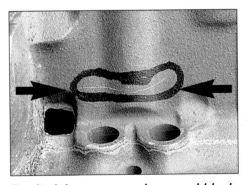

Don't sink any money in a used block until you have it pressure tested and Magnafluxed. Luckily, the owner of this block discovered these cracks in the valley (not that uncommon in small-blocks) and through the lifter bores before extensive machine work was performed.

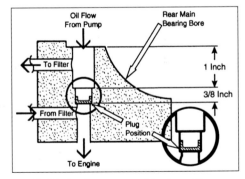

This is sometimes called the "forgotten plug." If it isn't removed before the block is pressure washed, the main oil passages will not be adequately cleaned. Remove the plug by inserting a ¼-inch diameter steel rod (found in hardware stores) into the oil-pressure access at the rear of the block. A few taps with a hammer will drive the plug out. It's a ½-inch type P5 plug available at any parts store. This plug must be in place for oil to flow to the oil filter. Do not drive the new plug in farther than ¼-inch or you risk restricting engine oil flow. Later model factory engines use a large steel ball instead of the plug.

block. If the hole is a blind hole and it carries some torque (e.g., main-cap bolts), it should be tapped with a bottoming tap to insure that threads reach all the way to the bottom of the hole. A bottoming tap can be made from an ordinary tap by grinding off the tip, which is normally used for starting the tap into an unthreaded hole. If any of the head-bolt holes are pulling out, wait until after the decking operation to repair them with Heli-Coil thread repair inserts.

A popular modification at this point is to tap the front three main oil galleries and install threaded pipe plugs. This procedure is unnecessary when the standard plugs are properly installed and staked in place, except in a NASCAR or long-distance application where vibration is severe. However, tapping the passages only takes a few minutes, so you may want to perform this modification even for street use. If you decide to give it a try, make sure you do not tap the gallery passages too deep. If the plugs screw in too far, they can restrict the oil feed passages to and from the front main journal.

There are two other small modifications that some experienced engine builders make in this area. One is to drill a tiny 0.030-inch hole in the face of the front cam bore boss, directly above the cam bore. It should be centered directly above the cam bore centerline and pass into the short oil passage leading from the main oil gallery to the front cam bearing. This hole will provide a constant source of lubrication for the cam drive gear thrust surface, reducing the chance of scoring the block or damaging the backside of the cam gear. It will also allow some air trapped in the oil galleries to escape, improving oil flow upon engine startup. Another modification is to drill a second 0.030-inch hole in the center of the middle oil gallery plug. This bleeds trapped air and ensures rapid front main bearing oiling. However, a second bleed can reduce idle oil pressure and may lead to front cover leaks on street engines, so restrict the second bleed to engines used for competition only. Finally, make sure that the bleed hole(s) is no larger than 0.030-inch or too much oil pressure will be lost.

You may also wish to give some consideration to the oil drain-back holes in the lifter valley. There are several holes located along the length of the valley and two large openings at the front and rear. The small holes should be drilled, tapped, and fitted with screw-in plugs even in a street application. In addition, for racing, the two large drain holes at the rear of the block should be gently rounded with a grinder and then tapped and

350/400 Displacement Combinations

350 Block with 400 Crank

Bore (inches)	Stroke (inches)	CID
4.001	3.750 (400 crank)	377 ci
4.030 (.030 over)	3.750	382 ci
4.060 (.060 over)	3.750	388 ci

When combining a 350 block with a 400 crankshaft, the 400 main bearing journals must be turned down to 2.450 inches, and shorter 5.585-inch 400 connecting rods must be used. This provides the increased reliability of the 350 block with the torque-producing characteristics of a long-stroke, short-rod, large-displacement engine. It's a good choice for tow packages, heavy vehicles, or other high-torque applications.

400 Block Combos

Bore (inches)	Stroke (inches)	CID
4.126	3.000 (302 crank)	321 ci
4.156 (.030 over)	3.000	325 ci
4.186 (.606 over)	3.000	330 ci
4.126	3.484 (350 crank)	372 ci
4.156 (.030 over)	3.484	378 ci
4.186 (.060 over)	3.484	384 ci
4.126	4.000 (special crank)	427 ci
4.156 (.030 over)	4.000	434 ci
4.186 (.060 over)	4.000	440 ci
4.126	3.250 (327 crank)	348 ci
4.156 (.030 over)	3.250	352 ci
4.186 (.060 over)	3.250	358 ci
4.126	3.750 (400 crank)	401 ci
4.156 (.030 over)	3.750	407 ci
4.186 (.060 over)	3.750	413 ci
4.126	4.250 (special crank)	455 ci
4.156 (.030 over)	4.250	462 ci
4.186 (.060 over)	4.250	468 ci

The 400-ci blocks should not be bored more than 0.030-inch oversize for high-performance applications, though you can go 0.060-inch over for moderate street performance, towing, or RV use.

Make sure the block you select has the correct flywheel/flexplate and starter alignment. The starter on the left is for the small-diameter (153-tooth) flywheel, while the one on the right mates with a large-diameter (168-tooth) flywheel. You can tell the difference by observing the location of the mounting bolts.

Another important consideration for block selection is the positioning of the clutch-linkage-mounting holes on the left side of the block. These vary, depending on the original application and can cause problems if mismatched in a stick-shift swap.

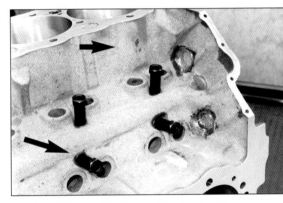

Solid mounts have been popular in drag racing, but they create torque stress in the cylinder walls next to the mounting bosses. A better plan is to use cushioned mounts and restrict engine movement with a torque strap at the front of the motor. The best overall engine mount is the GM locking mount. On the right is a cushioned mount with interlocking tabs to limit engine movement.

Note in the rear cam bearing bore housing there are three holes in the oil groove. The left and right holes feed the left and right oil galleries, respectively. Small plugs with drilled orifices are threaded into these holes to restrict the oil. Aftermarket aluminum restrictors can also be installed from the rear of each gallery to accomplish the same thing.

For racing applications, it's desirable to prevent drain-back oil from raining down on the spinning crank assembly. The drain holes in the lifter valley can be plugged so that oil is forced to drain at either end of the engine. This is also accomplished by using standoff tubes screwed into each drain hole. The tubes prevent oil from draining, but still allow crank case pressure to equalize.

plugged with pipe plugs. The left side will generally take a ¾-inch pipe plug, with a ⅜-inch pipe plug on the right. This eliminates the large volume of oil draining onto the large rear crank throw spinning directly below. Many racers carefully open up the drain holes at the front of the valley so that oil will drain more easily. With the rear holes plugged, a certain amount of oil will build up in the valley during a run, but it will quickly drain when the engine is shut off. The extra oil in the valley has no discernible effect on the operation of the lifters and pushrods, and oil draining at the front of the block never touches the rapidly spinning crank. It works!

There is, of course, no reason to install any of the plugs until final assembly, when all the major machining operations have been completed and the block has been thoroughly cleaned.

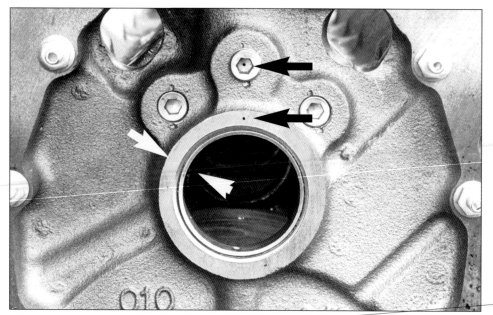

For any performance application, the bores should be finished on a Sunnen CK1 or equivalent power hone. Always instruct your machine shop to use torque plates with head gaskets during the honing process. Most modern engine shops are well versed in proper block honing techniques.

There are variations in the way block casting cores fit together during the casting process and in the way factory machine tools finish the block. For performance, using a "well-centered" block is desirable. One way to check for this is to observe the front cam bore. It should be centered in the machined surface (arrows). An off-center bore indicates the possibility of machine or core shift, but this doesn't necessarily preclude the use of the block for moderate performance use. The arrows indicate the location of two 0.030-inch pressure oiling holes that are drilled to improve oiling at the rear of the cam gear and to prevent oil starvation of the front main bearing during engine startup. The tiny hole in the center gallery plug bleeds air from the gallery at startup to prevent an airlock of the front main bearing oil supply. The hole in the face of the cam bore provides oil pressure to the backside of the cam gear.

Lifter bores are another good indicator of a dimensionally correct block. The bores should be evenly centered in the lifter bore bosses on the block.

Align Boring

Align boring is a highly touted procedure to straighten the alignment of the main bearing saddles. Align bor-ing should be reserved for special applications where the block has become warped or some unique mod-ification absolutely requires realign-ment of the crank bores. Most slight irregularities can be cleaned up with a simple align-hone operation, but even this is not generally necessary on the average used cylinder block. Main-sad-dle straightness can be checked with a machinist's straightedge and with a simple check that you can perform yourself. By laying a *straight crank* (make sure you check crank run out with a dial indicator before you per-form this procedure) into the block with properly clearanced bearings, you can check for binding by spin-ning the crank by hand. If it spins smoothly, the block is in great shape.

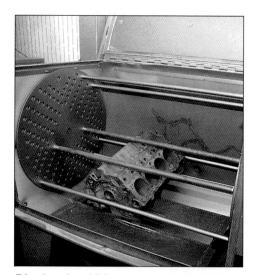

Blocks should be power washed at elevated temperatures with good agitation. Modern block cleaning equipment can make a block look brand new, and it can reveal any imperfections, flaws, or cracks.

Align boring is a valuable machining procedure when properly applied, but don't do it if it isn't necessary.

Align boring is a fairly straightfor-ward procedure, but it requires careful

Align boring isn't typically necessary for most engine rebuilds, or even for many minor performance buildups, but it's a great corrective measure for a block that is out of spec, or one that requires realignment because steel main caps have been installed.

Pressure checking is an essential part of cylinder block selection. A good machine shop will pressure test every block prior to performing any machining operations.

and very accurate machine setup and operation to achieve a first-class job. The standard procedure is to take a slight cut off the bottom (the parting-line face) of each main cap and to then mount them in place on the block. Then a carefully aligned boring bar is spun through the main bore, cutting new bearing saddles that are perfectly aligned, one to the other. It is important that a minimum amount of material be removed from the block saddles because the operation moves the crank centerline closer to the cam, creating extra slack in the timing chain, which

The 501/503/525-series race-prepared Bow Tie blocks are rich with features that make building a competition small-block much easier. The front camshaft-bearing flange incorporates a provision for a production thrust plate (arrows 1), eliminating the need for a cam bumper. Oil galleries have been extended to the front of the block and they are 0.070-inch thicker, allowing for oversize drilling (arrows 2). Pressurized oil may be fed directly to the mains via an external dry sump pump (arrow 3).

Decking cuts the deck surfaces so that they are perpendicular to the cylinder bores and parallel to the centerline of the crankshaft. The end result also establishes the distance from the deck to the crank centerline, an important dimension that must be carefully controlled to gain the desired piston-to-cylinder-head clearance.

This bypass transfer passage leads from the right cylinder head to the lower opening at the right side of the water pump. This passage is prone to leaking and some engine builders feel that it makes the number two exhaust valve run too cool. Some builders plug it for racing applications.

Standard Overbore Displacements

All small-blocks can safely be bored 0.030-inch oversized, providing the block does not suffer from core shift or other casting defects. Many can be safely overbored 0.060 inch, but this is risky with blocks produced after 1967. If even slight core shift occurs in late thin wall blocks, cylinder failure is likely. The same warning applies to all 400-ci blocks.

Engine 265			Engine 283		
Stroke	Bore	CID	Stroke	Bore	CID
3.000	3.750 (standard)	265 ci	3.000	3.875 (standard)	283 ci
3.000	3.780 (.030 over)	269 ci	3.000	3.905 (.030 over)	287 ci
3.000	3.810 (.060 over)	274 ci	3.000	3.935 (.060 over)	292 ci
Engine 302			Engine 307		
Stroke	Bore	CID	Stroke	Bore	CID
3.000	4.001 (standard)	302 ci	3.250	3.875 (standard)	307 ci
3.000	4.030 (.030 over)	306 ci	3.250	3.905 (.030 over)	311 ci
3.000	4.060 (.060 over)	310 ci	3.250	3.935 (.060 over)	316 ci
Engine 327			Engine 350		
Stroke	Bore	CID	Stroke	Bore	CID
3.250	4.001 (standard)	327 ci	3.484	4.001 (standard)	350 ci
3.250	4.030 (.030 over)	331 ci	3.484	4.030 (.030 over)	355 ci
3.250	4.060 (.060 over)	337 ci	3.484	4.060 (.060 over)	360 ci
Engine 262			Engine 305		
Stroke	Bore	CID	Stroke	Bore	CID
3.100	3.671 (standard)	262 ci	3.484	3.736 (standard)	305 ci
3.100	3.701 (.030 over)	266 ci	3.484	3.766 (.030 over)	310 ci
3.100	3.731 (.060 over)	270 ci	3.484	3.796 (.060 over)	315 ci
Engine 400			Engine 267		
Stroke	Bore	CID	Stroke	Bore	CID
3.750	4.126 (standard)	401 ci	3.484	3.500 (standard)	267 ci
3.750	4.156 (.030 over)	407 ci	3.484	3.530 (.030 over)	272 ci
3.750	4.186 (.060 over)	413 ci	3.484	3.560 (.060 over)	277 ci

(Measurements in inches unless otherwise noted.)

may subsequently cause valve-timing problems. It is also absolutely essential that the boring fixture is exactly aligned on the block, otherwise the crank bore may be higher or lower at one end or it may not be centered side-to-side in the block.

In addition to correcting a warped block, align boring is required for the installation of specialty four-bolt caps or when bearing spacers are being used to install a small-journal crank in a big-journal block (sometimes desirable to achieve unique bore/stroke combinations). Special four-bolt main caps can be added to any small-block case. They are available from many sources but all come with rough-cut bearing saddles. When a block is modified to accept such caps, it is essential that the main bores are accurately align bored.

Special extra thick main bearings are also available to fit small-bearing cranks into large-journal blocks without align boring. However, these bearings are expensive. Therefore, some engine builders prefer to use spacers for installing standard small-journal bearings.

Decking

Decking is a procedure whereby the deck surfaces are machined perpendicular (90 degrees) to the centerlines of the cylinder bores and equidistant from—and dead parallel to—the centerline of the crankshaft. This establishes the distance from the deck to the crank centerline, an important dimension that must be carefully controlled to gain the desired piston-to-cylinder-head clearance.

Ordinary street engines rarely receive this treatment, but there is some power to be gained from equalizing compression and cylinder volume through decking. When teamed with the use of assorted head gasket thicknesses, deck height and piston-to-cylinder-head clearance can be closely controlled. The most common procedure is parallel decking, which

Arrows indicate the drilled holes that route oil directly from the main oil gallery to the center main bearing saddles; the system is called Priority Main Oiling. Each priority feed passage barely intersects its cam bearing bore, necessitating the careful alignment of the cam bearing oiling hole with these intersecting passages. The blocks have thicker deck surfaces and blind-drilled and tapped head-bolt holes to improve gasket sealing and to prevent coolant leaks.

involves removing the minimum amount required to get both deck surfaces parallel to the crank centerline. Many engine builders use parallel decking as a starting point from which

they can establish desired piston-deck heights through additional block machining or piston-top machining. (Remember that deck height is the distance from the piston flat to the deck surface of the block. It is not the clearance between the cylinder head and the top of the piston. True piston-to-head clearance is established with a combination of head gasket thickness and deck height.) If you're rebuilding a used engine, it may be helpful to check existing deck heights before the engine is disassembled. By determining where the deck surface is in relation to the pistons, you may be able to avoid decking if things are close. As a last resort, some amount of piston top machining may be necessary to achieve the desired clearances.

Many engine builders like to push everything to the absolute limit, and with that in mind, a good rule of thumb for small-block Chevy engines is to maintain a minimum of 0.035-inch piston-to-head clearance with steel rods and 0.060-inch with aluminum rods. How you arrive at these figures is not particularly important except in all-out, high-compression

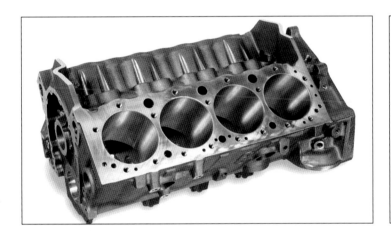

Dart's cast-iron Little M and Sportsman blocks illustrate how the aftermarket has stepped in to fill the performance needs of racers and high-performance street applications. The Little M block offers extra thick deck surfaces and cylinder walls, blind-tapped head-bolt bosses, standard external mounting bosses, priority-main oiling, scalloped water jackets, four-bolt fastening on all five main caps, and a choice of steel or nodular-iron caps. They are offered in both 4.00- and 4.125-inch bore sizes and with 350- or 400-ci mains. The rear main cap is configured for a standard oil pump and a two-piece, rear-main seal.

The Iron Eagle block from Dart incorporates all the features necessary to build big-inch small-blocks. The pan rails are spread 0.400-inch per side to increase clearance with stroker cranks. These blocks also come in standard 9.025-inch and tall 9.325-inch decks with dual starter mounts functional fuel pump boss, two-piece rear seal, and a raised camshaft for stroker clearance.

racing engines where you may be concerned with the amount of quench in the combustion chamber.

Cylinder Boring

The importance of straight, perfectly round cylinder bores cannot be overstated. You can't make power if you don't seal the cylinders, and you can't seal the cylinders without precision machining. It has become commonplace to simulate normal operating stress on the block during all boring and honing operations, the theory being that the cylinder needs to be round while the engine is running, and every effort should be made to duplicate normal operating conditions. Installing and torquing all the main caps simulates the stress imparted to the cylinders. Some engine builders also feel that a dummy oil pump should be torqued in place on the rear main cap to truly simulate distortion of the rear cylinders and the rear main bearing saddle. This is an important point to remember when align honing the block.

Torque plates have become *de rigueur* and the difference they make is measurable. They are used to simulate stress placed on the block when the heads are torqued in place. Head bolts cause a great deal of cylinder distortion, especially near the deck surface where the piston rings operate. To fully simulate normal operating conditions, you also need to use the proper head gasket under the torque plates. Many engine builders have their own pet theories on how thick a proper torque plate should be. Some like a very thick plate, on the order of four inches or more, while others are happy with a plate between two and three inches thick. Obviously, you can reach a point of diminishing returns with all of this, especially when you consider that the head bolts normally clamp a head that is made of cast iron and is full of ports and water passages. The clamping force exerted by a steel plate may (and probably *does*) cause a slightly different distortion pattern. Regardless of the subtleties, torque plates produce good results and all experienced engine builders use them. The best advice we can give you is to use the plates when building a racing engine and exercise your own good judgment for a street engine. If you can afford it, do it; if not, you may never notice the difference.

Since cylinder wall shape and condition significantly impact power output, thoughtful boring and honing procedures should be exercised. First, you have to ensure that the cylinders are bored 90 degrees to the crank axis. If the deck surfaces have already been cut parallel to the crank axis, a standard deck-referenced boring bar may be used. Otherwise, the block should be bored with a bar that references directly off the crank centerline. For honing, you should seek out a shop that uses a Sunnen CK-10 Cylinder King or similar power hone. Hand

ZZ Short Block *This is a partial short-block version of the 350-ci, 355-hp high-output ZZ4 engine. This engine assembly includes block, crankshaft, pistons, rings, and connecting rods.*

Partial 383 Engine Assembly *This is basically a GM 383 short block, which is also the core assembly for the GM 383 Crate engine PN 12497317. It is based in bare block assembly PN 88959106. Unlike conventional aftermarket 383 assemblies, this factory combination uses a 4.00-inch bore and a 3.80-inch stroke instead of a 3.75-inch crank with a 4.030-inch bore.*

honing has long been considered the path to maximum horsepower, but even the most prominent racers have come to love the CK-10.

The final honing procedure depends on the type of rings you are using. In nearly every case except a full race engine, there is little reason to use anything other than a standard-width ring set (with a moly-faced top ring) from a major manufacturer like Speed Pro or TRW. All-out racing engines may use thin,

Bolt Torque and Cam Bearing Specs

Unless otherwise indicated, the torque specs in this guide are for lubricated fasteners. While you can install fasteners dry, you will find that lubrication allows fasteners to screw in easier, prevents thread seizure, and gives more accurate torque readings. If you decide not to use lubrication, torque values can often increase by 10 to 25 percent. This higher torque value will not necessarily result in a "tighter" fastener. In fact, bolts installed dry may have less holding ability than lubricated fasteners tightened to the values shown here.

Unless otherwise noted, all Bow Tie four-bolt main blocks require 65 pounds on the inner bolts, 60 pounds on the outer bolts, and 40 pounds on the two ⅜-inch bolts at the front. All torque specs are for lubrication with engine oil.

Small-blocks use five cam bearings numbered from front to back. The numbers are stamped on the back of each bearing. "Late" refers to 1957 and later engines.

Bolt Torque For All Small-Block V-8s

Main Bearing Caps	Torque	Lubricant
	Inner 70 ft/lbs	Molykote/Oil
	Outer 65 ft/lbs	Molykote/Oil
Connecting Rod Bolt—3/8-inch	45-50 ft/lbs	Oil
Connecting Rod Bolt—11/32-inch	37-42 ft/lbs	Oil
Connecting Rod Bolt—7/16-inch	60-65 ft/lbs	Oil
Cylinder Head Bolt	65 ft/lbs	Sealant
Rocker Arm Stud (Late HP Head)	50 ft/lbs	Sealant
Camshaft Sprocket	20 ft/lbs	Oil
Intake Manifold	30 ft/lbs	Oil
Flywheel	60 ft/lbs	Oil
Spark Plugs (Conventional Gasket)	25 ft/lbs	Dry
Spark Plugs (Tapered Seat)	15 ft/lbs	Dry
Exhaust Manifold	25 ft/lbs	Antisieze
Oil Pan Bolt	165 inch/lbs	Oil
Front Cover Bolt	75 inch/lbs	Oil
Rocker Cover	25 inch/lbs	Oil

Cam Bearings For All Small-Block V-8s

	1	2	3	4
TRW	SH 290	SH 288	SH 287	SH 287
Federal Mogul	2021DR	2022DR	2023DR	2023DR
Michigan Bearing	230CS	231CC	232CS	232CS

	5 (early)	5 (late)	Complete Cam Bearing Sets
TRW	SH 289	SH 288	SH 287S (early), SH 290S (late)
Federal Mogul	2024 DR	2022DR	1145M (early), 1235M (late)
Michigan Bearing	233CS	231CS	73CS (early), 950CS (late)

350-ci Bare Block, 4.00-inch Bore
This standard-duty, bare block assembly was used on 1973–1985 Goodwrench 350-ci engines. It has straight, nonsplayed four-bolt mains, 4.00-inch cylinder bores, and two-piece rear main seal. It does not include oil gallery plugs or dowel pins. Next to a good used block, this is your best choice for building a high-performance 302-, 327-, 350-, or 383-ci small-block for street use.

plasma-moly, stainless steel, or chrome rings, but average street or bracket racing engines live quite happily with a standard ring set. For either application, the cylinders should be finished with a 400–500-grit hone and plenty of clean, filtered honing oil. A good shop will leave the block coated with honing oil when they are finished to prevent surface rust from forming. If you're not going to assemble the engine immediately, be sure to check the cylinders periodically and relubricate them if necessary.

Cam Bearings

Installing cam bearings is normally relegated to a machine shop (some shops even offer the service at no charge when they are performing other cleaning and machining operations for you), but you may wish to

350-ci Bow Tie Bare Block *Usable for 302-, 327-, and 350-ci engines, this block features siamesed cylinders that can be bored to 4.090 inches for displacements well over 400-ci. It is the same as cast-iron block PN 10051183 with the exception of straight, nodular-iron four-bolt main caps. Crankshaft diameter is 2.45 inches and it is machined for a one-piece rear seal. It replaces the older PN 366287 block and weighs 212 pounds.*

Bow Tie Sportsman, 400-ci Mains with 4.117-inch Bore *This is a fully CNC machined block from the HD 2.45-inch main; casting number 10051184 is machined for 2.65-inch mains. It includes nodular-iron main caps with four bolts on all five main caps. The outer bolts on the three center mains are splayed out 20 degrees. It offers priority main bearing oiling and a 9.025-inch deck height. Blocks are finished bored at 4.117-inch and can be taken out to 4.150-inch. This block uses a one-piece rear main seal, and the top of the lifter bores might require some clearance if using aftermarket roller lifters.*

tackle the job yourself if you have access to the tools. Machinists install these bearings all the time, so they'll probably get them in correctly, and doing it yourself can be a frustrating experience if you're a first-timer.

Bow Tie Sportsman, 350-ci Mains with 3.98-inch Bore *This is a fully CNC machined block from the HD 2.45-inch main, casting number 10051184. It includes nodular-iron main caps with four bolts on all five main caps. The outer bolts on the three center mains are splayed out 20 degrees. It offers priority main bearing oiling and a 9.025-inch deck height. Blocks are finished bored at 3.980 inch and can be taken out to 4.150 inch. This block uses a two-piece rear main seal and the top of the lifter bores might require some clearance if using aftermarket roller lifters.*

First of all, you can encounter real problems if you aren't aware that the cam bearings come in different sizes. When you put the bearings in the block, they must be installed in 1, 2, 3, 3, 2 sequence. Check the chart in this section to determine which bearing part numbers are intended for specific bearing bores. These numbers are standardized on all blocks since 1957. Earlier blocks use a different bearing set with wider rear (number 5) bearing.

A cam bearing installation tool can be purchased or rented depending on your particular requirements. Install the rear cam bearing first and work your way forward. Before you drive any bearings into place, be certain the impact edge of the bearing has a sufficient chamfer to allow its easy installation in the block and to prevent raising a burr on the bearing surface that can interfere with camshaft rotation. Drive the rear bearing in carefully until it rests just ahead of the rear cam-plug housing. The bearing oil holes and block passages must align on early 1955–1957 blocks, and this is good practice on all engines. The intermediate bearings will fit evenly into their housings and they should not hang out on either side. The front bearing should be driven in until it is even with the inner edge of the chamfer in the front bore. If you damage a bearing during installation, most machine shops will sell you a single replacement.

Cast-Iron Bow Tie Bare Block, 3.875-inch Rough Bore *This is a small-bore version of the heavy-duty cast-iron Bow Tie block. It can be bored and honed from 3.875 inch to a maximum recommended bore diameter of 4.030 inch. This block has two-bolt mains and is machined for a one-piece rear main seal. Extended oil galleries may interfere with some camshaft drive mechanisms so clearance should be checked prior to assembly. A boss below the bellhousing, behind the number eight cylinder, can be drilled and tapped for a lifter-valley oil scavenge line when the engine is equipped with a dry-sump oiling system.*

Cast-Iron Bow Tie Bare Block, 3.98-inch Rough Bore *This is alarge-bore version of Bow Tie block with many added features. Recommended for severe-duty competition, this block can be bored to a maximum size of 4.150 inches. These blocks weigh 181 pounds and are machined to accept late style one-piece rear seal crankshafts. Two-piece seals can be used with adapter PN 10051118.*

Cast-Iron Rocket Block *The Rocket Block was developed by Oldsmobile as a corporate component. It is precision machined to within ±0.001-inch on all dimensions. Extra thick siamesed cylinder walls offer a minimum 0.275-inch cylinder-wall thickness with a 4.125-inch bore. Blocks can be bored to a maximum of 4.155 inch, and still retain standard 4.400-inch bore centerlines. Two deck heights are offered: 9.025-inch standard (PN 22551788) and 9.325-inch tall deck (PN 22551790).*

Cast-Iron Bow Tie Block, 3.750-inch Semifinished Bore *This Bow Tie block is the late version of the PN 101343311, fully blueprinted block designed for professional competition. It features priority main oiling and a maximum bore size is 4.030 inches. It incorporates all of the features of the previous version and even adds to the package with a reduction in weight of about 20 pounds.*

All five mains use 8620 steel main caps. The bores must be finish-honed to remove about 0.007-inch by the engine builder. Designed to accept dry-sump oiling, the rear cap has a provision for an internal oil pump and wet-sump oiling system. This is a two-piece rear seal design.

Core (Freeze) Plugs

Anytime you have an engine completely torn down for a rebuild, it's a good idea to replace all the freeze plugs and the rear cam bearing plug. This is a simple task that is easily accomplished right on the engine stand prior to final assembly. These plugs are reasonably foolproof, but it's possible to get a leaker if you're not careful. A large-diameter socket is ideal for tapping in the plugs. Each plug should be coated with sealer before you install it and it should be carefully driven straight into the block. Take particular care when driving the cam plug because it is thinner and shallower and prone to

Block Preparation Checklist

1. Remove all freeze plugs, oil gallery plugs (including the pressed-in plug located under the rear main cap), drain cocks, cylinder-head dowels, cam bearings, and any miscellaneous bolts.
2. Pressure clean the block to remove dirt and sludge. Some blocks are very grimy, so don't hesitate to have it done twice if necessary.
3. Visually inspect the block for cracks in the cylinder bores, main webs, and lifter bosses. Check closely for indications of prior abuse, including broken main caps and mounting bosses, stripped bolt holes, and cracks in the block surfaces around the lifter gallery.
4. Have the block pressure checked and Magnaflux inspected.
5. Deburr the block, making sure to break all sharp edges and radius all corners.
6. Carefully check all critical block dimensions to ascertain any need for special corrective machining. Write everything down in a notebook.
7. Machine all the areas that are out of spec. Align bore if required.
8. Bore and hone for the correct piston-to-wall clearance. Use torque plate for all high-performance engines.
9. Chase all head bolt and main cap bolt holes. Use a bottoming tap on all blind holes.
10. Only install top-end oil restrictors if the engine will use roller-bearing rocker arms; never restrict oil to conventional ball-and-trunnion rockers.
11. Using the trial assembly method, check the block for adequate crankshaft counterweight and connecting-rod clearance. Grind if required.
12. Steam clean the block at the local car wash after all machining is completed.
13. Lubricate all machined surfaces with light oil to prevent surface rusting.
14. Install new cam bearings and blow out any small chips that may be lodged from the bearings.
15. Install new oil gallery plugs (including the plug under the main cap), rear camshaft plug, and all freeze plugs. Be sure the front oil gallery plugs are adequately staked or replaced with screw-in plugs.
16. Do not store the block in a clean plastic trash bag until it has dried at least three or four hours after washing.

Aluminum Block, 3.986 Semifinished Bore The bare aluminum block weighs only 146 pounds and is cast from A-356 aluminum that has been heat treated to T6 specifications. Main bearing diameter is 2.45 inches, and wall thickness has been increased for added strength. The 0.620-inch thick deck surfaces have blind-tapped head bolt holes to improve sealing. Cylinder sleeves are semifinished at 3.986 inches and will finish at 4.150 inch. 8620 steel main bearing caps on all locations will clear standard oil pans, and the block is configured for the early two-piece rear seal. These blocks are designed for wet-sump oiling, but can be converted to dry sump by plugging the hole in the rear main cap.

leaking if it's distorted. Wipe off the excess sealer around each plug, but try to leave a nice bead to help give a good seal. Do not drive plugs in too far or they will fall into the water jackets. They should only be driven in until flush with the block surface. Most applications will make use of cup plugs in either steel or brass that may last longer when corrosion problems are anticipated. You'll also find specialty bolt-in plugs that have rubber seals, but they are not significantly better than a standard plug (and the rubber may deteriorate). They are, however, easier to replace when the engine is in the car, and this may be something to consider.

Final Block Prep

Once the block has been decked, the edges of the deck surfaces should be deburred and a chamfer should be cut at the top of each of the head-bolt holes. (This prevents the top threads from contacting the head surface when the bolts are torqued.) Wash the

Tall-Deck Aluminum Block *This tall-deck block has a 9.525-inch deck height. It can be bored to 4.160 inches and stroked to 4.250 inches with major modifications. The deck surface is 1.125 inches, and it can be machined as low as 9.00 inch. Bores start at 4.119 inch. The camshaft is raised 0.391 inch and the pan rails are spread 0.400 inch per side to accommodate large strokes. This a four-bolt main block with splayed center caps and a 400-style two-piece rear main seal (Fel Pro PN 2909). It's a dry-sump design with no provision for an internal oil pump. The oil filter boss is removed so the starter can be mounted on either side.*

blow the block dry immediately. Even before the cylinders are dry, apply a thin film of lubricant to protect them. Lightweight engine oil, automatic transmission fluid, or WD-40 are good choices.

Cylinder block preparation is as vital as any other step in high-performance engine building. It can make a vast difference in performance, one way or the other. Before you begin final assembly of your engine, check off the items on our block prep checklist. And you may wish to refer to the S-A Design book *How To Rebuild The Small-Block Chevrolet* for complete step-by-step engine prep and assembly instructions.

Factory Block Choices

Chevrolet has implemented many cylinder block revisions, with the end result being a full lineup of specialized Bow Tie blocks designed to meet the specific needs of a broad range of racing and high-performance applications. Following is a current list of Chevrolet high-performance block features and availability.

block down with clean solvent and scrub it thoroughly with *warm* water and laundry detergent (warm water promotes less rust than hot water but still cleans effectively). Scrub brushes and a rifle-bore cleaning kit are entirely permissible for this operation and you should wield them with a vengeance. Plan on getting yourself good and wet and try to use a source of pressurized warm water. One of the most convenient methods of cleaning a block is to cart it down to your local self-service car wash and have at it with a handful of quarters. In any event, be sure to have plenty of clean lint-free towels for drying the machined surfaces. If at all possible, take along a small air tank so you can

Aluminum Block, 4.117-inch Semifinished Bore *Same as PN 10185075, except with larger bore and 2.65-inch (400-ci) main bearings.*

CRANKSHAFTS

Crank Identification

All small-block Chevrolet crankshafts are made from two basic materials. Prior to 1963 all cranks were made from forged steel alloys, but nodular iron has long since become the standard crankshaft material. Forged cranks are generally preferred for performance work, but for most street engines the use of a forged crank is purely a luxury. Nodular iron is a very stable material that provides good service in any street or bracket-racing engine. It has the ability to flex under load and withstand considerably more punishment than you might expect.

In 1967, the factory began making available forged cranks with a special surface-hardening treatment called Tufftriding. Tufftriding is a chemical hardening process that imparts a very tough surface to the bearing journals. It does offer a significant decrease in friction, but again, it isn't really necessary in a performance street engine. The best advice we can give you is not to search for a Tufftrided, forged crank unless you are putting together a very serious engine.

Crankshaft science has progressed significantly, and you really can't go wrong with a well-prepped factory

It's not difficult to tell a forged crank from a cast crank if you know what to look for. A cast crank will have a thin parting line down the front of the first throw, while a forged crank will have a wide forging mark (finger).

crank or on any of the top aftermarket brands. Stock cranks were available in stroke lengths of 3.00, 3.25, 3.48, 3.80, 3.75, and 3.10 inches, the latter two being offered only in nodular iron. These cranks are not all interchangeable. Some of the cranks have main-bearing journals and/or rod-bearing journals of unique size to accommodate special engineering requirements. Currently, there are three different main-bearing diameters and two different rod-bearing diameters. The vast majority of available cranks have the current "standard" main and rod journals, but the

small-block builder must be aware of the many combinations to ensure his combination is correct.

The 3.00- and 3.25-inch cranks are the only ones available with small main-bearing journals, although some later versions were also made with large main and rod journals. The 3.10-, 3.80-, and 3.48-inch cranks are only available with the now-standard large main-journal size. The 3.75-inch crank uses a totally unique, even larger, main-journal size. The small main-journal 3.00- and 3.25-inch cranks also had small-diameter rod journals, while all the rest, including the 3.75-inch

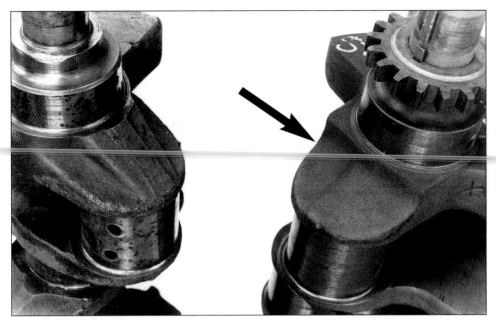

Large-journal steel cranks in the 350- and 327-ci configuration are not always easy to find, but if you happen to spot some, there's an easy way to tell them apart. The rare 327-ci crank has a large dip or notch (arrow) in the front arm. The steel 350 crank has no notch.

crank, have the now-standard large rod journals.

As a point of reference, a small-journal crank has 2.30-inch mains and 2.00-inch rods, a large-journal crank features 2.45-inch mains and 2.10-inch rods, and the 3.75-inch crank (400 ci) has 2.65-inch mains and 2.10-inch rods. There are also early 3.00-inch stroke cranks available with large journals (1968–1969 302-ci Z28), and 3.25-inch cranks with large journals (1968–1969 327-ci and 1968–1973 307-ci).

Small-journal, 3.00-inch stroke cranks all have round counterweights, relative to the crank centerline. The Tufftrided, 3.00-inch, large-journal 302 cranks have the fan-shaped counterweights, similar to late 327- and 350-ci cranks. Cranks manufactured prior to 1968 all had a round flywheel flange, while those made in 1968 and later had irregularly shaped, counterweighted flywheel flanges.

There are some cast 3.00-inch cranks around, and they are usually found in 1966 and 1967 283-ci engines and a few late 1965 283-ci engines. Forged 3.00-inch cranks were still made during this period, but most of them were used in truck motors. The cast 283 cranks should only be used in 1962 and later engine blocks, because the front counterweights interfere with the front main bearing webs.

Rod length is consistent in all engines except the 400 (3.75-inch stroke). Therefore, stroke changes must be accompanied by piston compression-height changes. Piston compression height must always be matched to the stroke of the crankshaft, except in the unique 400, where a shorter connecting rod compensates for the increase in stroke. All 400-ci pistons have the same compression height as

All production cranks from 1955 to 1985 have a 3.58-inch diameter flywheel bolt pattern on the flange. In 1986 however, the flange bolt pattern diameter was reduced to 3.00 inches to facilitate the use of a one-piece rear seal (left). This pattern is easily seen in the accompanying flexplate photos. The flywheel bolt pattern on the late-model flexplate (left) is clearly smaller in diameter and tighter than that on the early model unit (right) with a larger bolt pattern.

Since 1986, all production small-blocks have used a one-piece rear main seal that mounts in an aluminum adapter bolted to the rear of the block as shown here. Late crankshafts were redesigned for the one-piece seal and incorporate a large round flange. Late-model cranks are not compatible with early blocks. However, GM crankshaft seal adapter P/N 10051118 permits the installation of early-style two-piece rear seal cranks into blocks machined for the late-style one-piece rear seal.

Mic the crank journals to make sure they will finish grind to no smaller than 0.030-inch undersize. If the journals are already 0.030-inch undersize or greater, you may not find bearings suitable for performance work. Most bearings for 0.040 or 0.060-inch undersize journals are not designed for performance work and should be avoided. Find another crank.

If you will be using a manual transmission, make sure the crank has been drilled to accept a pilot bushing.

350-ci pistons, which allow the 350 internals to be installed in a 400 block rather easily. The late model 383 crank is a 4340 steel crank with a 3.80-inch stroke. It has a one-piece rear seal.

Having covered the basics of small-block crankshaft identification, we can now look at some of the less noticeable differences that set them apart. To begin with, there is absolutely no difficulty in identifying a forged crank from a cast crank. You don't have to worry about casting numbers or plink-

ing cranks with a hammer. On all cast cranks, the flashing marks are readily distinguished as a thin seam along the edges of the counterweights. It is most noticeable on the front arm of the crank. Forged cranks have a wide flat rib on the front arm. The flashing along the edges of the counterweights is ground off, so they also have a very smooth, even surface compared to the rough, grainy surface of a cast crank.

You can also look for specific clues and use the process of elimination.

Remember that there are no large-journal, 3.00-inch stroke cast cranks; no 3.25-inch stroke, small-journal cast cranks; and no small-journal 3.48-inch cranks, forged or otherwise. All 3.75-inch cranks are cast, as are the 3.10-inch cranks. All 3.80-inch cranks are forged. If you have a 3.00-inch crank without notches in the full round flywheel flange, it is one of the original 283 forgings. A round flywheel flange with two balancing notches indicates an early 327 crank

Basic Crankshaft Specifications

Prior to 1963, all small-block cranks were made from forged steel alloys, but nodular iron is now the standard material for production engines. GM currently offers several forged crankshafts for performance applications, as well as unmachined forgings that can be finished to builder's specifications.

Crankshaft Specs (in inches)

Stroke	Main Journal Diameter	Rod Journal Diameter	Engine	Year Installed
3.100	2.450	2.100	262 ci	1975-'76
3.000	2.300	2.000	265 ci	1955-'56
3.484	2.450	2.100	267 ci	1979-'81
3.000	2.300	2.000	283 ci	1957-'67
3.000	2.300	2.000	302 ci	1967
3.000	2.450	2.100	302 ci	1968-'69
3.484	2.450	2.100	305 ci	1976-'94
3.250	2.450	2.100	307 ci	1968-'73
3.250	2.300	2.000	327 ci	1962-'67
3.250	2.450	2.100	327 ci	1968-'69
3.484	2.450	2.100	350 ci	1967-'94
3.750	2.650	2.100	400 ci	1970-'72
3.750	2.650	2.100	400 ci	1973-'80

Current Factory Crankshaft

Except as noted, all crankshafts are forged & nitride-treated and are designed for the early, 2-piece seal.

3951527	3.75-inch stroke (400), cast nodular iron, non-nitrided
14088527	3.48-inch stroke, cast nodular iron, non-nitrided, 1-piece rear seal (installed in 350 SP engine)
3941180	3.48-inch stroke, 1053 steel, non-nitrided, 2-piece rear seal
3941184	3.48-inch stroke, 1053 steel, nitrided, 2-piece rear seal
14096036	3.48-inch stroke, 1053 steel, 1-piece rear seal, 350 HO, non-nitrided, requires counterweighted fly wheel for proper engine balance (used in the ZZ3, 350 HO engine)

Raw Unmachined Forgings

10185100	3.46-3.50-inch stroke, for 2.100 rod journals, S38 micro alloy steel, 2-piece rear seal
10051168	3.20-4.00-inch stroke, vacuum degassed 4340 steel, non-twist forging, can be ground to 400 main size, large circular counterweights, no machining pads, lightened rod pin arms
24502460	Same as 10051168 except with larger crank snout that can be machined for big-block damper size

(3.25-inch), which is further distinguished by a wide front arm and flattened counterweights to clear the pistons. A 3.00-inch, 302 crank will have a round flange with a single balancing notch, and a narrow front pin arm. The counterweights are also round and not flattened, since piston clearance is not required with the 3.00-inch stroke.

Inspection and Prep

Once you have located several choices that will serve your purpose, a careful inspection is in order to determine the best of the bunch. The final criterion for crankshaft suitability is an absence of cracks. This should only be determined by a thorough Magnaflux inspection. Most cracks occur

Magnafluxing is another essential step in crank inspection. This procedure locates tiny fatigue cracks and is cheap insurance against premature engine failure.

in the radius where the rod journal joins the throw, and they are sometimes difficult to pinpoint. If the crank is intended for street use and the crack is small, it can sometimes be removed when the crank is reground. This is a determination you will have to make in collaboration with your crank grinder.

In any instance, there are several checks you can make prior to Magnafluxing to determine the suitability for your particular application. The bearing journals should all be carefully mic'ed to ascertain their present size. Each journal should be examined for evidence of excessive wear or discolored surfaces, which would indicate metal-to-metal contact. If any of the journals are badly nicked or peppered, move on to another crank. Check each journal radius fillet for obvious signs of damage. The nose and keyway section should be relatively free of damage, although minor damage is usually repairable. Inspect the thrust surfaces of the rear main journal for damage or excess wear and determine if the crank will accept a pilot bushing. Some early cranks produced for use with Powerglide-equipped cars were not drilled for pilot bushings. If the crank survives these preliminary checks and you find it free of cracks, it will usually provide excellent service with only minimal preparation.

Prior to finish-grinding the crank, there are a number of steps you can take to ensure its integrity. Regardless of the intended use, have it hot tanked to remove grit and grime. Then attack the oil holes with a small wire brush. Rifle-bore kits have the right kind of brushes, but similar brushes are also available over-the-counter from reputable speed shops or machine-shop suppliers. Use a medium file or heavy grit paper to carefully deburr the counterweights and be sure to break the

Prior to final assembly, the crankshaft should receive a thorough cleaning, including a vigorous attack of all the oil holes with a small cleaning brush.

edges of any holes that are not on the journals. The oil holes on each journal should receive a very slight chamfer; nothing big, just chamfer the edges approximately 0.030- to .060-inch. Don't grind a giant trough around the hole. All you're doing is reducing the load-carrying surface and wasting your time.

For street use, it is perfectly acceptable to cut a crank undersize as long as the shop maintains an adequate radius on each journal. Undersized bearings provide excellent service in thousands of street and bracket racing engines. Problems are rare if the crankshaft grinder is reputable. Sure, top engine builders check every clearance fifteen times, but thousands more competent assemblers just install 'em and run 'em—and they live. If you're not building an all-out racing engine and you can trust your crank grinder, it will save a lot of time.

There are two things you never do to a small-block engine, regardless of its application. If your machinist suggests grooving the crank journals, find another machinist. The same goes for grooved bearings. Never use fully grooved bearings in a small-block engine. The correct bearings are only

Oil supply holes on the rod and main journals should be lightly chamfered to promote good oil distribution to the bearings. Don't get crazy, just open up the edges approximately 0.030 to 0.060 inch.

grooved on the upper half. The lower half carries an incredible load and there's no sense in reducing the amount of load-carrying surface. Cross drilling is an acceptable practice, but it's old technology. Keep in mind how many millions of small-blocks provide heavy-duty service every day with perfectly stock oiling systems.

Identifying Nodular-Iron Crankshafts

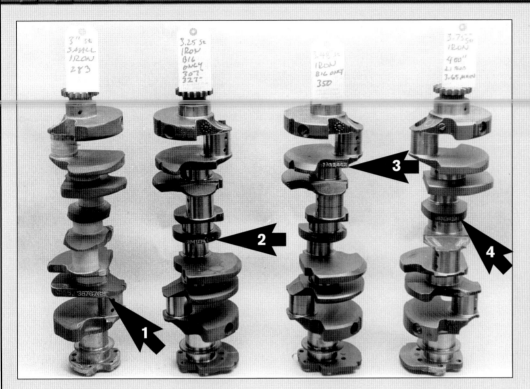

One of the easiest ways to identify iron castings is through the location of the casting number. There may be some exceptions to these generalities, but the number on the 3-inch crank is on the front arm of the rear rod throw (arrow 1). The 3.25-inch crank has the number on the front arm of the number three throw (arrow 2). The 3.48-inch crank has the number on the rear arm of the front throw (arrow 3), and the 3.75-inch crank has the number on the rear arm of the number two throw (arrow 4).

Beginning at the left, we have a comparison of 3.00-, 3.25-, 3.48-, and 3.75-inch stroke cast-iron cranks. The 3-inch small-journal crank (arrow 1) has a narrow front arm and a full-circle flywheel flange. The 3.25-inch cast-iron crank (arrow 2) is available only in a large-journal configuration. The front arm is much wider than the 3-inch crank. Note the thin casting seam that readily identifies all cast-iron cranks. The 3.48-inch cast-iron crank (arrow 3) is available only with large journals. It is difficult to tell the 3.48-inch crank apart from the 3.25-inch cast cranks, but the

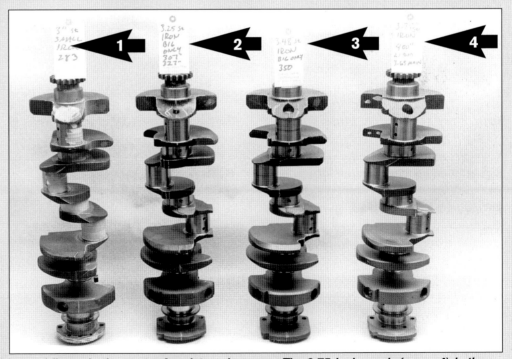

counterweights are generally wider and flatter in the center for piston clearance. The 3.75-inch crank (arrow 4) is the only long-stroke crank available. It has unique 2.65-inch mains, a slightly wider front arm, and a larger flywheel flange.

Identifying Large-Journal Crankshafts

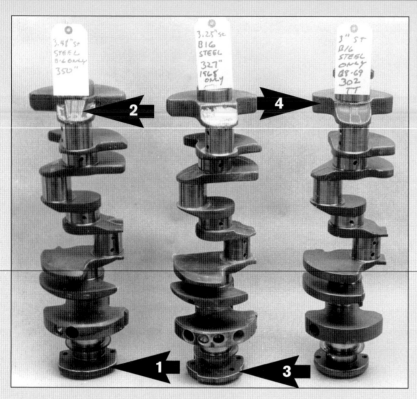

From left to right we have a comparison of the 3.48-, 3.25-, and 3.00-inch steel forgings, all with 2.45-inch main journals. The easiest way to identify these cranks is through an inspection of the flywheel flange counterweight. The 3.48-inch crank (arrow 1) has a large, square-shaped weight. Note that on the 3.48- and 3.25-inch cranks, some of the counterweight edges are tapered for piston clearance. The 3.48-inch crank (arrow 2) has a distinctive rib forged into the front rod-throw arm. The rear flange counterweight on the 3.25-inch crank is circular (arrow 3), but there is definitely some extra material added, compared to the completely round 3.00-inch crank flange. The front arm of the 3.25-inch crank does not normally have a rib and it is has a squared-off face. The 3.00-inch crank (arrow 4) is very easy to spot. There are some forging marks on the front arm, but no rib; the weights all have square edges and the flywheel flange is round.

A back side view of the large-journal cranks shows that these forgings are very similar. Again we can see that the flywheel flange is the easiest variation to spot. The counterweight/throw arms of the 3.48-inch crank are wider and stronger, as can be seen on the rear arm of the number four throw. (arrow 1) On the forward arm of the number-four throw you can see the wide forging line that easily identifies all forged cranks. The 3.48-inch steel crank is available only with 2.45-inch mains. The 3.25-inch steel crank (arrow 2) was available only in 327-ci engines in 1968. The Tufftrided 3.00-inch large journal crank (arrow 3) was available only in the 302-ci Z28 engines in 1968–1969.

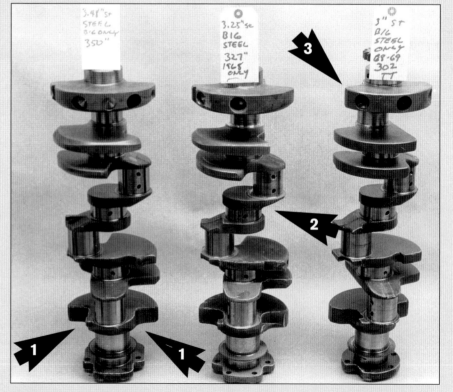

Balancing

In the great majority of engine rebuilds it is advisable to have the operating components rebalanced to ensure smooth operation and longevity. Critical balancing is helpful in a high-performance engine, but the greatest benefits are derived from achieving a smoother, longer-lasting engine. If you are rebuilding your street engine and you've changed pistons, you should get the machinist to weigh your old pistons and pins to determine the difference between them and your new ones. Even when the new piston is an exact duplicate, it should be checked. Sometimes a forged replacement piston will be slightly lighter than the cast piston it replaces because of the absence of the thermal expansion struts. In these cases, you may find that the manufacturer has tried to keep the weight constant by using a heavier wrist pin. This is a noticeable difference in some of the TRW 400-ci replacement pistons.

From a racing standpoint, balancing takes on a different character. Naturally, the lightest overall reciprocating weight (e.g., the weight of the rods, pistons, rings, etc.) is desirable, but this must be tempered by strength and reliability requirements. Balancing reciprocating weight is extremely important, because it minimizes rod, crank, and bearing stress. The rotating weight of the crankshaft transfers load across the main saddles to each end of the crankshaft, where the flywheel and the balancer help control crankshaft pulses. Many engine builders feel that overbalancing the entire assembly is an important step. Overbalancing is adding one to two percent extra bob weight during the balancing process. It is thought that this helps smooth out a high-RPM engine. Balancing is an important step, and you should always consider it for a high-performance engine.

Straightening a crankshaft is a simple process. Pressure is applied to the crank to bend it in the right direction. Fix it in place with a hammer blow. This procedure does not shorten crankshaft life, but it has become relatively unnecessary with the broad availability of inexpensive aftermarket cranks.

You should also check the stroke and straightness of your crank prior to balancing the internal engine assembly. Most cranks will not require straightening, but when you do run across a bent crank, it will usually be off by quite a bit. To determine the condition of your crank, mock it up in the block with the front and rear bearings installed and lightly lubed. Torque the main caps to the correct spec and then arrange a dial indicator so it can read off the center main bearing journal. Make certain the journal is free of oil and debris and then slowly rotate the crank while observing the dial indicator. The crank should be straightened if it has more than 0.003-inch of run-out. This is a relatively simple procedure that can be handled by most competent crank grinding shops. You should make certain they don't try to straighten it in a hydraulic press. A knowledgeable crank man will use a large hammer to straighten a crank.

For street applications, you can install the crank just as you would for final assembly, with all the bearings in place and the main caps torqued (leave out the rear main seal for this check). Then try spinning the crank by hand. If you're able to easily spin the crank by hand, it will work just fine on the street.

Many racers prefer to have their cranks checked for perfect throw indexing, but in most cases this is an unnecessary step. The idea is to make certain that each crank throw is exactly 90 degrees from the next and that they are all in the proper relationship to the keyway on the crankshaft snout. More importantly, you should make sure the stroke lengths are equal. Sometimes a crank can be straight and properly indexed, but some of the throws will actually be slightly longer or shorter. This is an important determination to make before the crank is ground and balanced.

Identifying High-Performance Steel Crankshafts

These are the most common short-stroke, small-block steel cranks. This comparison shows the relative strength and bulk of the small-journal 3.25-inch cranks (arrows 2 and 3) compared to the large-journal 3.25-inch crank (arrow 1) and the large-journal 3.00-inch crank (arrow 4). The small-journal 3.25-inch crank is the heaviest steel small-block crank made by Chevrolet. A careful examination shows that the counterweights and rod throw arms are sturdier than the other examples. We have shown two of the 3.25-inch cranks to illustrate the difference in the front rod throw arm; some are drilled (arrow 2), some are not (arrow 3). Either is suitable for any application.

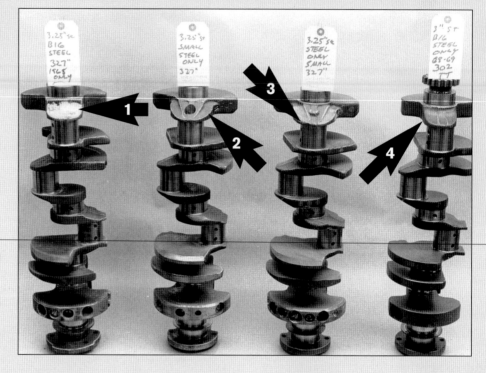

A backside view of the large-journal 3.00-(arrow 3) and 3.25-inch (arrow 1) cranks compared to the small-journal 3.25-inch (arrow 2) crank again illustrates the relative strength of the small-journal crank (arrow 4). Note in particular that the rear portion of the small-journal crank is much heavier than either of the other examples. The rear counterweight arm of the front throw (arrow 5) is not relieved as is the large-journal crank (arrow 6). The 3.00-inch crank on the right has been turned slightly to show the forging number on the front arm, another way of identifying this crank.

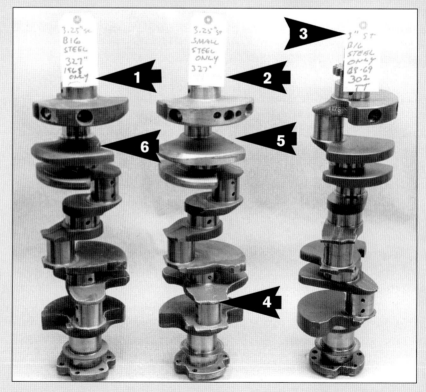

Identifying 3-inch Steel Crankshafts

The 3.00-inch steel cranks are the most difficult to tell apart. These photos indicate the notable visual differences. The old 283-ci small-journal, 3.00-inch crank (arrow 1) is one of the lightest cranks. It is the only one with a completely round flywheel flange. The later small-journal forging used in the 1967 302-ci Z28 engines has a notch in the flywheel flange (arrow 3) and is otherwise identical to the early crank except for some minor variations in the shape of the counterweights. The large-journal 3.00-inch steel crank from the 1968–1969 302 also has a notch in the flywheel flange, but note that the counterweight on the rear arm of the front throw (arrow 4) has straight sides, and the square chucking pads for factory machining remain.

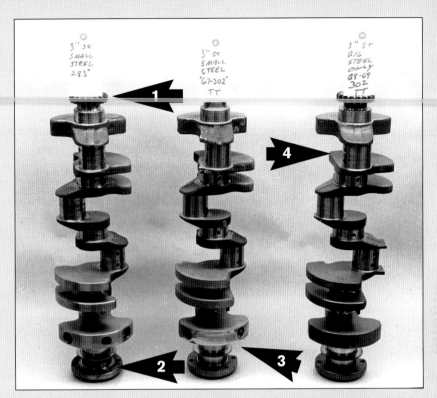

This view of the 3.00-inch cranks shows the distinguishing notch ground in the flywheel flange on the late steel cranks. The forward sections of these cranks are virtually identical. Balancing notches and drilled holes will vary according to the individual forging requirements. Major differences are found in the rear sections. The forward arm of the number three throws on the small-journal cranks (arrows 1) are rounded, while this arm on the large-journal crank (arrow 2) is square.

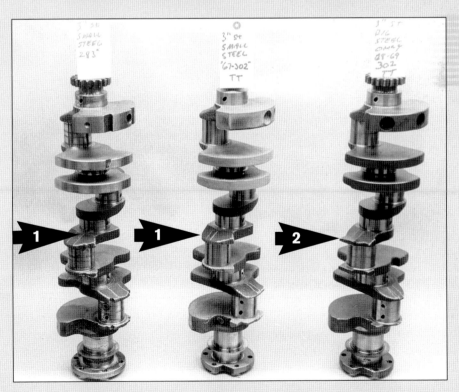

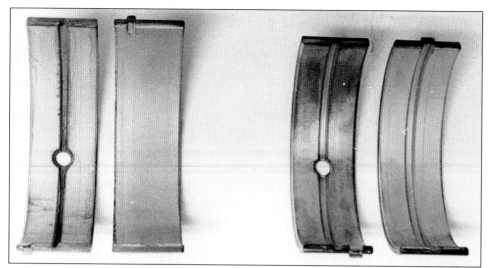

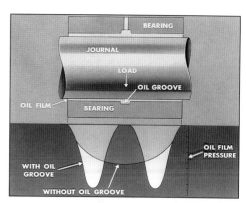

As illustrated in the previous pressure diagram, never use fully grooved bearings as shown on the right. Good high-performance bearings (left) will only be grooved on the top half, leaving the full width of the lower bearing to maintain oil film and minimize oil-film pressure.

It's common practice to use grooved bearing shells in the block but ungrooved bearings in the caps. This practice improves bearing life by reducing oil film pressure in the cap bearings. The original research was done by GM years ago and is illustrated in this diagram. Note that when the lower bearing is grooved, the oil film pressure is almost twice as high and much more likely to permit metal-to-metal contact.

Grooved main bearing shells are installed in the block. Main caps receive the ungrooved half to ensure long bearing life.

Bearings

The type of bearings you use in your engine should complement the intended use. Since bearings are designed with various characteristics according to application, it's important to use the right ones. All engine bearings have different degrees of fatigue strength, corrosion resistance, and surface behavior built into them. You need to determine which of these criteria is most important to your application and select bearings on this basis. A high-performance street engine needs a high-strength bearing with corrosion resistance and surface behavior a secondary consideration. Speed Pro, TRW CL-77, and GM Moraine 400 bearings all share this characteristic. They do, however, require frequent oil changes since they have poor embedability, and the crankshaft can be easily scored by foreign particles.

In a strictly drag race application, corrosion resistance and fatigue strength are less important because of the short duration of severe service. The most important considerations are embedability and conformability under stress. Moraine 400 bearings are a good choice here, but Speed Pro bearings are even better. With clean oil under adequate pressure, bearings should appear nearly new, even after severe or extended use. It's all in using the right bearing, the right oil, and proper clearance.

For street use, small-block bearing clearances should be kept absolutely stock. Chevrolet spent a bundle working out the ideal clearances, and who are we to argue with their obvious success? For high-performance and drag

Plastigauge is a common and surprisingly accurate method of checking bearing clearances when you don't have proper measuring equipment.

Rod and Main Bearing Clearances

Many racing mechanics apply the tried-and-true rule of using 0.001 inch for each 1 inch of shaft diameter as the minimum operating clearance. Multiply this amount by 1.5 to determine maximum bearing clearance.

Engine Application	Rod Bearing Clearance (inches)	Main Bearing Clearance (inches)
Stock Street	.0017 – .003	.002 – .0035
High-Performance Street	.002 – .003	.0025 – .0037
High-RPM Racing	.0025 – .0035	.0032 – .004

strip use, clearance adjustments are necessary. Many engine builders do not distinguish between large- and small-journal engines when setting clearances, but there are significant differences. The main difference is that small-journal cranks generally require slightly more clearance, because they tend to "whip" or flex more than a large-journal crank.

You'll never be far off if you set them up with main-bearing clearances between 0.003 and 0.0035 inch. Optimum rod-bearing clearances should be kept between 0.0022 and 0.003 inch. Large-journal cranks are more stable, so you can generally tighten up the clearances 0.0005 inch. Understand that these clearances are preferred, but you don't have to hit them right on the money. If you're within 0.0005 inch either way, you're in good shape. Just remember to give the small journals a tad more room to allow for increased flex.

It's highly unusual to experience bearing problems in a small-block Chevy. If you have trouble, retrace your steps and more often than not, you'll uncover the problem. Remember also that bearing life is contingent on well-prepared, round crank journals and round, well-aligned bearing bores. More often than not, clearances

All small-blocks take crankshaft thrust on the number-five rear-main bearing. It receives direct pressure oiling and rarely causes problems. Thrust clearance should be maintained between 0.005 and 0.007 inch. Before checking the clearance, set the crank by driving it forward and backward with several raps from a brass hammer or a regular hammer cushioned by a small block of wood. Then set a dial indicator to read fore and aft movement at the front of the crank. To simulate crank thrust, pry it back and forth with a large screwdriver. Small-journal cranks require slightly more clearance than large-journal cranks because they tend to whip more. Clearances should be checked vertically in the bearing bore: 0.0025 to 0.003 inch for large journals, 0.003 to 0.0035 inch for small journals. If the thrust clearance on the rear main bearing is too small, increase it by installing the bearing halves in the rear main cap and sanding them against fine wet-dry paper on a surface plate.

Crankshaft Prep Checklist

1. Visually inspect thrust surface and crank journals for obvious signs of damage, excessive wear, or pilot bearing bore not drilled (needed for stick-shift applications).
2. Inspect front keyways for loose or damaged slots.
3. Magnaflux to locate cracks.
4. Pressure wash and thoroughly clean oil holes with small brushes and solvent.
5. Cross-drill main journals if desired.
6. Deburr rod throws and counterweights.
7. Shot-peen if desired.
8. Grind and micropolish crank and rod journals for proper clearance and correct index.
9. Balance for chosen components. If heavy metal is needed for balancing, always install slugs parallel to crank centerline so centrifugal force will not work metal loose.
10. Only use neutral balance flywheels for stick-shift racing applications.
11. Install new pilot bushing if required.
12. After thorough cleaning, lubricate the crank with light oil (e.g., WD-40) and store in a plastic bag.

Here are two 1053 forged-steel cranks from GM. Both are 3.48-inch stroke and have 2.100-inch large rod journals. The crank with the large round rear flange (left) can only be used in late-model blocks with a one-piece seal. The other crank with the squared-off rear flange (right) is designed for early blocks with a two-piece rear seal. However, it can be used in late blocks when they are equipped with PN 10051118 adapter, the PN 10121044 two-piece seal, the PN 12337823 retainer gasket, the PN 9441003 dowel pin, and a 1986 or later oil pan.

will be the last thing to cause problems. Whenever you're not sure about something, think stock, and 9 times out of 10 it will work just fine.

High-Performance Chevy Crankshafts

350 Forged Steel Crankshaft, PN 3941184
This 1053 steel crank has been nitrided to increase journal hardness; it carries

forging ID number 1182. It is still a two-piece rear seal crank.

350 Cast-Iron Crankshaft, PN 14088527
This crank is used in the 300- and 330-hp 350-ci special performance service engines with identification code "SP." It requires a one-piece rear seal or a two-piece rear seal adapter.

350 Forged Steel Crankshaft, PN 14096036
A 1053 steel crank used in 1986 and later 350 engines. It has a 3.48-inch stroke and 2.10-inch rod journals and requires a one-piece rear seal. This crank is used in the ZZ3 engine assembly.

Crankshaft Forging, PN 10185100
This is the same raw forging used to make crankshaft PN 3941184, except it is forged from S38 micro alloy steel. It can be machined for a 3.46- to 3.50-inch stroke.

Crankshaft Forging, PN 24502460
This unmachined crankshaft gives engine builders the ability to customize their stroke to work in a particular class or build up. It has a large front section for machining to big-block or small-block balancer size, and it will accommodate finished strokes from 3.20 to 4.00 inches. The 2.900-inch diameter main bearing journals can be ground to fit 400-ci small-block main bearings. This crank is forged from vacuum-degassed 4340 steel, which provides exceptional strength and durability. This is a "nontwist" forging, meaning all rod throws are forged in place. The large, circular counterweights are engineered to minimize bearing loads. The rod pin arms are lightened, and the machining pads found in production cranks are eliminated.

Crankshaft Seal Adapter, PN 10051118
This adapter permits the use of early style two-piece rear seal crankshafts

Torsional Balancers and Accessories

All dampers listed in the chart are eight-inch diameter, except as noted. Pre-1969 timing marks are 2 degrees advanced relative to the keyway centerline—late timing marks are 10 degrees advanced.

Factory Torsional Balancers

6272221	6.75-inch cast iron damper used on most '69 and later production 305/350 engines with late timing mark
3817173	1963 and later high-performance damper, 1-11/16-inch thick. Also used on 1967-68 302s and 327s with early timing mark
6272224	1970-74 LT-1, Z/28 & L-82 with late timing mark, 1-11/16-inch thick
3947708	1969 Z-28, large journal 302ci, with late timing mark, 1-5/16-inch thick
364709	Malleable iron, recommended for competition classes where stock balancers are permitted, late timing mark, outer ring marked "MALL"
6272225	Stock balancer for 400 engine, used with externally balanced engines with 400 crankshaft

GM/Fluidampr

12341632	6.25-inch, 7.9 lbs., neutrally balanced, do not use with external balance applications, degreed from zero to 50°
10051170	7.25-inch, 13.9 lbs., neutrally balanced, do not use with external balance applications, degreed from zero to 50°

Timing Covers & Accessories

12342088	Chrome plated timing cover with Bow Tie emblem, all applications
12341904	Chrome timing cover pointer for use with 12342088 cover with 6.75-inch late timing mark dampers
12341915	Chrome timing cover pointer for use with 12342088 cover with 8-inch late timing mark dampers
3923290	Timing cover for 8-inch balancers with early timing mark
3991433	Timing cover for 8-inch balancers with late timing marks
3991436	Bolt-on timing tab for using 1969 and later, 8-inch balancer on any engine with any timing cover (stock timing tab removed)

in late model one-piece real seal type blocks. It's also used for installing a heavy-duty crankshaft in a Bow Tie block machined for a one-piece rear seal. It includes a two-piece aluminum seal retainer and related hardware, but does not include a gasket or two-piece seal.

Harmonic Balancers

All street and bracket racing engines should be operated with a good harmonic balancer. Without one, the crankshaft will surely crack. For a low-output, small-inch small-block, the stock 283 balancer PN 3861970 works well. Never use it on a larger engine that will be revved to high RPM. The 302/327 high-performance balancer (PN 3817173) is a good choice for any engine. These large, eight-inch balancers are the best ones to use, and there are several of them. In 1969, there was a slight change in the position of the timing mark, so you should use one that matches your engine, unless you are planning to make up your own timing marker. Use damper PN 3947708 for the 1969–1975 engines. A special damper with a nodular-iron outer ring is offered for engines that will operate continuously at high RPM. It is offered as PN 364709, and Chevrolet recommends the outer inertia ring be pinned to the inner casting to prevent it from working forward or backward. All 400-ci engines are externally balanced with special balancers and flywheels. When building a 400-based engine, you have to use the special 400 balancer, PN 6272225. The 400 also uses a specially balanced flexplate, which is available as PN 340298.

Harmonic balancers should be pulled onto the crankshaft with the proper installation tool; never beat one onto the crank with a hammer. Most cranks made after 1967 had the nose drilled to accept a large balancer retention bolt. Early cranks do not have this feature, but it is a simple job for a competent shop to drill the crank snout. If

Raw forging P/N 10051168 is the current factory choice for machining high-performance cranks with stroke lengths from 3.20 to 4.00 inch.

Most 1969 and later balancers have the timing mark 10 degrees advanced from the keyway centerline; the timing mark on earlier balancers was only 2 degrees advanced. To avoid any possible mismatches and timing errors, always check the accuracy of the timing indicator with a piston stop tool during preassembly fitting.

The harmonic balancer is a precision part of the engine and it should be carefully installed. Beating it on with a large hammer is not the answer. Commercially available installation tools screw into the front of the crank and let you pull the balancer gently onto the crank snout.

you're serious about keeping your engine together, bolt the balancer on; it can and will come off if you rely on the press fit. Never use a balancer where the rubber mating surface between the hub and the outer ring is damaged. Treat the balancer as if it were another precision part of the engine—it is!

Note: Many of the part numbers listed here are out of production. They are provided as a reference for restoration efforts. Consult the GM Performance Parts catalog for current production damper availability.

6.75-inch Torsional Damper, PN 6272221

Used on most late 1969 and later production 305 and 350 small-blocks. Recommended for V-6 90-degree engines and V-8s with limited clearance. The timing mark is 10 degrees before the keyway centerline. Use with chrome timing pointer PN 12341904.

8-inch Torsional Damper, PN 3817173

Originally used on high-performance 302s and 327s produced from 1962 to 1968. The cast inertia ring is 1¹¹⁄₁₆ inches wide, and the timing mark is 2 degrees before the keyway centerline. The damper ID number is 7173 and it has the pre-1969 timing mark, so don't use it with chrome timing pointer PN 12341904 unless you adjust the top dead center (TDC) mark.

8-inch Torsional Damper, PN 3947708

1969 302 Z28 damper. Features the 1969 and later timing mark location with a 1⁵⁄₁₆-inch-wide inertia ring and the timing mark located 2 degrees before the keyway centerline. Damper ID number is 7708, and it can be used with the chromed pointer.

8-inch Torsional Damper, PN 6272224

1970–1974 350, Z28 and L-82 damper. A cast-iron balancer with a 1¹¹⁄₁₆-inch-wide inertia ring and 1969 and later timing mark. Damper ID is 2224. Use with chrome timing pointer PN 12341904.

8-inch Torsional Damper, 400 small-block, PN 6272225

Counterweighted balancer requires corresponding counterweighted flywheel for 400-cubic-inch engine or proper balance on 383 small-blocks. The timing mark is 10 degrees before keyway centerline, and it can be used with chrome timing pointer PN 12341904.

Heavy-Duty 8-inch Torsional Damper, PN 364709

Off-highway damper for competition use where production dampers are permitted. Features a nodular iron inertia ring and high temperature rubber for durability. The hub is balanced separately before the unit is balanced together. The heavy-duty damper carries ID number 4709 and the outer ring is marked "MALL" 0. The timing mark is 10 degrees before the keyway centerline, and it can be used with chrome timing pointer PN 12341904.

High-performance applications will want to use GM torsional damper PN 24502535. It's tuned for 9,000-rpm usage, comes fully degreed for your convenience, and is drilled and tapped for standard accessory drives. The damper is 7.74 inches in diameter and weighs 8.95 pounds. This same damper is available for a larger 1.598-inch blower crank snout under PN 24502535.

Torsional Damper—Standard Hub PN 24502534

Specially tuned dampers for use up to 9,000 rpm. They fit all small-blocks with standard size hub diameter; 70 durometer O-rings are used to dampen crankshaft vibrations. The black outer ring is fully degreed with contrasting white marks to simplify ignition timing and valve lash adjustments. The hub is drilled and tapped for standard pulleys and accessory drives. This damper is 7.74 inches in diameter and weighs 8.94 pounds (4.5 pounds inertia weight).

Torsional Damper—Large Hub PN 24502535

Same damper as PN 24502534 except for use with large-diameter 1.598-inch crankshaft nose, which is the same size as a big-block Chevy.

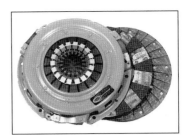

This heavy-duty 11-inch diameter diaphragm clutch assembly PN 3884598 is a high-performance unit recommended for use with 14-inch flywheels PN 39911469 and 3986394.

Factory Flywheels and Flexplates

If you apply a few simple rules, you'll have no trouble choosing a small-block flywheel or automatic transmission flexplate. Refer to this table for common GM part numbers and the text for selection guidelines.

Manual Transmission

Part Number	Outside Diameter (in.)	Year	Crank Flange Bolt pattern	Clutch Diameter (in.)	Starter Ring Gear Teeth	Notes
14085720	12-3/4	1955-85	3.58	10.4	153	Weight approximately 15 pounds. This GM nodular iron flywheel was designed for 2-piece crank seals.
3986394	14	1970-80	3.58	11	168	This flywheel is designed for the 400-ci small-block V-8 and is externally balanced. Compatible with balancer PN 6272225.
3991469	14	1955-85	3.58	10.4, 11	168	For 2-piece seal cranks.
10105832	14	1986-up	3.00	11, 11.85	168	For 1-piece seal cranks.
14088646	12-3/4	1986-up	3.00	10.4, 11	153	Weight approximately 16 pounds. A lightweight nodular-iron wheel for 1-piece seal cranks.
14088650	12-3/4	1986-up	3.00	10.4	153	Production-weight flywheel for 1-piece seal cranks.

Automatic Transmission

Part Number	Outside Diameter (in.)	Year	Crank Flange Bolt pattern	Clutch Diameter (in.)	Starter Ring Gear Teeth	Notes
471598	14	1970-85	3.58	10.75, 11.50	168	Use with crankshafts that do not require external balancing and have the early 2-piece rear seal.
471578	14	1970-80	3.58	10.75, 11.50	168	Use on externally-balanced 400cid engines. Compatible with balancer PN 6272225.
471529	12-3/4	1969-85	3.58	9.75, 10.75	153	Use with crankshafts that do not require external balancing and have the early 2-piece rear seal.
10128412	12-3/4	1986-up	3.00	10.75	153	Use on externally-balanced late-model cranks designed for the 1-piece rear. This is the flexplate specified for the 350HO engine.
10128413	14	1986-up	3.00	11.50	168	A heavy-duty flexplate for externally-balanced late-model cranks designed for the 1-piece rear.
10128414	14	1986-up	3.00	10.75, 11.50	168	Use on externally-balanced late-model cranks designed for the 1-piece rear.

*NOTE: Torque converters for TurboHydro 350 and TurboHydro 400 transmissions are manufactured with both 10.75- and 11.5-inch converter bolt patterns. To identify the proper pattern, measure the distance from the converter centerline to an attaching bolt hole, then multiply by two.

CONNECTING RODS

Small-block Chevy connecting rods are typically available in two standard lengths. The vast majority of production small-block rods are 5.700 inches long when measured from the center of the piston-pin hole to the center of the crank-journal hole. The second type production rod is exclusive to the 400-ci small-block engine. Due to the longer stroke and the reduced compression height of the 400 engine, the connecting rod was shortened to 5.565 inches. It is nearly unheard of for either of these rods to cause problems in ordinary service. There are undoubtedly many small-block connecting rods that have more than a half-million miles of service. They will literally last forever with normal usage.

There are numerous rod designs within the 5.700-inch family, as well as a number of special factory heavy-duty rods. As with any other small-block component, you have to determine which specific piece will best fulfill the requirements of your particular application. Selecting the right rod for a high-performance or racing application is more important than you might think. Connecting rods are the most highly stressed components in the entire engine. They have the unenviable task of hanging onto the pistons while they're slamming up and down in the cylinder bores. Contrary to popular belief, it isn't the force of combustion that places the most stress on the rod. The point of maximum stress occurs at the top of the stroke when the entire mass of the piston must be stopped and instantly reversed. The forces at work here are incredible, and the connecting rod must absorb them. Fortunately, the aftermarket has graced us with an enormous selection of quality connecting rods.

The trick is to select the optimum piece for the best price. In a pure stock

From the very first small-block connecting rod, the 5.700-inch length has been a standard for all production engines–except the 400-ci, which uses 0.135-inch shorter rods.

The 5.565-inch 400 rod on the left has shorter rod bolts that are countersunk deeply into the rod shank. This prevents interference between the rod bolts and the block or camshaft with the longer 3.75-inch stroke.

A closer look at the rod bolt fit on a 400-ci rod shows how the shorter bolt is seated deeply into the rod shoulder. On these rods, the notch between the bolt seat and the rod beam is usually much larger and often very rough. It is advisable to smooth and detail them with a small file or grinder prior to shot-peening.

situation, use whatever you have, as long as it is in good condition. Unlike crankshafts, almost all Chevy connecting rods are made of forged steel, so you don't have to distinguish between cast and forged pieces. They are all, therefore, very tough. In most cases, the major consideration is the need for a large- or small-journal rod, with either a pressed or full-floating piston pin. Street applications will generally use a pressed pin, but full-floating pins are desirable for racing engines. Beyond this, there are a number of choices, depending upon your budget and application.

In 1994, powdered metal (PM) rods emerged with new technology. Some forged rods were still being used, but the PM rods gradually filled the pipeline on LT1 and LT4 engines. Unlike typical PM "cracked" rods (where the rod is one piece and the big end is broken in half, creating unique

mating surfaces that lock together), Gen II rods can be reconditioned, since the parting faces are machined. They are all 5.7-inches in center-to-center length with standard 2.100-inch journals. The small end accepts the standard .927-inch, pressed-fit wrist pin.

GM offers the 5.7-inch Corvette PM rod (PN 10108688) in a kit of eight rods under PN 12495071. They suggest limiting horsepower to 500 with these rods, but we have seen them live in many 500–600 horsepower engines. This is particularly true if you limit engine speed to 6,500 rpm. For odd combinations, the late-model L99 4.3-liter or 265-ci rod can be used. Its 5.94-inch length offers some versatility for unique piston and rod combinations. They can be used for street or competition up to 500 horsepower. Single rods are offered under PN 10108697, or get a complete set under PN 12495072.

Another 5.7-inch PM rod was designed for the 383 GM crate motor. These rods (PN 12497624) are 5.7 inches long and are machined to clear the camshaft in longer stroke engines, such as the 383. A set of eight rods is available under PN 12497870. If you are not using an aftermarket rod, this may be your best bet on any stroker application under 500 horsepower.

Early Small-Journal Rods

There's really no reason to use the early 265/283 small-journal rod unless you happen to have a set in good condition and you're not building a high-output engine or you're restoring an original engine. In a small-journal application you should always try to use the 327-ci rod, which was first made available in 1962. It is easily identified by the teardrop configuration around the pin hole and slight bulge in the side facing, right next to the head of

the rod bolt. Early 327 rods retained a fully circular configuration around the big end of the rod. All small-journal rods use $\frac{11}{32}$-inch rod bolts that work just fine in a moderate street engine. If you plan on buzzing it pretty high, it's imperative that you install good rod bolts in these rods. Popular ARP bolts are made from a superior metal and are an excellent choice.

The 1967 Z28 rod is a small-journal piece identical to the late 327-ci rod, but it receives additional attention at the factory. It is Magnaflux-inspected, heat-treated, fully shot-peened, and selected with an eye for the best possible rod-to-cap parting surface. The Z28 rod was offered as PN 3927145, while the standard 327-ci rod was PN 3864881. Both are no longer available, so you'll have to work with used rods if you're striving for authenticity.

If you're going to work with used rods, it's best to take no chances. Replace the bolts and have the rods completely reconditioned. Many of the 1966–1967 small-journal rods still had the oiling slot in the rod cap. These rods are perfectly acceptable, even though GM determined that the slot was unnecessary and eliminated it in 1967. There are a lot of small-journal 327 rods around without the oiling slot, but they aren't necessarily Z28 forgings. These are excellent small-journal rods and will give good service with proper preparation and specialty bolts.

Large-Journal Rods

In 1968 and 1969, the 302-ci engine received a large-journal rod with factory installed full-floating piston pins. These rods receive the same special attention as the early Z28 rod. The part number for these rods was PN 3946841; the big-journal pressed-pin rod used in 1970–1979 Z28 engines

Identifying Small-Block Factory Rods

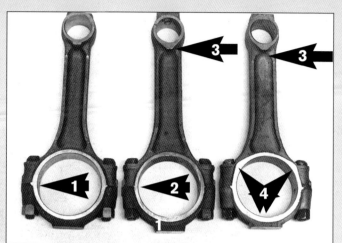

The big end on the early 283-ci rod (arrow 1) is completely round and has a very narrow beam width. It is quite similar to the early 327-ci rod (arrow 2), which is also round on the big end, but has a thicker section across the beam. The early and late 327-ci rods have the teardrop shape on the small end (arrow 3), but the later rod had beefier shoulder bumps on the big end (arrows 4). You should avoid the narrow 283-ci rod, even for mild performance engines. Of these three, select the late 327-ci rod for all small-journal performance applications.

Unless you have a 350-ci rod for comparison, it's difficult to spot the 0.135-inch shorter 400-ci rod. Look at the small bumps on the rod shoulders. While standard rods also have these bumps, the 400-ci rod has notches in the centers from the countersunk bolt seats (see arrows).

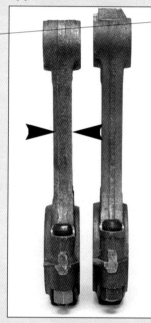

A side view illustrates the very narrow beam of the early 283-ci rod (arrows). This rod is unacceptable in any application, but the late 283/early 327-ci rod may be used successfully for all stock or mild 265/283-ci rebuilds.

All small-journal rods use tiny $^{11}/_{32}$-inch rod bolts (left), while large-journal rods use $^3/_8$-inch bolts like the one on the right. The unique 400-ci rod (center) is shorter, but uses $^3/_8$-inch bolts.

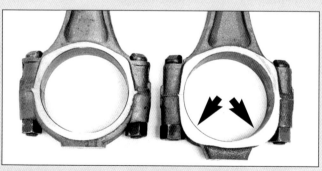

For the inexperienced, it can be difficult to tell a small-journal rod from a large-journal rod. The difference is only 0.100-inch and identification is generally easier if you use visual clue; like the strengthened caps (arrows).

Checking Critical Rod Dimensions

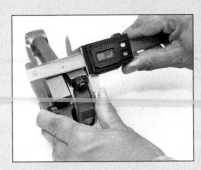

Checking big-end bore diameter with the caps torqued in place will verify bearing crush. Small-journal rods should measure 2.1250 inches, plus 0.0002 or minus 0.0003 inch. Also, make sure the bores have no more than 0.0002-inch taper and that they are no more than 0.0005 inch out-of-round.

Rod side clearance can be measured with vernier calipers or with feeler gauges when the rods are assembled on the crank through. Clearance for stock steel rods should be 0.008 to 0.012 inch for steel rods in stock engines, 0.008 to 0.015 inch for steel rods in high-performance engines, and 0.032 to 0.060 inch for aluminum rods (consult rod manufacturer for exact specs).

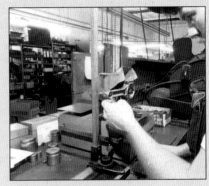

Rod balancing is a complex operation that sets the pin-end weight, the big-end weight, and the overall rod weight. Find a machine shop that takes pride in doing quality machine work; a cheap balancing job is not what you're looking for!

While measuring rod length is important, a more revealing measurement is deck height and its variation from cylinder to cylinder due to rod-length variations. This measures the accuracy of the block machining, rod length, crank stroke, and piston pin position. Variations should be less than 0.0025 inch for performance work.

Below right: A wide variety of specialty connecting rods are available. Standard-length street rods to extra long fully machined forgings offer light weight and excellent durability. Quality rods are offered by Crower, Oliver, Callies, Scat, Carrillo, Cunningham, Eagle, and other specialty rod manufacturers.

High-performance fastener manufacturers such as ARP offer extremely strong bolts with rolled threads and ground underhead radii. Rod bolts are subjected to stress and loads that far exceed all other engine fasteners. This is especially true when heavy steel rods are run at speeds above 7,000 rpm.

On stock type rods, the notch between the bolt seat and the rod beam should be gently radiused to prevent stress cracks. If the bolt seating surfaces are in poor condition, it is wise to have them spot faced, but this must be done by a competent machinist who can get them perpendicular to the bolt centerline while removing as little material as possible.

was listed as PN 3973386. These large-journal rods were fitted with stronger ⅜-inch rod bolts, which are adequate for any street application and some automatic transmission bracket cars. Here again, if you want to run the engine at high RPM, install ARP bolts to avoid early failure.

The current standard large-journal, pressed-pin rod (usually referred to as a 350 rod) is PN 14096846. It is

the "Pink" rod used in the 350 HO engine. A heavier-duty version of the same rod is PN 14095071. This rod is also the well-known heavy-duty 1038 steel "Pink" rod, but it is Magnafluxed, shot-peened, and heat treated. Both of these rods have ⅜-inch-diameter rod bolts. The "Pink" rod was used in the 1970–1972 LT1, 1970–1974 Z28, and all L82 350s. A floating-pin version of this rod for 1969–1970 Z28s is available under the original part number PN 3946841 as listed above.

Heavy-Duty Rods

Other factory-built, heavy-duty connecting rods are called Bow Tie rods. Bow Tie rods are made from 4340 vacuum-degassed steel for maximum strength. Dedicated forging dyes are used for each rod length to help minimize rod weight. Bow Tie rods have been tested to 10 million cycles at racing loads without failure. They are equipped with heavy-duty aircraft-quality ⁷⁄₁₆-inch-diameter bolts threaded directly into the rod forks, and the rod caps are positively located by alignment sleeves. All Bow Tie rods are machined for 2.1-inch-diameter rod journals and pressed-fit wrist pins. They're shot-peened to ensure durabil-

ity. Chevrolet recommends that they be lubricated with 30-weight engine oil and torqued to 70 ft-lbs with a recommended bolt stretch of 0.005 to .006 inch.

Bow Tie rods are available in two lengths: 5.7-inch (PN 14011090) and 6.0-inch (PN 14011091). Bow Tie rods are also available with profiled beams, which reduce rod weight by approximately 50 grams. A typical profiled 5.7-inch Bow Tie rod weighs 739 grams, with 529 grams on the big end. Chevrolet suggests that the profiled rods are more uniform in weight and thus easier to balance in sets. These rods are also shot-peened after machining. Profiled 5.7-inch rods are available under PN 14011082, while 6.0-inch profiled Bow Tie rods are PN 14011083.

Aftermarket Rods

For racing engines, there are numerous specialty connecting rods available. They offer many advantages, including superior strength, lighter weight, and in some cases, greater durability. Steel racing rods are available from reputable companies such as Crower, Oliver, Callies, Scat, Eagle, Cunningham, Manley, and Carrillo.

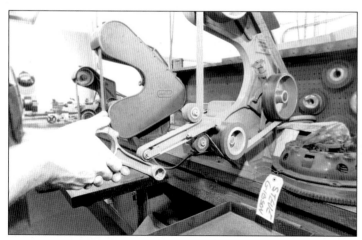

Polishing the rod beams on stock rods is a procedure that removes the forging line and grinds away potential stress risers. Some shops use carbide grinder bits to cut away the forging line and then apply a belt sander to polish the beam before shot-peening. Make sure the bolt head contact surface is not damaged during the procedure.

Rod Assembly and Installation Tips

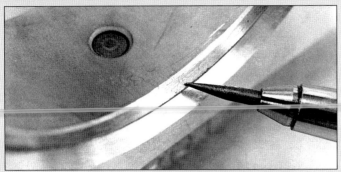

Some racing crankshafts are ground with a large radius that requires a chamfer on the edge of the bearing and sometimes the rod. Make sure your rod bearings do not contact the crank journal radii.

Assembling the pin without adequate lubrication is a common mistake for amateur and first-time engine builders; the result is immediate damage to the pin and pin bores. Apply plenty of lube to the pin, pin bushing, and piston.

If you check rod bearing side clearance with plastigauge, use a spacer or feeler gauges to prevent the rod from twisting as you tighten and loosen the bolts.

Always use protectors over the rod bolts when installing the rods. The slightest contact between the rod bolt and crank will raise a burr on the journal surface that will damage the rod bearing.

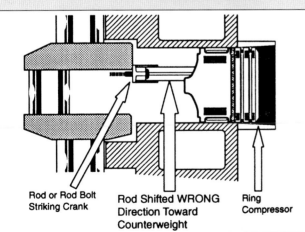

Rod or Rod Bolt Striking Crank   Rod Shifted WRONG Direction Toward Counterweight   Ring Compressor

Make certain you have the rods correctly aligned as shown here. The large flat faces should face each other and the offset with the radius for the crank journal should face the crank throw.

Note how the bearing is located well away from the crank radii and the rod chamfer has plenty of clearance.

Rod side clearance is best checked between the rods with a feeler gauge.

For serious drag racing, aluminum rods are the norm. The extra bulk around the big end of the rod ensures the dimensional integrity of the bearing housing bore at very high engine speeds. Most aluminum rods are not significantly lighter than a stock rod; they are simply much sturdier without the increased weight penalty incurred when beefing up steel rods. Aluminum rods are not exotic by any means, but they should be considered so when building a street engine. Some determined street machiners and bracket racers have had great success with aluminum in limited-use applications, but it is really unnecessary.

The same advice applies to other specialty rods that aren't made of aluminum. Other materials used to make high-strength rods include stainless steel and titanium. These rods are designed exclusively for severe-environment endurance racing, but nothing else. They are very high-quality pieces and they work extremely well, but they have no place in anything less than a full-competition engine being raced in recognized and formally sanctioned competition.

Rod Preparation

For more ordinary street purposes, factory steel rods are always preferred, and their preparation is important. Chevrolet has published specific recommendations for the preparation of factory connecting rods. These guidelines are mostly dimensional recommendations, but there are standard procedures you can follow when preparing a set of used rods.

The first step in any rod prep scheme should always be Magnafluxing to determine if cracks are present. Magnafluxing is not overly expensive. If the rods are going to be used in a relatively serious racing engine, you should consider having them X-rayed

Rod Prep Checklist

1. Visually inspect for obvious signs of damage.
2. Magnaflux to determine condition.
3. Deburr rod and polish side beans if desired.
4. Shot-peen rod and cap.
5. Install new bolts and recondition to low side of factory specs.
6. Check and correct side clearance.
7. Install bushing for floating pin if desired.
8. Adjust center-to-center length with pin bushing.
9. Drill pin oiling holes from bottom of pin boss.
10. Check and straighten rod if required.
11. Balance end-to-end.
12. Clean rod in solvent and store in plastic bags until ready for assembly.

to determine their true condition. Used rods can also be improved by an at-home stress-relieving procedure. Simply pop them into the kitchen oven for eight hours at 450 degrees. This accomplishes the same effect as your taking a nice hot bath to relieve tension.

Polishing the rod beams is a popular procedure, but again it isn't really necessary for a street engine. There is certainly no harm in doing it just for fun, and many part-time engine builders favor it. Polishing is necessary to remove the forging line down the side of the rod and expose potential stress risers. If you're going to do it, be sure all grinding is done lengthwise and not from side to side. Most shops use carbide cutters to remove the forging line and small sanding discs to polish the beam before shot-peening. It's important to blend your grinding smoothly at each end of the rod. At the top of the rod, the beam should contour smoothly into the area around the wrist pin hole.

You can't successfully grind a set of rods without removing the bolts. You have to get them out in order to successfully blend the side of the rod into the rod bolt seating surface. Don't

cut down the surface at the notch where the bolt seat begins. The notch itself should be gently radiused; you may have to do this with a hand file. After the beams are polished, the rods can be shot-peened prior to reassembly. Rather than tape the piston-pin hole, simply insert an old pin that has been turned down slightly in a lathe. The pin will prevent any shot from damaging the pin bore.

If the bolt seating surfaces are damaged or not perpendicular to the axis of the rod bolt bore, you should consider having them spot-faced. This is a delicate procedure, and only a very minor amount of metal should be removed. Be sure you can trust your machinist before committing to this work. The nut surface on the cap should receive the same treatment. When you consider that all the engine power output is contained by these bolts, it makes sense to give them a fair chance. A "cocked" rod bolt is on its way to an early failure.

Side Clearance

To promote good oil control, it's also important to closely control the amount of side clearance between each pair of connecting rods. If this clearance is too great, an excessive amount of oil will be deposited on the cylinder walls where it can overpower the rings and possibly reach the combustion chamber to cause detonation and a loss of power. Side clearance can be premeasured by checking a pair of rods with a set of dial calipers and comparing the dimension to that measured between the crank cheeks with a snap gauge.

Generally you'll have plenty of side clearance available, but in those rare cases where it is insufficient, you can increase it by facing the big end sides of the rods on sandpaper laid against a flat surface. Some shops use a large rotary sanding disc, but you have to be careful because they take off a lot of material in a short time. Naturally, you'll want to look for another set of rods if the side clearance is way too large.

Rod Bore Sizing

Measuring the inside diameter of the rod bearing bores is important. This size must be within tolerances to ensure proper rod bearing crush. If the bores do not fall within the recommended tolerances, the bores should be resized.

Resizing of the big end and pin fitting are jobs best left to your machinist. Proper big end sizing is accomplished by removing the rod bolts and taking a surface cut across the parting faces. Some shops try to expedite the procedure by only cutting the rod cap and leaving the bolts in the rod. This procedure sounds questionable, but it seems to produce good results as long as the rods are only applied to street engines. If you're constructing a competition engine, be certain to check your machinist's procedure and insist that the work is done right.

After the parting surfaces are cut parallel, the rod is reassembled with new bolts. They are pressed in with a hydraulic press, and don't let anyone tell you it is okay to knock them in with a hammer. The rods are then torqued to the same specs used for final assembly. This should only be done in a rod vise that holds the rod firmly. You can build a simple device for removing the nuts after you get your rods home by cutting two 1½x5-inch strips of 0.250-inch aluminum. These can be used to clamp the rods in an ordinary bench vise for easy disassembly.

When torquing rod bolts, it is generally conceded that a three-step approach is best. For example: if the torque spec is 42 ft-lbs, you should start by pulling the nuts up to 25 ft-lbs first. Then alternating from side to side, pull them to 35 ft-lbs and finally to the desired spec. Splitting it into thirds ensures even bolt torque and promotes proper bearing crush.

For best results, the big end should be finished to the low side of factory tolerances. This will help ensure good bearing crush and guard against spun bearings. Some shops like to put an exceptionally smooth finish on the big end bore to help promote better heat transfer from the bearing. This is easily accomplished by wrapping the rod hone with 400-grit sandpaper for final polishing. It's a simple procedure that really works.

Pin Bushings

At this point, the machinist will fit the wrist pin bushings if you are going to run floating pins. These bushings are normally made from bronze or naval brass, although the factory rods receive a special coating and are used without a bushing. Pin clearance should be maintained between 0.0008 and 0.0012 inch. The machinist will

Here are two schools of thought regarding budget pin oiling ideas on stock rods. The rod on the right shows the oiling hole drilled from the top. Alternate thinking suggests that two holes be drilled from the bottom to take advantage of splash oiling from the crank.

also take this opportunity to place the pin hole in the proper location to equalize center-to-center length on all the rods. This spec is normally finished to factory tolerances, but in a competition engine, you may wish to lengthen or shorten this dimension to accommodate any unforeseen problems with regard to deck height. This is why many aluminum rods are prefinished at 5.690 inches instead of the stock 5.700 inches.

Rod Bearings

Selecting rod bearings for your freshly prepped rods is not a difficult task if you adhere to the theory of combination and application. The crankshaft chapter has a section that describes the various properties of bearing materials and how they affect your selection. These are small numbers here. For the average small-block, 0.0025 to 0.0030 inch is the universal clearance. You'll never have a problem with it. If you want to get more specific, small-journal rods are thought to

Factory Connecting Rods

Except as noted, all of these factory are forged, large journal, 5.7 inches long, machined for pressed pins, and come as a complete assembly w/nuts & bolts.

14011059	Big-block 427, L88, 4340 steel unmachined raw forging (less cap). Can be used to make ultra-HD small-block custom-length rods. Crankpin hole will machine 2.1- 2.2-inch, rod center-to-center from 5.7- to 6.135-inch. (GM no longer stocks bolts.)
3963571	Unmachined cap blank for above.
14011090	"Bow Tie" 5.70-inch rod. Magnafluxed & vacuum degassed 4340 steel, 7/16 HD capscrews.
14011091	6.0-inch length version of above.
14011082	Same as PN 14011090, but profiled beam for reduced finished weight; Magnafluxed after profiling.
14011083	6.0-inch length version of PN 14011082.
14096846	HD "pink rod." 1038 steel , Magnafluxed, shot-peened & heat-treated. Uses 3/8 bolts. 350-HO version.
14095071	Original HD "pink rod." Used in '70-'72 LT1/'70-'74 Z28/all L82.

Some engine builders believe that stock rods will benefit from low-temperature stress relieving. Simply bake them for eight hours at 450 degrees.

need slightly more clearance than large-journal rods. A small-journal rod bearing in a steel rod should be fitted at about 0.003 inch for a racing engine, but you can snug it down to around 0.002 inch in a street motor. A large journal rod needs about 0.002- to 0.0025-inch clearance, but can be run at 0.0015–0.002 inch in OEM applications.

This stuff is not as critical as some people would have you believe and you should never open up clearances any more than absolutely necessary. Since small-journal cranks tend to whip around a bit more, they need just a slight bit more clearance to prevent the crank from biting the bearing. It's that simple. If you're going to be running aluminum rods,

open up the clearance a little more than usual to allow for rod growth. Generally, something in the neighborhood of 0.0035 to 0.004 inch is acceptable. We've seen plenty of success with 0.0035-inch clearances, but 0.004 inch is more than usable, even though it does sound a bit large.

During one of your trial assemblies, you should take time to observe the rod-bearing-to-crank-throw relationship. Sometimes the crank grinder will leave a very large radius on the crank throw and it is possible for it to interfere with the bearing. Most bearings are already clearanced to avoid this problem, but sometimes it isn't enough. If you look at a stock bearing as it comes right out of the box, you will note that the edges are already slightly chamfered. In most cases this will suffice, but be sure to determine whether or not the bearings will contact the crank fillet and correct the problem if necessary.

If there appears to be only a slight interference, the chamfered edge of the bearing can be increased slightly by hand with a bearing knife. In extreme cases, where the crank has been reground or has been specially ground with very large radius fillets (for added strength), the bearing chamfer may have to be substantially increased by machining in a lathe. This will happen only in very rare cases, and should be avoided because it will decrease the area of the bearing.

Properly prepared small-block rods almost never fail in ordinary use. They even live under less than ideal conditions, but you can hurt them through carelessness. Don't cut corners on rod preparation. Follow the rod prep checklist provided here, use the correct bearings and see to it that they are oiled correctly. Follow the procedure closely and rod failure is the last thing you'll have to worry about.

PISTONS

Years of research and development by piston manufacturers, top engine builders, and dedicated racers have developed a wealth of good information concerning piston design and application for small-block Chevys. In fact, there is so much information available that it's easy to become confused when trying to make a piston selection.

Factory Pistons

Factory pistons offer a good starting point for high-performance applications. There have been several types of pistons used in the small-block engine: permanent-mold cast aluminum, modern Hypereutectic, and forged or "impact extruded" aluminum pistons. Prior to 1962, all small-block pistons were cast aluminum with either flat tops or $1/8$-inch pop-up domes. The 1962 340-hp, 327-ci engine received the first factory-designed forged pistons, and thereafter they were offered in high-performance 327, 302, and 350 engines. The 327-type dome was used through 1967 on all high-performance 327 engines and in the 1967 302-cid Z28 engine. Later forgings featured a larger dome used in 1968

and later 302 and all high-performance 350 engines.

Small-block pistons from different displacements are generally not interchangeable. Other than differences in bore size, the major difference between pistons is the compression height (also called pin height: the distance from the centerline of the piston pin to the deck surface of the piston). Rod length and block height are standardized (except in the 400 and in tall-deck racing blocks), so changes in stroke length are accommodated by raising or lowering the position of the pin in the piston. However, there are some notable exceptions: the 400 uses a shorter rod, thereby maintaining the same compression height as the 350; and the 307 piston has the same compression height as the 327 piston because it has the same stroke as the 327, though it has a 283 bore size.

Your piston selection must always complement the stroke of the crankshaft; otherwise you'll end up with the piston sticking out the top of the block or only partly up the cylinder at TDC. With properly matched components, the piston deck will always be very close to the deck surface when the piston is at TDC. It should appear flush with the deck surface if you're

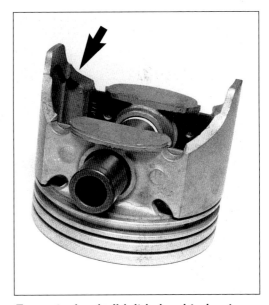

For a stock rebuild, it is hard to beat the economy of cast pistons like those offered by Silvalite, Triplex, or Badger. They don't require special preparation, and the price is very reasonable. They are a much better choice than trying to salvage used pistons. Note the thermal expansion struts to control dimensional integrity (arrow).

eyeballing it, but in actuality it must be a slight distance down the bore when checked with proper measuring equipment. This distance is the deck clearance specified in factory blueprints.

The difference in piston compression height is illustrated here. Even though many small-blocks share the same 4.00-inch bore size, there are several different stroke lengths. Because rod lengths and deck heights remain constant (except on the 400-ci engine), piston compression height must be matched to the stroke of the crankshaft. This is what happens if you install a 327-ci piston in an engine with a 350-ci crankshaft. The piston protrudes out of the bore by approx-imately ⅛ inch at TDC. This is about half the difference in stroke length between the 327 ci and the 350 ci.

Some high-performance piston kits include rings and others don't. It depends on the type of pistons and the application.

Selecting Pistons

When selecting pistons, it's important to honestly evaluate your requirements. Your favorite Pro/Stock racer may use special high-compression forgings that are ultralight and double trick, but that doesn't mean you need the same thing for your street performance car. Remember that many of the factory high-performance cars provided exceptional performance with nothing more than cast, flattop or newer hypereutectic pistons. You can often save big bucks by choosing a low-compression piston that is compatible with lower-quality fuels, but is still quite capable

of delivering exhilarating performance when combined with the proper power components.

Factory (or factory-type) cast or hypereutectic pistons have inherent advantages over forged pistons, including greater dimensional stability. This prevents the piston skirts from expanding greatly during normal operation and allows a relatively small "cold" piston-to-wall clearance (something on the order of 0.001 to 0.002 inch). The tighter piston fit reduces cold-start engine noise, ring wear, and oil consumption.

These pistons are also designed to use press-fit wrist pins, eliminating the

potential problem of pin retainer failure. And the pins in these pistons are offset by 0.060 inch to help minimize piston slap, reducing engine noise and improving ring life.

Factory pistons provide excellent results when engine speeds are kept below 6,000 rpm. However, skirt clearance should be increased slightly (to 0.0025 to 0.003 inch) if higher engine speeds are anticipated. Remember that a good street engine should produce the broadest possible torque curve, allowing it to develop substantial power at or below peak engine speeds. At higher engine speeds, tight clearances invite engine seizure because of increased friction and higher temperatures. In nearly every case, it's best to keep clearances tight, peak speeds below 6,500 rpm, and religiously avoid detonation that can crack rings and distort ring lands.

Another point of concern is piston balancing and lightening. Weight removal is something that can help engine performance in some respects although there is substantial evidence that this is not always the case. While the ability of the engine to rev faster is improved when the reciprocating mass is lessened, most modern racing pistons are now about as light as you can make them anyway, so further machine work is usually not recommended.

Current Factory Pistons

You'll find that GM currently has cast, hypereutectic, and forged pistons for 350 performance engines. Some dealers may still have stock replacement pistons for other engines such as the 327, 305, and 400, but you may be better off purchasing special aftermarket pistons for these engines.

GM Performance also offers a large selection of special racing pistons for 4.00-inch bore 350s. They are

Piston Materials and Applications

Cast pistons have been the standard automotive piston for decades. They are inexpensive and easy to produce. They have a thermally stable crystalline grain structure and often incorporate cast-in steel expansion struts that allow them to fit tightly in the bore for optimum stability and ring seal. Under normal use they will stand up to well to tens of thousand of miles of use. However, they have limited speed, thermal, and detonation resistance. They should only be used in moderate performance engines where speed is limited and detonation is strictly avoided.

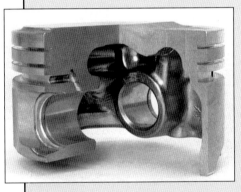

Hypereutectic pistons are castings but have nearly 2½ times the silicon of a standard cast piston for increased hardness and greater resistance to higher temperatures and cylinder pressures. They are dimensionally stable and require very little skirt clearance. In some instances they can be operated with less clearance than standard cast pistons. This feature keeps the pistons and ring package well stabilized in the bore and improves sealing and blow-by control. While hypereutectic pistons are well suited to street performance applications, they do not have the detonation and temperature resistance of forged pistons. They should not be used with more than very light nitrous oxide injection loads, or with high-pressure turbo- or supercharging systems.

Forged pistons are manufactured with a forging die from a solid slug of heat-treated aluminum alloy. They possess the dense grain structure and metallurgical properties to stand up to severe use, including a degree of detonation resistance. However, forged pistons have less dimensional stability and require greater skirt clearance for reliable operation. Forged pistons remain the top choice when strength and durability are required for racing, turbocharged, supercharged, or nitrous oxide-injected applications.

all designed to produce 12.5:1 compression, and are forged aluminum for severe-duty applications. They are available for both 5.7- and 6.0-inch rods in standard and oversize bore diameters, and they're machined for ⅟₁₆-inch top and second rings. Each piston comes with round wire pin retainers and a pin machined specifically for these locks. These pistons come in sets with asymmetrical domes designed to fit Chevy combustion chambers. Piston ring sets are also available from GM or some aftermarket manufacturers.

There is also a wide variety of specialty pistons available from several manufacturers. Some of these are remanufactured and should be avoided, but many provide an excellent base from which to construct a true budget engine. The thing you really want to avoid is used pistons or locally reconditioned pistons with knurled skirts and spacers to reduce the ring side clearance. Used pistons are always going to have excessive ring side clearance and very often they will have too much back clearance behind the ring because the engine rebuilder has been in there with his ring groove cleaner and removed another 0.010 to 0.020 inch of metal. With good pieces available at reasonable prices, there is no reason you should ever have to resort to used pistons.

Hypereutectic pistons now available from GM and from aftermarket manufacturers such as Keith Black are another great alternative. These pistons were developed specifically to provide a stronger piece that would withstand punishment without requiring an expensive forging. They are more expensive than replacement cast pistons, and they definitely are not bulletproof, but they offer an added measure of strength and performance in engines where cylinder pressure, detonation, and fuel quality are controllable.

Here are four replacement pistons for the 400-ci engine. A high-compression racing piston is in the rear while different stock-type pistons are arrayed in front. Each has a different dish volume as was used by the factory to adjust compression ratios in different years.

Forged Pistons

When your plans include serious racing or hot street engines, forged pistons provide the additional strength and performance you need. Forged pistons are made by forming aluminum slugs into pistons with enormous presses (forging). This procedure creates a dense metal grain structure, making the pistons stronger without incurring a substantial weight penalty.

Consider for a moment the incredibly tough job a high-performance piston must perform. Few mechanical pieces of any sort operate under such severe conditions. The piston has to accept the full force of combustion and transmit it to the rod and crankshaft assembly with little or no distortion. It must further withstand the additional ravages of pre-ignition and detonation, while maintaining efficient cylinder sealing and preventing excess oil from reaching the combustion chamber. Moreover, it has to cope with speeds up to and sometimes exceeding 4,500 feet per second. To do this it has to maintain structural integrity so that the piston rings maintain their seal against the cylinder wall. In addition, the piston has to dissipate a significant proportion of

Hypereutectic pistons have been the rage for about 15 years now, and Speed Pro makes some of the best ones. They are available in all popular configurations.

the heat of combustion through the rings and skirts.

A forged piston is more able to handle these conditions because of denser grain structure and lack of porosity. This is especially important when it comes to ring land distortion. The piston must precisely retain and stabilize the piston rings if the engine is to make good power. Forged pistons are generally considered superior in this respect, but the degree of success depends upon the specific design of the piston. A great deal of investigation has gone into piston alloys and skirt design. While a forged piston is much tougher, it's still aluminum and therefore has difficulty dealing with heat. Because of the greater density of forged alloys, expansion from heat is greater, resulting in a piece that has to be fitted with significantly greater skirt clearance.

The cam-shaped skirt and the barrel contour of the skirt face are typical characteristics of TRW/Speed Pro pistons and slipper skirt pistons in general. The shape of these pistons is elliptical (as viewed from the top of the piston), which reduces expansion and concentrates thrust against the strongest part of the skirt. The barrel contour (as viewed from the side, along the pin axis) reduces friction and stabilizes the piston by reducing

the amount of skirt material in contact with the cylinder wall. Only a small portion of the skirt contacts the wall, but it's enough to stabilize the piston, while the ring package keeps the piston centered in the bore. This technique offers significant reductions in friction, which translates to improved power and lower temperatures. This leads back to our original requirement: To be an efficient piston, it must effectively support the rings so they can seal the cylinder and prevent charge contamination as the piston moves in either direction. In a nutshell, fuel mixtures and cylinder pressure must be contained above the rings, and oil must be kept out of the combustion chambers.

Compression Ratio

When you get down to selecting the pistons for your engine, it becomes a matter of obtaining the desired compression ratio for the engine application, given the selected cylinder heads and the octane rating of fuel. First of all, remember that the very act of increasing the bore size will increase the compression ratio. This occurs because you are squeezing a larger volume into the same combustion chamber. You should also consider that flattop pistons promote efficient combustion and increase engine efficiency. Domed pistons may still have a place in the overall scheme of things, but many racing engines are now built with flat tops and combustion chambers sized to control the compression ratio. For a general performance street engine, 9:1 compression is a great place to start.

Top Super Stockers run pretty hard with the stock compression ratio and flattop pistons, but they are allowed to snug everything up to minimum specs. With the allowable overbore and minimum combustion chamber

Chevrolet Small-Block V-8 High-Performance Pistons

These GM pistons are designed for 4-inch-bore small-blocks. They produce compression ratios from 9 to 11:1. All are forged aluminum unless otherwise indicated. All use ⁵⁄₆₄-inch top and second rings with ³⁄₁₆-inch oil rings. Pin location and dome shapes vary with application.

Part Number	Engine	ID#	Size	Pin Type	Compression Ratio	Head Chamber Volume	Notes
10104455	350	10104458/ 14096277	Standard	Pressed	9.8:1	58 cc	Hypereutectic (high silicon alloy) used in 350-ci HO engine assembly. First design incorporating "ZZZ" ID.
10104456	350	10104459	0.001 Oversized	Pressed	9.8:1	58 cc	Hypereutectic (high silicon alloy) used in 350-ci HO engine assembly. First design incorporating "ZZZ" ID.
10104457	350	10104460	0.030 Oversized	Pressed	9.8:1	58 cc	Hypereutectic (high silicon alloy) used in 350-ci HO engine assembly. First design incorporating "ZZZ" ID.
10181389	350	10105168/ 10172749	Standard	Pressed	9.8:1	58 cc	Hypereutectic (high silicon alloy) used in 350-ci HO engine assembly. Second design with ZZ1, 2, 3, ID.
10181390	350	10105168/ 10172749	Standard High Limit	Pressed	9.8:1	58 cc	Hypereutectic (high silicon alloy) used in 350-ci HO engine assembly. Second design with ZZ1, 2, 3, ID.
10181392	350	10105169/ 10181388	0.030 Oversized	Pressed	9.8:1	58 cc	Hypereutectic (high silicon alloy) used in 350-ci HO engine assembly. Second design with ZZ1, 2, 3, ID.
12520264	350	10046106/ 14075651/ 14093679	Standard	Pressed	9.1:1	64 cc	350 ci/300-hp engine
12520265	350	NA	0.001 Oversized	Pressed	9.1:1	64 cc	350 ci/300-hp engine
12520266	350	NA	0.030 Oversized	Pressed	9.1:1	64 cc	350 ci/300-hp engine with SP ID.
3946876	302	3927173	Standard	Floating	11:1	64 cc	1968-'69 Z-28.
3946882	302	3927176	0.030 Oversized	Floating	11:1	64 cc	1968-'69 Z-28.
3942543	350	3942548	0.030 Oversized	Pressed	11:1	64 cc	1969 L-46.
474190	350	336747 464664/ 464692	Standard (Piston O.D. 3.998 to 3.999.)	Pressed	9:1	76 cc	1971-'80 L-82.
474192	350	464695	0.030 Oversized	Pressed	9:1	76 cc	1971-'80 L-82.
3989051	350	3949464	0.030 Oversized	Pressed or floating	11:1	64 cc	1970 LT-1.

Calculating Compression Ratio

In its simplest form, compression ratio is calculated by dividing the volume enclosed in the cylinder when the piston is at bottom dead center by the volume enclosed in the cylinder at top dead center. The only tricky part is measuring these volumes. To calculate compression ratio, the following volumes must be measured or calculated: Swept volume of the piston; the displaced volume of the piston dome and valve notches; the head gasket volume; and the volume of the combustion chamber.

Calculating the swept volume of the piston is quite straightforward. The following formula calculates the volume of a simple cylinder:

Volume (inches to ccs) = (Bore/2)^2 x 51.49 x Stroke

This formula also includes a factor that converts the inches of bore and stroke to the cubic centimeters (cc's) of volume.

The displaced volume of the piston dome and valve notches is more complex. The dome can be raised, causing an increase in the compression ratio, or it can be dished, lowering the compression ratio. Even if the piston has no dome (a flat top), it can pop out above the deck surface at TDC or end up below the deck. If the piston has valve notches, they will always reduce the compression ratio by some amount. The combination of all these factors is the "displaced dome volume."

Fortunately, there is a relatively easy way to measure this variable. By moving the piston a precise amount down the bore from TDC (often ½ or 1 inch) and sealing it with grease or Vaseline, you can fill the space with water dispensed from a burette. With the bore covered by a plastic plate (also sealed), the volume can be measured to within ¹⁄₁₀cc. By comparing this volume with the calculated volume of a cylinder of the same height (½ or 1 inch), the difference is the net vol-

ume displaced by the piston dome. A sample calculation uses the same formula as before, except the distance the piston is lowered in the bore (½ inch) is substituted for the stroke:

Volume = (4.030/2)^2 x 51.49 x .5 = 104.53 cc

104.53 cc (calculated) - 99.8 cc (measured) = 4.72 cc

The measured volume using the burette of 99.8 cc is subtracted from the calculated volume of 104.53 cc. In this case, the result is positive, indicating that the displaced dome volume is 4.72 cc, which would raise the compression ratio.

The compressed head gasket volume is often provided by the gasket manufacturer. If it isn't, you can calculate it using the same volume formula, except that you substitute the compressed gasket thickness (0.035 inch in our example below) for the stroke and the inside gasket circle (4.1 inches) for the bore:

Head Gasket Volume = (4.1/2)^2 x 51.49 x 0.035 = 7.57 cc

The final volume is the space in the combustion chamber. It is measured using the water and burette method. Make sure the valves are sealed (a little grease on the valve seats helps) and the spark plug is installed. Use a plastic plate to seal the head surface. Typical chamber volumes run from under 60 cc to over 80 cc.

Now that all of the enclosed volumes have been measured or calculated, it's just a matter of adding or subtracting them and doing the final division to determine compression ratio. Here's the formula:

CR = (C - P + G + V) / (C - P + G)

Where CR = Compression Ratio

C = Combustion Chamber Volume

P = Displaced Dome Volume

G = Compressed Head Gasket Volume

V = Swept Volume in the Cylinder

Let's plug in some typical small-block 350 numbers:

CR = (78 - (-4.2) + 7.57 + 727.5) / (78 - (-4.2) + 7.57) = 9.1:1

Note that the formula requires subtracting the displaced piston dome volume, but production 350s have negative dome volumes (flattop pistons with valve reliefs). As you may remember from math class, two negatives make a positive.

Here's one more example using a 302-ci race engine with positive dome displacement:

CR = (68 - 7.1 + 7.57 + 627.2) / (68 - 7.1 + 7.57) = 10.2:1

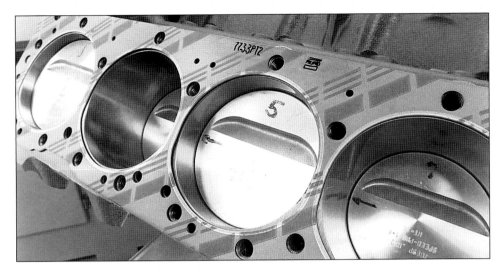

This is the quench area found on all small-block pistons. It rises under the flat part of the cylinder head, immediately adjacent to the combustion chamber. The quench area is very important to effective combustion in a wedge-type engine. The arrows indicate how the mixture in the quench area is squished into the combustion chamber when the piston rises. This causes turbulence in the chamber and promotes better flame travel.

Nine-to-one compression ratios are just about the safest limit with today's fuel, although EFI has allowed us to push that up above 10:1. On the plus side, the lower compression ratios allow the use of flattop pistons that offer superior combustion characteristics. Always use top-quality head gaskets like these from Fel Pro. Installed properly, they are reliable and will never require retorquing the head bolts.

sizes, the true compression ratio is usually higher than the figure quoted by the factory.

In some cases, high-dome pistons must be used, even at the expense of flame travel efficiency. The wedge design of the small-block engine makes use of a significant amount of quench area to increase turbulence in the combustion chamber. If you examine the small-block head, you'll see that the combustion chambers are not completely round, but more like a bathtub with a wedge-shaped chamber. Nearly a third of the cylinder bore is capped by the flat surface of the head. This area matches the flat pad or quench surface of the piston. It is this area where piston-to-head clearance is often measured, and it is also the area that creates turbulence in the chamber. When the piston rises rapidly in the bore during compression, mixture squeezed out of the quench area creates vortices of turbulence inside the chamber. This usually improves mixture quality and flame travel. When the piston has a dome that can interfere with this process, it has been found that careful shaping of the piston dome and a generous fire slot across the dome are the straightest paths to horsepower.

For a hot street engine or a bracket racer, you don't need a gargantuan dome that matches the shape of the combustion chamber. If you start with a standard TRW/Speed Pro piston and lower the dome by machining ⅛ inch from the peak, you'll still achieve a substantial compression ratio. Cut a slight trough in the area of the spark plug leading across the dome. This will ensure that the dome does not mask the flame

Speed Pro's LW series lightweight pistons are forged pistons with maximum performance designed into them. They are lighter than the standard forgings and they have special performance features such as enlarged oil slots, pin oilers, lightweight pins, high-performance skirt coatings, and a wide range of piston-top configurations.

These race-modified pistons sport gas-port holes that direct combustion pressure to the back of the ring to force it against the cylinder wall.

After the valve reliefs are cut to the proper depth, all sharp edges are smoothed and blended and the piston top is coated with a heat-reflective coating.

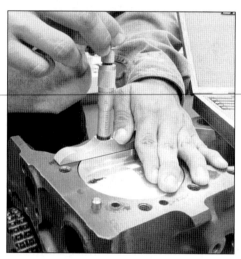

With the piston precisely at TDC, a critical examination of deck heights should include checking deck heights at various locations around the perimeter of the piston. This will ensure that small amounts of piston rock will not reduce piston-to-head clearance below minimum for reliable operation (typically 0.045 inch with steel rods).

This piston illustrates a well-finished dome configuration from the old school of thinking prior to the high-efficiency of flattop pistons and smaller combustion chambers. The dome has been radiused and fitted with a generous fire slot. The valve reliefs have been cut quite deeply to allow for adequate valve-to-piston clearance with a high-lift, long-duration cam. All sharp edges on the dome are generously radiused, the dome is hard sanded and the top is glass-beaded.

front. After altering the dome, blend and smooth all sharp edges. The trough should be carefully blended into the general shape of the dome. Consider having the piston crowns glass beaded. This leaves them with an excellent finish, but make sure the rest of the piston is masked with heavy tape. Thoroughly clean each piston with solvent and compressed air when you're finished.

Valve Clearance

For most street engines, piston-to-valve clearance will not be a problem, but it's something you should always check as a matter of course. It is more of a concern in a bracket-type engine where you may be using a healthy camshaft with lots of lift. Checking piston-to-valve clearance involves assembling the actual pieces to be used in the

engine and using light replacement springs on the valves or modeling clay on the piston tops to determine the distance from the valve to the piston when the piston is in the vicinity of TDC. For absolute assurance, the clearance should be checked at all points for 10 degrees on either side of TDC. The closest proximity may occur at a point just before or after TDC, depending on the phasing of the cam in relation to the crankshaft.

If you determine that the clearance is less than 0.100-inch on either valve, the pistons will have to be flycut to deepen the valve reliefs. This operation will have to be performed for you by a competent shop with the right equipment. Your job is to accurately determine where and how much material needs to be removed. On a car with an automatic transmission, you may be able to reduce the intake clearance to about 0.080-inch—but no less. Take care to remove no more material than is necessary, because you're also reducing compression ratio. In any case, this procedure should be followed by sandpaper blending and glass beading.

Piston Pins

Piston pin retention is another matter of wide debate. For most performance engines, it's safe to say that a pressed pin is the only way to go. Full-floating pins have not been found to have significant advantages over pressed pins. They make engine assembly easier, but in a street engine they are just another potential trouble spot. In most cases, pressed pins are your best bet.

If you choose to work with floating pins, other factors need to be considered. One of the most important things to check is connecting rod side clearance. If side clearance exceeds 0.018 to 0.022 inch, too much movement may subject the pin to greater stress. Even

With the piston at TDC, a dial indicator bridge is used to check deck height at various locations on the piston top. By adjusting the indicator to zero when the tip is resting on the deck surface, any deviation is registered when it is placed on the piston top.

Placing dabs of modeling clay in the valve pockets performs the old-school method of checking piston-to-valve clearance. The engine is then rotated with the heads in place and the valves properly lashed. The heads are removed and the thickness of the clay is checked with vernier calipers. While this method has many long-time followers, the dial indicator method described in the adjacent photo is more accurate and preferable.

After the cam is installed and degreed, a head is installed and the valves are held shut with light checking springs. As the engine is rotated in two- or three-degree increments, the rocker arm is opened as far as possible against spring travel. Stem travel is measured with a dial indicator, giving a direct readout of piston-to-valve clearance.

In floating-pin configurations, the pin is usually retained by a Spirolox (two on left), Tru-Arc (two on right), or round wire retainers (not shown). Everyone has their own particular favorite, but most engine builders seem to favor the Spirolox and round wire retainers.

more important is floating-pin end clearance. If this clearance is too great, it can allow the pin to hammer the retaining locks right out of the pin bores! Make sure end clearance falls between 0.001 and 0.008 inch. In any case, you should ascertain that there is not an interference fit, which would actually place constant pressure against the locks and just about guarantee removing them the hard way.

Pin clearance should be 0.0006 to 0.0008 inch in the piston and 0.0008 to 0.0010 inch in the rod. These clearances have to remain tight to prevent the pin from knocking in the rod and causing virtually instant failure. Although floating pins have been successfully operated without using bronze bushings in the rods, there is always a danger of pin seizure. They rarely give trouble when a bronze bushing is pressed in the rod small end. The most important aspect of all this is proper pin lubrication. If the

piston does not have a hole leading from the oil ring groove to the wrist pin bore on either side, you'll have to provide it by drilling intersecting holes in the ring groove and the pin bore. Some engine builders prefer to oil the pin with a small groove around the piston just above the oil ring. Oil collects in this groove and is drawn to the pin through oiling holes by a properly functioning vacuum system. Most of these features are now included in modern racing pistons.

Oiling the pin bushing in the rod is also a matter of considerable debate. It has long been accepted that the pin oiling hole should enter from the top of the rod. Then many respected engine builders began drilling two smaller holes from the bottom of the pin boss, on either side of the rod beam. This has

Piston Clearance Recommendations

Setting piston-to-cylinder wall (skirt) and ring end-gap clearances are critical steps in building a reliable small-block. Use these charts as a starting point, and discuss your specific application with your machine shop.

Piston Skirt

Piston Source	Piston Type	Street and Performance Clearance (in inches)	Competition Clearance (in inches)
Chevrolet	Cast Aluminum	.0015-.0025	Not Recommended
Chevrolet	Forged	.004-.006	.0055-.0065
Chevrolet	Hypereutectic	.0015-.0020	Not Recommended
TRW/Speed Pro	Hypereutectic	.0015-.0020	Not Recommended
TRW/Speed Pro	Forged	.003-.0055	.0055-.0065

Ring End-Gap

For 5/64 & 1/16 Ductile Iron Top Rings & .043 & .031 Pressure Back/Head Land Top Rings		For Regular (Plain) Iron Second Rings	
Using Special Fuels:			
Supercharged/injected nitro engines	.022/.024	Supercharged/injected nitro engines	.014/.016
Supercharged/injected alcohol engines	.018/.020	Supercharged/injected alcohol engines	.012/.014
Using Gasoline:			
Supercharged/injected gasoline engines	.022/.024	Supercharged/injected gasoline engines	.012/.014
Oval track rectangular rings	.018/.020		
Oval track head land rings	.024/.026	Oval track	.012/.014
Oval track pressure back rings	.020/.022		
Pro stock, comp eliminator, modified production, etc.	.018/.020	Pro stock, comp eliminator, modified production, etc.	.012/.014
Super stock	.018/.020	Super stock	.010/.012
Stock	.016/.018	Stock	.010/.012
Street engines	.016/.018	Street engines	.010/.012

Note: These Speed Pro end gap recommendations will be appropriate in most cases. They stress that this chart should be used as a guide to normal ring fitting, and that the ideal end gap may be different for specific combinations. If you're ever in doubt, check with other engine builders or add .002 inch to the recommended gap. Racers with plenty of experience often close up the gaps rom .002 to .004 inch, but you have to be willing to sacrifice a motor if you guess wrong.

become popular, but many people still cling to the older single-hole method. It's difficult to say which is better, but you have to consider that there probably is more oil located below the pin than above it. We have also seen rods fitted with holes on both the top and the bottom, which seems to have no affect on rod strength, at least in most performance applications.

An interesting fact that you may have observed concerns the subtle difference between various pins. Close inspection of most pins will show that they are bored in one operation. This yields a smooth notch-free bore through the center of the pin. However, some pins appear to be bored from both ends and the bores never match up correctly. There is often a step right in the center of the pin, exactly where the greatest loading occurs. This presents no particular problems in a street or bracket-racing application, but any severe service application, such as a supercharged or

This view shows a typical pin oiling strategy. On the left, you can see how the oil is taken from the oil ring groove and routed to the wrist pin. In some cases, pin oil is also aided by oil recovered from an accumulator groove between the oil ring and the compression rings. This groove provides some place for excess oil to go so it won't migrate past the rings into the combustion chamber.

Pin-to-piston-pin bore clearance should be 0.0006 to 0.0008 inch. This clearance has to be tight to prevent the pin from knocking in the piston and causing instant failure of the pin bore. Insufficient clearance can be corrected by honing the pin bores. Excess clearance can also be corrected by installing oversized pins.

turbocharged engine, should be fitted with smooth-bore pins.

Piston Rings

Piston ring selection can make or break your project. Ideally, you want a ring set that provides excellent cylinder sealing, good oil control, and minimum frictional drag. This is a tall order when you consider the operating environment. On one hand, you have the heat of combustion trying to melt the top ring and leak by it, while the second ring and the oil ring are trying desperately to prevent oil from entering the combustion chamber and contaminating the mixture. On the other hand, you have the cylinder walls, which are trying to grab the rings and bring everything to a standstill.

Many experimental ring designs have been used to meet the specific requirements of different racing environments. For the average street or bracket-racing engine, ring combinations are fairly standardized, and the best plan is to stick with proven pieces and procedures. The conventional three-ring layout works exceptionally well when the rings are gapped and installed correctly in properly honed cylinders.

Stock Chevrolet pistons generally have 5/64-inch top and second rings with either a 1/8-inch or 3/16-inch oil ring. The factory ring sets are an excellent choice for street performance, as are TRW and Speed Pro replacements. Engines that aren't required to operate at very high engine speeds work extremely well with wider rings, because they stabilize the pistons and the wide face provides a better seal at low engine speeds. For high-performance work, you should consider lighter and thinner rings. They are more able to seal the engine at high speeds because they resist ring flutter and the subsequent loss of seal. Thinner rings also reduce frictional drag, which skyrockets at high engine speeds.

The choices are clearly defined: A wider factory-type ring will seal the cylinder better at any engine speed up to 5,500 rpm; above this, thinner 1/16-inch rings do a better job until engine speed approaches 8,000 rpm; beyond that, you'll need extra thin rings and special sealing techniques that exceed the spirit of even most bracket-racing engines. This is pro-racer stuff, and you probably don't need any of it!

There is no reason to use anything other than a single-moly or plasma-moly ring set in any hot street engine or bracket racing powerplant. Chrome rings may still have a place in environmental conditions where engines are prone to ingesting a lot of dirt and grit, but the moly ring is the absolute best choice in nearly every other case. For a turbocharged engine, plasma-spray moly rings are the hot tip since they resist flaking under severe detonation conditions.

The conventional three-ring system for general street and high-performance use consists of a high-strength ductile iron top ring with a moly-coated surface. The temperature resistant moly is usually embedded in a thin channel on the face of the ring.

Setting Ring End Gaps

Properly setting the end gap on oversize (gapable) ring sets can be a tedious, error-prone process. However, done precisely, it almost certainly will improve horsepower, reliability, fuel economy, and extend engine life. Done incorrectly, it can take the fine edge off an otherwise excellent engine, or in the worst case, result in severe ring damage and greatly shortened engine life.

To properly gap rings, you must do two things: 1. Remove the precise amount of material (exact to the thousandths of an inch) from the end of each ring, and 2. Ensure that the resulting gap is parallel and have no burrs or sharp edges that can scratch the bore. Until recently there were two common ways to gap rings, both of them less than satisfactory. Filing while holding the ring in a vise is one common practice. So is using a simple cutting-wheel tool made by several manufacturers, including Perfect Circle, K-D, and others. Both of these methods require substantial experience and manual dexterity. And even with experience, it's easy to ruin a ring or two. (Luckily, most machine shops will sell individual rings at a reasonable price.)

There is also a tool from ABS Products that uses a rotating table and a dial indicator to make gapping rings the precision process it should be. In fact, using

the ABS tool, it's possible for an experienced builder to gap all 16 top and second rings in about 15 to 30 minutes. And with only a little care, each ring gap will be exactly the right width and dead parallel.

However, the ABS tool is rather expensive. Fortunately, many machine and engine shops now use ABS gapping tools. We strongly recommend that you have your rings gapped by one of the shops that use this tool. Since it takes them so little time to gap a set of rings, the cost should be reasonable. If you are determined to do it yourself (and you don't want to buy the ABS tool), consider the Huggins E-Z Gap ring support and gapping tool as an alternative to the K-D type of cutting wheel. Available from Taylor Engines (310-698-7231), the Huggins E-Z Gap is an inexpensive tool that includes a file, feeler gauge, and instructions. While it does require learning the proper technique, you may have better luck with this tool than other low-cost methods.

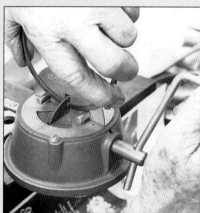

The simple cutting wheel tool made by Perfect Circle, K-D, and others requires a steady hand and a good deal of practice and is still good at chewing up rings. Luckily, there are good alternatives.

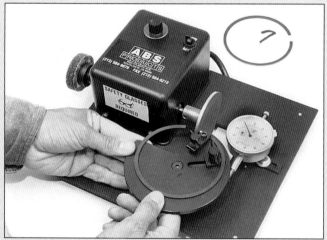

ABS Products ring gapping tool uses a rotating table and a dial indicator that makes gapping rings a precision process. Using this tool, it's easy to remove just the right amount of material to achieve a perfect gap every time.

Consider the Huggins ring-gapping tool. This inexpensive kit requires mastering the proper technique, but some have had better luck with this tool than other basic methods.

Using a matched ring set from a major manufacturer ensures maximum quality. You can get a standard set that is already pregapped for end clearance, or you can purchase a file-fit set that will require custom fitting to each bore. Speed Pro now incorporates special skirt coatings on most of the high-performance pistons.

It is important that the ring is dead parallel when it is being checked in the bore. This is necessary to prevent false end-gap readings and/or partial butting when the engine reaches operating temperature.

Optimum End-Gap Positions

Install all piston rings with end gaps staggered as shown here. With properly gapped rings and properly honed cylinder walls this procedure will provide the best cylinder sealing and most efficient oil control. Install rings on pistons with the proper expander tool whenever possible.

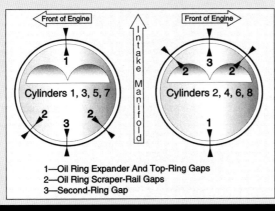

```
  Front of Engine                    Front of Engine

         1                                  3
                         I
                         n
                         t
                         a
    2         2          k        2                2
                         e
       3                 M                1
                         a
  Cylinders 1, 3, 5, 7   n    Cylinders 2, 4, 6, 8
                         i
                         f
                         o
                         l
                         d
```

1—Oil Ring Expander And Top-Ring Gaps
2—Oil Ring Scraper-Rail Gaps
3—Second-Ring Gap

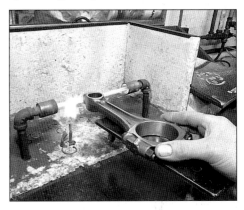

Pressed pins are installed using après and a rod heater to expand the small end of the rod during pin installation.

Second rings are standard or low-tension (for racing only) cast iron. They have a tapered face and no coating. The second ring acts primarily as a backup to the top ring and helps transfer combustion heat to the cylinder walls. Three-piece oil rings have stainless steel rails and an internal expander to provide good oil control with a minimum of friction.

There is also a double-moly ring set where the second ring also has a moly inlay. These rings work well in a competition environment, but they are not necessary in a street engine since they do not provide a substantial

benefit for day-to-day operation, and the low-tension second ring used in most double-moly sets does not provide good, long-term oil control.

All of the rings available from TRW/Speed Pro are offered in standard oversizes and also in special sets that have an additional 0.005-inch oversize to allow for individual fitting to the bores. Careful ring fitting to the individual bores is an important procedure that can virtually guarantee more horsepower from your engine. In a well-sealed engine, the end gap is the only path through which combustion gases can escape to the crankcase. It is

therefore desirable to close the gaps as much as possible to prevent the passage of gases in one direction and oil in the other direction.

Standard ring sets are manufactured so they may be easily fitted with little consideration given to the end gaps. Generally, they're pregapped slightly on the wide side so that rebuilders can stay out of trouble while flat rating their way through your engine. The special oversize sets require that each individual ring be gapped to its particular cylinder. It's important that the gap be kept small enough so that there will be

Piston Prep Checklist

1. Make sure you have the correct pistons, including left and right sets when using domed pistons.
2. Magnaflux pins and Zyglo-test pistons if they are used.
3. Check ring groove, skirt, pint-to-bore, and pin-end clearances.
4. Determine what machine work will be required, and measure and record critical piston dimensions prior to any machine operations.
5. Mock up engine assembly and check deck height.
6. Check piston-to-valve clearance while engine is preassembled.
7. Machine valve reliefs (if necessary) and perform machining and dome blending.
8. Drill pin holes if required.
9. Deburr piston and glass bead deck and dome surface.
10. Balance pistons.
11. Clean in solvent, blow dry, and store in plastic bags until assembly.

This view illustrates the difference in compression heights and the effect it has on pin location. When longer rods are used in a given combination, the pin is moved higher in the piston. In extreme cases the pin gets into the ring package and shorter pins have to be used for clearance.

Experienced engine builders often install rings by carefully wrapping them onto the piston. If you premark each piston with the cylinder location and an arrow indicating the front of the piston, you can quickly arrange end gaps in the proper orientation.

There is quite a range of piston-top configurations for the typical small-block. Clockwise from the left rear, we see a dished or reverse deflector dome, a moderate-performance dome, a racing dome, flattop with two valve reliefs, and a flattop with four valve reliefs.

Special installation tools can also be used to install rings. These require more care because it is possible to expand the ring too far and break it during installation.

Piston Ring Checklist

1. Visually inspect for signs of damage or mispackaged rings.
2. Set end gaps; keep ends parallel. Keep rings square in bores when measuring end gaps.
3. Send one set of rings to your machine shop with other assembly pieces to aid in balancing.
4. Clean with solvent and store until final assembly.
5. Install rings carefully with end gaps properly positioned.

minimum gas leakage when the engine reaches operating temperature. You have to be careful here, because a ring that has insufficient clearance will butt in the cylinder, scuff the bore, and immediately end the possibility that your engine will deliver top-notch performance and longevity.

It's also essential that the end-gapping procedure be performed properly. Not only do you have to set them at the right clearance, you must keep the ends square and free of burrs or sharp edges. Furthermore, when you check a ring in its bore, make sure that it is straight and dead parallel with the deck surface. A false reading will be obtained if the ring is not positioned properly. If your engine is used for bracket racing and you tear it down from time to time, be sure to check the end gaps for signs of butting. If they are shiny after extended usage, it may indicate they have been in contact with one another.

Pistons and rings are very important parts of your engine, whether it's a pure stocker or a full-race piece. Their selection and preparation should be the subject of careful consideration. Don't buy over your head, but don't buy budget parts if you're building a race motor. A little forethought here will save you money and grief, and go a long way toward ensuring that you build a strong, reliable small-block!

Piston Assembly and Clearance Checking

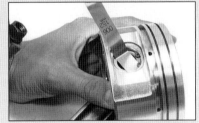
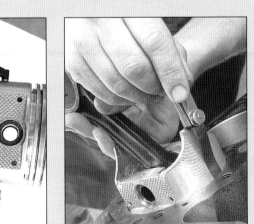

Oil the pin bores in the rods and pistons lightly. Then, following all the applicable orientation rules, assemble (or check the assembly of) all rods and pistons. If you have press-fit pins, proceed to the next step. For floating pins: You don't need to install the pin-lock rings for preassembly. However, you should check endplay on at least one piston (preferably the entire set). Use snap-ring piers for standard pin locks, while Spirolox can be worked in one loop at a time with a probe or small screwdriver. Make sure the lock rings are fully seated in the pistons. Then check pin endplay with either feeler gauges or vernier calipers. Endplay should be 0.001 to 0.008 inch; clearance outside this range can force the locks out during engine operation!

You can check piston-to-cylinder wall (also called "skirt") clearance with micrometers, or you can use feeler gauges with very little, if any, loss in accuracy. To use micrometers: Use an outside mic to measure a piston skirt at the position indicated by the manufacturer. Then measure the minimum bore diameter in the matching bore. Subtract piston diameter from bore diameter to obtain skirt clearance. To be certain of your figures, repeat the measurements several times for each piston. To use feeler gauges: Insert a piston upside down into the appropriate bore with feeler gauge strips between the skirt and the bore. Start with feeler gauge strips that are 0.001 to 0.002 inch too thin and increase in 0.001-inch steps. When the piston just becomes snug in the bore, the skirt clearance is 0.001 inch less than the gauge thickness.

CAMSHAFTS

Selecting a camshaft is one of the most important decisions you'll face when building a high-performance small-block for street or bracket racing. In many ways, the camshaft is the command center of the engine. Your cam calls the shots—and if it calls them wrong, you lose the ball game, even though the rest of the team may have been playing well.

Cam Selection

So much has been written about camshaft selection and design that it is very easy to get confused. How can anyone make an intelligent selection when confronted with such conflicting data? Your favorite hero racer endorses Hu-Mon-Gor cams because "they really work for me," and he might even be telling the truth. The lobes are so high they're snow-capped and his engine really flies on the big end, but that doesn't mean it will work for you. His combination works for exactly that reason; it's his combination. Now unless your vehicle and application are identical to his, why in the world would you expect it to work for you?

A successful profile is always based on two simple things: combi-

Major manufacturers such as COMP Cams and Crane offer an extensive lineup of high-performance camshafts to suit every application. These cams are available individually or in various kits that may include only lifters, or complete kits that also have timing chains and gears, pushrods, valvesprings, retainers, and more.

nation and application. You can't have one without the other, and you can't mismatch them without encountering dramatic loss of performance. When selecting a cam, you will be confronted by an intimidating battery of facts and figures and a sprinkling of little white lies. It's not the intention of the cam manufacturers to deceive you, but they do have to present their products in the best light possible when compared with the competition. The "more is

better" syndrome is still prevalent and it is more the fault of the consumer than the manufacturer. A substantial number of cam buyers still seek the biggest, meanest stick they can buy, regardless of their combination and application. Because of this, cam manufacturers still use "advertised" duration figures, which add to the confusion.

For the benefit of the knowledgeable consumer, most cam makers also publish duration figures measured at

If you compare a roller cam (foreground) to a flat-tappet cam, the difference is considerable. Rollers are made from steel billet cores. Rollers can generally achieve more aggressive cam profiles that can live on the street. Solid rollers are most prevalent, but the popularity of hydraulic rollers has risen dramatically in recent years.

The cam is driven at one half of the engine speed, as shown by the timing dots on this billet gear set. The camshaft and the crankshaft are properly aligned when the timing dots are aligned as shown here (arrow). This billet timing set is adjustable via the adjusting nuts so that timing may be varied up to eight degrees advanced or retarded.

Small-block camshafts are located in the cam tunnel directly above the crankshaft in conventional fashion. The lobes are splash lubricated from oil coming off the lifters.

some fixed point of valve lift, generally 0.050-inch. Always remember that the advertised duration is purely theoretical and it does not usually represent the actual time (in crankshaft degrees) that the valve is off the seat. To gain a further understanding of all the factors at work, let's examine the various components and how they relate to each other.

Cam Drive Basics

The camshaft is driven off the crankshaft via a 1:2 ratio so that the camshaft rotates once for every two crankshaft revolutions. To arrive at the proper timing sequence, the cam and crank gears have marks that are aligned when the timing chain is installed. With this arrangement, it is possible to alter the relationship between the cam and the crank to fine tune the combination. This can be done by installing a special offset bushing in the cam gear or by using an offset Woodruff key on the crank gear. In addition, most chain and gear manufacturers offer crank gears cut with multiple keyways that allow you to easily advance or retard the cam in 2-degree increments up to 6 or 8 degrees. There are also a variety of other timing alteration methods, including an adjustable cam gear bushing (using a hex key) from Cloyes that makes altering timing easier than ever. Any of these methods allow you to rotate the cam ever so slightly with respect to the crank, either advancing or retarding cam timing. And sometimes there are advantages to this procedure, but in almost every case you will want to first run the cam in the "straight-up" position to determine whether a timing alteration is really necessary. The shape and location of each lobe on the camshaft determines when the valves are opened and closed, how far and how fast they open and close, and how long the valves stay open. Let's take a close look at how these functions are related and why they occur when they do.

Valve Events

There are a variety of interrelated factors that determine how valvetrain events are timed. Their occurrence is expressed in degrees of crankshaft rotation. Keep in mind that a full stroke of each piston requires 180 degrees of crank rotation and a total of 720 degrees is

Camshaft Basics

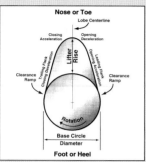

Camshaft terminology can be confusing, so here's the lowdown. To start off, the camshaft is a round shaft incorporating **cam lobes.** The **base circle diameter** is the smallest diameter of the cam lobe and is shaped perfectly round. **Clearance ramps** begin the transition from the round base circle to the **flanks** of the lobe. As the cam turns, the lifter is smoothly lifted by the clearance ramp and flank and continues to rise as it approaches the **nose.** The lifter's rate of lift decreases to a stop as it reaches maximum lift at the **lobe centerline.** Maximum **lifter rise** is determined by the height of the tip of the cam lobe from the base circle diameter. The lifter then slides or rolls back down the other side of the nose, ramp, and flank, closing the valve. Valve **duration** is the number of crankshaft degrees that the lifter is held above a specified height by the cam lobe (usually 0.006, 0.020, or 0.050 inch). A **symmetric lobe** has the same lift curve on both the opening and closing sides; an asymmetric lobe is shaped differently on each side of the lobe. A **single-pattern cam** has the same profile on both the intake and exhaust lobes; a **dual-pattern cam** has different profiles for the intake and exhaust lobes.

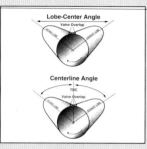

Lobe-center angle is the angle measured in camshaft degrees (multiply by two for equivalent crankshaft degrees) between the maximum-lift points on the intake and exhaust lobes for the same cylinder. The lobe-center angle is ground into the cam when it is manufactured and cannot be changed (unless the cam is reground). As the lobe-center angle is decreased, the valve overlap period (when both intake and exhaust valves are open) is increased. This usually results in a rougher idle, reduced low-speed power, and increased high-speed power. The lobe **centerline** is the angle measured in crankshaft degrees between the point of maximum lift on the number one intake lobe (usually) and TDC. This value is determined by the indexing of the cam to the crankshaft. A reduced centerline angle (less than the lobe-center angle) indicates that the cam is advanced.

When the cam is aligned, the crank key and the camshaft dowel pin will be in the approximate position shown here.

needed to complete the intake, compression, power, and exhaust cycles.

Consider first the opening and closing of the valves. To begin the first (intake) cycle, the intake valve opens to admit the air/fuel mixture. For efficient cylinder filling it is advanta-geous to open the intake valve early (before TDC). This allows the relatively slow moving intake charge more time to get moving before the piston starts down the cylinder. Just how early it should open is a function of engine speed, induction efficiency, and desired power output. The intake valve can be opened to efficiently produce power. This is because the fuel charge has inertia, and while it's hard to get it moving, once it reaches reasonable speeds, it will continue moving. So opening the valve early allows the already-moving charge to enter the cylinder before the piston begins to move down the bore on the intake stroke.

Augmenting this effect is the relatively late closing of the exhaust valve. It is left open after TDC (top

This is a typical nonadjustable, double-roller timing set available from most major camshaft suppliers. This type of cam gear can still be adjusted by installing an offset dowel pin bushing.

dead center) to improve intake flow (among other reasons) by allowing the low pressure that follows the rapidly exiting exhaust gases to draw additional intake charge into the cylinder. If the camshaft is well matched to the engine, significant cylinder filling will occur before the piston has moved very far down the bore (from early intake opening and late exhaust closing). Ideally, the exhaust valve will close just as fresh intake charge moves across the chamber. By that time, the piston has gained sufficient speed to continue filling the cylinder.

Thus far, we have opened the intake valve early and closed the exhaust valve late in an effort to aid cylinder filling at higher engine speeds. One might think that the intake valve should be closed at BDC (bottom dead center) so that compression can begin immediately, but the dynamic function of the engine offers an opportunity to continue to pack the cylinder with air and fuel. While the crankshaft is swinging the connecting rod from one side to the other, the piston experiences a certain dwell time at BDC. It is momentarily motionless, and afterward, once the piston begins to rise in the cylinder, it takes a while before it reaches substantial speed. This leaves

In addition to rearward thrust, roller cams and other racing cams can produce forward thrust that causes ignition timing variations and can damage the cam lobes and lifters. A thrust bumper or cam button like this one provides an effective means of controlling forward thrust.

These offset bushings are used to adjust cam timing on a standard nonadjustable cam gear. They are available from all cam manufacturers.

COMP Cams also offer this three-piece aluminum timing cover that allows cam changes and adjustments without having to remove the cover from the engine. With the top portion of this cover removed, you can make cam adjustments and even change a cam.

For high-performance applications, some timing sets are equipped with a Torrington roller bearing behind the cam gear to absorb thrust loads from roller cams.

A high-performance camshaft kit generally includes most of the components necessary to set up a good compatible valvetrain. Most include valvesprings, retainers, locks, pushrods, seals, flat-tappet or roller lifters, a timing set, and distributor drive gear.

It's a good idea to deburr the cam gear and any mating surfaces prior to installation in any application.

Wet or dry belt drives like these from Comp Cams have become the norm in high-performance and competition engines. The belts are bulletproof and they resist stretching, so timing remains rock solid at all engine speeds.

Flat tappets are still the most prevalent type of valve lifters in use. They are simple and very reliable as long as you maintain an adequate supply of clean, filtered oil.

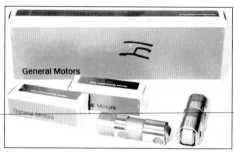

Hydraulic roller lifters are currently used in all GM production engines. These lifters have proven reliable for very long periods, just like their flat-tappet brothers.

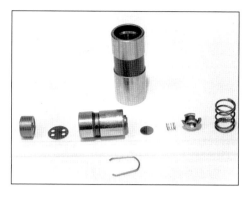

Flat-tappet hydraulic lifters have an internal spring and plunger assembly designed to act as a shock absorber while eliminating the need for clearance ramps. When you adjust the preload on these lifters, you are compressing the spring and changing the internal oil volume.

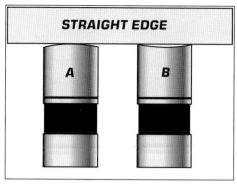

As shown here, all flat-tappet lifters have a slight taper to the surface, which allows them to rotate on the camshaft lobe. If the taper is incorrect or worn convex, the lifter and the lobe will fail quickly.

even more time for the inertia of the intake charge to continue filling the cylinder. The piston is now well into the compression stroke before the intake valve closes. It continues to rise in the cylinder, continuing the compression stroke until the mixture is ignited by the spark plug. The ignition point signals the beginning of the power stroke.

The events leading up to the power stroke are very important. Changes here have the greatest effect on the engine's torque curve, but it's still important to examine all events, including the exhaust valve opening point. Conventional thinking would again wait until the power stroke is completed before opening the exhaust valve, the idea being to obtain maximum effect from combustion pressure. In practice, however, the mechanical advantage of cylinder pressure on the piston, rod, and crank arm greatly diminishes as

the piston moves down the bore making it advantageous to open the valve well before BDC. In fact, by the time the piston has reached midpoint in its downward travel, it has already transferred nearly all of the available work to the crankshaft, and from there on it's just along for the ride.

Once the work has been done, you have to clean up the mess, and the early opening exhaust valve helps make the job easier. Since there is still considerable pressure in the cylinder, it will rapidly vent as soon as the valve begins to open. This allows the exhaust charge to build inertia before the piston starts chasing it up the cylinder. Once again, because of these same dynamic forces, when the piston begins the exhaust stroke, much of the pressure has already been relieved, reducing pumping losses. The valve is also well off the seat as the piston begins to rise, and it is relatively easy for the piston to push out what's left. Because of this and the physical ramming effect of the rising piston, it's easier to drive exhaust gasses out than it is to draw intake charge into the cylinder. For this reason, exhaust event timing is

often less critical than intake event timing. The piston reaches a momentary low pressure, which helps to draw in the next intake charge, and the four cycles begin again.

By examining some factory cams we can better understand how the timing of these events change as we move from a low-RPM street cam to a high-RPM race cam. By keeping in mind what we have just learned about flow dynamics, we can see how event timing, flow dynamics, and engine speed are all closely related. Study the chart below and find the 3896929 hydraulic grind; a cam that has been used as standard equipment in everything from the low-horsepower 283 to the medium output 350-ci engine. It's a perfect example of the ideal street cam for production vehicles. The timing is versatile enough to work in a wide variety of engines without hurting performance in any of them. Notice that it follows the game plan by opening the intake valve early: 26 degrees before TDC to be exact. This gets things moving and we can start adding up event timing to arrive at the number of degrees (duration) that the intake valve is open. To the initial 26 degrees of crankshaft rotation before TDC, we

Solid roller lifters are still preferred for all serious racing applications. Roller lifters can take plenty of abuse and they can be made extremely light to reduce valvespring requirements.

can add 180 degrees for the entire intake stroke and 90 more degrees for the amount of time the valve remains open after BDC. The total of these figures is 296 degrees, and that's listed as duration (in crankshaft degrees) at the lash point. This actually means the number of degrees between the point at which the valve lifts off and then returns to its seat. It is not, however, the true effective duration of the intake event. At extremely low valve lifts there is little significant flow, so we have to look at the timing from a point where the charge actually begins to gather momentum. Manufacturers disagree on just where this point occurs. This is understandable, since this initial point can be affected by a variety of factors, the most obvious of which are carburetor venturi area, intake manifold design, and cylinder head efficiency. It is generally agreed that significant flow begins somewhere between 0.010- and 0.050-inch valve lift and most manufacturers use a figure in this range as their reference checking point. The most common figure is 0.050 inch, although 0.020 and 0.030 inch are sometimes used for published specs.

At 0.050-inch valve lift, the intake event on the 3896929 cam is reduced to only 195 degrees. But this is not as bad as it seems. Recalling that the theoretical intake stroke is only 180 degrees, it provides an additional 15 degrees of duration in which significant flow can continue to fill the cylinder. And all is not lost with the low-lift flow, because the valve is physically off the seat during this period and some charge movement does occur (a certain amount of lead-time inertia is established for each event).

The 0.050-inch checking point is an excellent means of comparing camshafts, but only if the published figures for each cam are rated at the same 0.050-inch figure. If they differ, it will be difficult to arrive at a meaningful comparison without physical testing. If we move down the chart to one of the early race profiles (PN 2927140, for example) we can observe how the timing events are realigned to work at higher engine speeds. Where the hydraulic street cam opened the intake valve at 26 degrees BTDC (before top dead center), the 2927140 cam opens it at a much earlier 44 degrees BTDC. You have to remember that as engine speed increases, there is less time for each event (cycle) to occur. Therefore, a longer period (in crankshaft degrees of duration) is used to make up for it. You may notice that while the intake opening is significantly earlier, the closing point is nearly the same. This is because the designers wished to maintain a flat torque curve since this cam is intended for use in short-track racing, where superior torque is required to accelerate heavy cars out of low-speed turns. Cams listed below the 2927140 cam have a later closing point because they are intended for longer tracks and higher speeds where it is beneficial to move the torque curve higher in the RPM range.

When you examine the chart you will find that the 0.050-inch

Both of these studs are designed to screw into the cylinder head, as opposed to press-in studs used in many production small-blocks. The ⅜-inch stud on the left has a ⁷⁄₁₆-inch base thread, while the ⁷⁄₁₆-inch stud on the right is the same size both top and bottom for greater strength. The ⅜-inch stud generally uses a jam nut as shown, while ⁷⁄₁₆-inch aftermarket studs are usually used with poly locks. Poly locks for both sizes are available from the cam companies.

specification for the 2927140 cam provides 48 degrees more duration that the 3896929 cam. This is a significant breathing increase for the faster running engine. All of this is, of course, general and any cam grinder will tell you that the success of the overall combination depends greatly on the compatibility of the rest of the engine components and even the gearing, tire diameter, car weight, and a hundred other factors. With the basic information offered here, you should be able to study various cam profiles and observe how each is designed for a particular application. It may take considerable study before you are able to approximate the timing required for your engine. But before you get too engrossed, there are several other factors that can affect your selection. Chief among them is the lobe displacement angle, sometimes called the "lobe-center angle."

Original Small-Block Camshafts

Most of the camshafts listed here are still available from Chevrolet. Refer to these profiles as they relate to the discussion in the text. You can also use them for comparison against the more modern cams.

Part Number	Lifter Type	Cam Lobe & Running Valve Lash	Crankshaft Duration @ Lash Point	Crankshaft Duration @ .050 Tappet Lift	Maximum Lift with 1.5:1 Rocker Ratio	Lobe Center-lines	Remarks
3736097	Mechanical	.012/.018	287°/283°	222°/221°	.381/.380	110°	Used in pre-'64 Corvette; excellent torque and RPM
361995	Hydraulic	1/4 turn down from zero lash	289°/310°	187°/202°	.372/.410	114°	Used in 305-ci V-8; high torque and good fuel economy
3896929	Hydraulic	1/4 turn down from zero lash	296°/310°	195°/202°	.390/.410	112°	Used in 305-ci V-8; good high-torque street cam
3849346	Mechanical	.030/.030	313°/313°	236°/236°	.447/.447	115°	Used in 1964-'65 Corvette and 1967-'69 Z/28
3863151	Hydraulic	1/4 turn down from zero lash	320°/320°	221°/221°	.447/.447	114°	1965-'67 327-ci Corvette; good torque and power
3896962	Hydraulic	1/4 turn down from zero lash	320°/320°	222°/222°	.450/.460	114°	1969-'81 L-46 & L-82 350-ci Corvette; good power
3972178	Mechanical	.024/.030	307°/319°	229°/237°	.432/.452	116°	1970-'71 LT-1 Corvette & Camaro
3927140	Mechanical	.024/.026	316°/323°	243°/254°	.455/.481	112°	First racing design, good short track, use spring #3927142
3965754	Mechanical	.024/.026	324°/324°	249°/258°	.483/.503	112°	Second racing design, good short track, use spring #330585
366293	Mushroom	.025/.025	325°/335°	254°/262°	.560/.575	107°	Third racing design, good medium and long track

Lobe Centers

Imagine a line passing from the center of the cam directly through the highest point on the lobe. This is the geometric centerline of that particular lobe. To avoid confusion when comparing cams, remember that lobe-center angle is measured between the centerlines of the intake and corresponding exhaust lobes, while lobe centerline is the angle measured between the center of the lobe and TDC. Lobe-center angle is fixed and cannot be changed once the cam is ground. The lobe centerline can be altered by advancing or retarding the cam. When you do this, you are effectively moving the intake lobe centerline closer to or farther from TDC.

In terms of engine performance, the lobe-center angle is significant.

A larger angle yields less valve overlap (the period when both valves are open). This permits the cylinders to begin building pressure sooner and that boosts low-speed torque. Decreasing the angle yields greater valve overlap and moves the torque curve higher in the RPM range. This narrows the engine's effective powerband.

For most street applications, always select a cam that will build as much torque as possible. Generally you want valve events that produce a wider lobe-center angle, decreasing valve overlap. One of the advantages of the new high-velocity factory and aftermarket street roller profiles is that you have good idle quality by using wider 112 to 115 lobe centerlines, but you also have a high-RPM boost with more aggressive lobe profiles (increased effective duration). The result is a broad torque curve that is ideal for street use.

Turbocharged or supercharged engines should avoid cams with too much overlap, since the pressurized intake system already provides effective cylinder filling and forced exhaust scavenging. In these applications, long overlap can be detrimental, since some of the intake charge can be blown right through the engine without being burned.

For the average street and strip enthusiast, all of these factors are taken care of by the cam manufacturer. Their vast experience lets them provide you with a cam that they know will work. The worst thing you can do is let your friends pick your cam. The best thing you can do is call the manufacturer and talk with their technical assistance rep. The price of the call is more

High-performance applications using stock-type ball rocker arms should be equipped with grooved rocker-arm pivot balls. The grooves hold additional lubrication to prevent galling under severe conditions. Exhaust rockers always run hotter than intake rockers and they should always have grooved pivot balls even if the engine is nearly stock.

A cam lock plate as shown here is used to positively retain the cam gear bolts. After the bolts are torqued, the small tabs are bent up to prevent the bolts from backing off.

than worth the help you'll receive. If the tech rep is friendly, sincere, and asks a lot of questions, chances are he really has your interests at heart and will supply you with a cam just right for your needs.

While you're discussing cam specs with the tech man, you might keep some other factors in mind. Depending on the application, you'll probably be using either hydraulic or solid lifters. For a variety of reasons, roller cams are an excellent choice, but many people still rely on flat-tappet grinds. Camshaft companies now offer great

Roller-type rocker arms offer numerous advantages over stock-type ball pivot rockers. On the right is an aluminum full roller rocker arm from Crane Cams, while on the left is a budget-style roller-tip, ball-pivot combination rocker from Comp Cams.

street roller profiles with either hydraulic or solid roller lifters that offer more performance than virtually any streetable flat-tappet cam.

Current Factory Camshaft Kits

In addition to standard Chevrolet factory camshafts, GM also offers a variety of specially prepared camshaft kits designed and manufactured by Crane Cams. Each kit consists of a matched camshaft and lifter set and carries the endorsement of Chevrolet. They are listed here by part number and application.

PN 12353915

This cam works for all 1981–1987 small-blocks with computer control and nonroller camshafts except the HO 305. This is a hydraulic flat-tappet cam kit designed to boost midrange torque in cars and light trucks with optional factory gearing and/or automatic transmissions. It produces excellent low-speed torque for 305 and 350 engines running between 1,800 and 2,600 rpm.

Duration @ 0.050-inch lift: Int. 194 degrees, Exh. 204 degrees

Most roller rockers use a poly lock positive locking nut to maintain the adjustment. When the correct lash is set, the hex nut is snugger and the jam nut is tightened against it to lock the setting.

Lift: Int. 0.401 inch, Exh. 0.403 inch
Lobe-Center Angle: 104 degrees

PN 12533914

This cam works for all 1981–1987 small-blocks with computer control and nonroller camshafts. It's a special grind for high torque in full-size passenger cars and trucks. This kit designed for extra high torque on 267-, 305-, and 350-ci engines.

Duration @ 0.050-inch lift: Int. 180 degrees, Exh. 194 degrees
Lift: Int. 0.378 inch, Exh. 0.0401 inch
Lobe-Center Angle: 104 degrees

PN 12533923

This strong hydraulic camshaft works for all 1955–1966 small-block V-8s in California, 1955–1968 engines with federal emissions controls, all nonemission trucks, and 1966–1992 off-highway applications. This cam is optimized for 9.5 to 10.5:1 compression ratios and 3,000–4,000-rpm cruise speeds. Power range is from 2,200 to 5,700 rpm. You can run this cam to 6,500 rpm with performance springs and proper lifter adjustment.

Duration @ 0.050-inch lift: Int. 224 degrees, Exh. 234 degrees
Lift: Int. 0.465 inch, Exh. 0.448 inch
Lobe-Center Angle: 114 degrees

Different types of cam bumpers are available for adjusting the endplay on the camshaft. Roller-type buttons come in fixed lengths, while the nylon buttons can be trimmed and filed to achieve the exact clearance you are seeking.

Lash caps are used to provide a larger contact surface for the rocker-arm roller tip. They are often useful for achieving a proper roller-tip-to valvestem relationship and proper rocker-arm geometry.

One of the most critical clearances to check is retainer-to-guide or retainer-to-seal clearance. If you cam's lift is too great, you may have to trim the top of the guides to prevent contact and instant damage to the cam lobe and the lifter. Most builders try to leave at least 0.060 inch of clearance.

Valvespring shims typically come in .015-, .030-, and .060-inch thickness and in all types of inside and outside diameters. They are stacked as required to achieve the correct valvespring pressure on each valve.

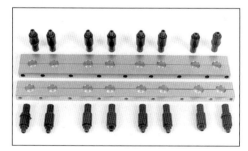

Stud girdles are as commonly used today as they were in the past. They are a good way to lock in your valve lash settings while stabilizing the valvetrain.

PN 12533918

This cam is meant for "marine" and off-road small-block applications with compression ratios from 8.75 to 10.5:1 and a 2,600-3,000-rpm cruise speed. The power range is from 2,000 to 4,500 rpm. It works well to 6,500 rpm with good springs and proper lifter adjustment.

Duration @ 0.050-inch lift: Int. 214 degrees, Exh. 224 degrees
Lift: Int. 0.442 inch, Exh. 0.465 inch
Lobe-Center Angle: 112 degrees

PN 12533917

This cam will work in 1955–1966 small-blocks used in California, 1955–1968 with federal emissions requirements, all nonemission trucks, and 1966–1992 off-highway applications. This is a hydraulic cam kit for 8.0 to 9.5:1 compression ratios and 2,200–2,600-rpm cruise speeds. The power range is from 1,500–4,000 rpm, though it can operate to 6,500 rpm using performance springs and proper lifter adjustment.

Duration @ 0.050-inch lift: Int. 204 degrees, Exh. 214 degrees
Lift: Int. 0.420 inch, Exh. 0.442 inch
Lobe-Center Angle: 112 degrees

PN 12533916

All small-blocks from 1981 to 1987 with computer controls and nonroller camshafts. This is a special grind for cars equipped with HO 305 and 350 engines that cruise above 2,600 rpm. Also recommended for 350 trucks.

Duration @ 0.050-inch lift: Int. 204 degrees, Exh. 214 degrees
Lift: Int. 0.423 inch, Exh. 0.446 inch
Lobe-Center Angle: 110 degrees

Lifter Types

The flat-tappet solid lifter is the earliest design and is still a very effective piece. There are basically two types available for the small-block, and they are referred to as "edge-orifice" and "inertia-valve" designs. (The latter is also called a

Modern Factory Camshafts

These camshafts are the latest profiles from Chevrolet for street and racing use. Included are three hydraulic roller profiles originally supplied in 1987 and later high-performance vehicles and engine packages. These roller cams could produce up to a 3.5 percent increase in fuel economy and five more horsepower than comparable flat-tappet cams.

Part Number	Lifter Type	Cam Lobe & Running Valve Lash (inches)	Crankshaft Duration @ Lash Point Intake/Exhaust	Crankshaft Duration @ .050 Tappet Lift Intake/Exhaust	Maximum Lift with 1.5:1 Rocker Ratio Intake/Exhaust (in.)	Lobe Center-lines	Remarks
14093643	hydraulic roller tappet	1/4 turn down from zero lash	294°/294°	202°/206°	.403/.415	115°	1987 350-ci Corvette & IROC-Z Camaro
1013334	hydraulic roller tappet	1/4 turn down from zero lash	336°/336°	235°/235°	.480/.480	114°	5.7L HO, ZZZ, and ZZ2 engines. Use with spring PN 10134358
10185071	hydraulic roller tappet	1/4 turn down from zero lash	N/A	208°/221°	.474/.510	112°	ZZ3 5.7L HO engine
14088843	hydraulic flat tappet	1/4 turn down from zero lash	294°/294°	202°/206°	.403/.415	115°	1983-'86 305-ci Z28 and L69 Camaro
3863151	hydraulic flat tappet	1/4 turn down from zero lash	320°/320°	221°/221°	.447/.447	114°	1965-'67 327-ci Corvette and Chevy II L-79 engine
3896962	hydraulic flat tappet	1/4 turn down from zero lash	312°/312°	222°/222°	.450/.460	114°	1969-'81 L-46 & L-82 350-ci Corvette
3972178	mechanical flat tappet	.024/.030	300°/312°	242°/254°	.435/.455	116°	1970-'71 LT-1 Corvette and Camaro
3927140	mechanical flat tappet	.024/.026	316°/323°	256°/268°	.469/.483	112°	First racing design, good short track cam, use with spring #3927142
3965754	mechanical flat tappet	.024/.026	318°/327°	262°/273°	.488/.509	112°	Second racing design, good short track/ road racing, use spring #330585
24502476	hydraulic flat tappet	zero lash	N/A	212°/222°	.435/.460	N/A	300-hp 350-ci SP engine assembly #12355345

"piddle-valve" lifter.) The difference is in the way they meter oil to the rocker arms.

The inertia-valve lifter, PN 5232695, meters overhead oil via an internal inertia (flapper) valve, while the edge orifice lifter, PN 5231585, meters oil based on the lifter-to-bore clearance. The 5232695 lifter was used in the early 302-ci Z28 engines and is currently recommended for applications equipped with production-type rocker arms or heavy-duty valvesprings. The more commonly used edge-orifice lifter (585) was installed in the early high-performance 283- and 327-ci engines and later 302- and 350-ci engines. The 5231585 lifter reduces upper engine oil circulation by up to 20 percent. It should be used with aftermarket roller rocker arms or production light-tension valvesprings. It should be avoided with stock rocker arms, because it may restrict enough oil to cause ball-pivot galling. Edge-orifice lifters are commonly used in dry-sumped engines or those with limited oil pan capacity.

During the useful life of the camshaft, each lifter should remain matched to the lobe to which it was originally mated, or almost certain failure will occur. A new cam should always receive new lifters. Unless you are really down and out, it is always better to replace the cam and lifters rather than individual pieces.

Hydraulic lifters should receive equally kind treatment to prolong their useful life. Many enthusiasts don't fully understand the true benefits of a hydraulic lifter. A hydraulic lifter acts as an effective shock absorber, allowing an oil cushion to absorb the load transmitted through the lifter. This makes it considerably easier on the entire valvetrain. For street applications, they are the only way to go. Hydraulic grinds are available to match all but the nastiest racing lobes and in the overall scheme of things, they provide equal performance and often last longer. Modern anti-pump-up hydraulic lifters will perform as well as any streetable solid-lifter grind.

Checking spring seat pressure is an essential step in valvetrain preparation. An inside micrometer (shown here) makes the job easy. Install the micrometer with the retainer and keepers adjusted to the exact installed spring height. After removing the micrometer and readjusting it to the same height, it's used as a stop to compress the valvespring to the proper height to read seat pressure.

Another important clearance that is easy to forget is the clearance between the rocker-arm slot and the stud. Stock rockers frequently encounter interference at this point with high-lift cams. Long-slot rockers are available from the cam manufacturers to cure this problem. You should also check this relationship when using roller rockers.

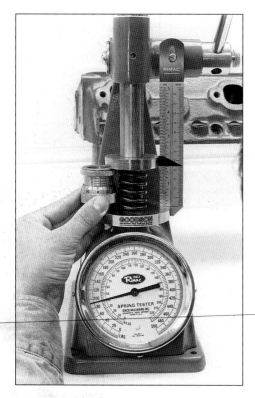

Light-tension checking springs are used to check piston-to-valve clearance and to install the valves when flowing cylinder heads.

The current production hydraulic flat tappet valve lifter is PN 5232720. It should be used in all regular production and high-performance hydraulic flat-tappet camshaft applications. The exception, of course, is aftermarket hydraulic cam kits, which are supplied with the correct lifters.

Since 1987, production engines have been equipped with hydraulic roller tappets. Roller tappets improve fuel economy and performance by reducing internal engine friction. The roller tappets also permit more aggressive cam profiles without the loss of engine idle vacuum and idle quality, essential for computer controlled engines. Factory hydraulic roller tappets are 0.630-inch taller than standard flat-tappet lifters, and they must be used with induction hardened camshafts. They also require shorter pushrods (PN 10046173), special lifter guides (PN 14093634), guide retainers (PN 14101116), and a camshaft thrust plate (PN 14093636). Factory hydraulic roller cams and roller tappets can only be installed in 1987 and later production blocks that are designed to accept the taller roller tappets and lifter guides.

Chevrolet continues to offer mushroom-style flat tappets for use with the mushroom-lifter camshaft PN 366293 that is now discontinued. These lifters can be used with aftermarket camshafts ground for mushroom lifters. Mushroom tap-pets have a larger 0.960-inch footprint than standard 0.843-inch lifters. The larger footprint permits more aggressive camshaft grinds and higher valvetrain velocity than standard lifters. They are only used where class rules prohibit roller tappets. Roller tappets offer the same advantages and they should be used whenever possible.

Valvesprings

Valvesprings have a major influence on the way your engine runs. They must provide enough seat pressure to prevent the valve from bouncing when it closes and enough open pressure to keep the lifter on the lobe throughout the entire intake or exhaust event. Contrary to popular belief, there is only one standard valvespring for the small-block Chevy engine. You may have heard reference to a guy running Z28 valvesprings, but there is no such thing. The same basic spring was fitted to all production cylinder heads.

Easy Valve Lash Adjustment

Hydraulic Lifters: Hydraulic lifters are normally adjusted one turn down from zero lash (the point at which all lash has been adjusted out of the valvetrain with the lifter on the base circle of the cam). To improve high-speed performance, cam manufacturers sometimes recommend an adjustment of only one-quarter turn or less. Hydraulic lifters can be adjusted with the engine running, although it can be a messy job since oil can splatter over the engine, but it only takes a few minutes or so to adjust each bank. Loosen each rocker arm adjusting nut until you hear a clicking sound that persists longer than a few seconds. Then tighten the rocker back down until the clicking just stops. Tighten the nut one-quarter additional turn (one full turn for the standard factory setting). Turn the adjustment in slowly so the lifter can compensate for the change.

Solid Lifters: Valve lash is necessary in a solid-lifter valvetrain to allow for thermal expansion. (With hydraulic lifters, adjustments happen automatically so lash is not required.) Solid-lifter and roller-lifter cam profiles offer some latitude for experimentation to locate the lash that produces the best performance. Tightening the lash can improve top-end performance slightly (increases lift and duration). Increasing the lash makes the engine stronger at lower speeds. As a rule of thumb, cams can handle about 0.008-inch tighter lash, but only 0.003 or 0.004 inch more on the loose side. If you have to make changes greater than this to get what you're looking for, it means that the cam is not well suited to the engine. Make sure you allow for the reduced piston-to-valve clearance that will result from decreases in valve lash.

Setting Lash on New Installations: Regardless of the type of lifter, you can set the valves quickly and accurately using the tried and true exhaust opening/intake closing method. This method allows you to work independently on any given cylinder, or you can work your way down one side and up the other. You can't get lost with regard to where the piston is, and it's almost impossible to make a mistake. You work on one cylinder at a time. Pick a cylinder to start with and, using a suitable starter motor switch, bump the engine over until the exhaust rocker arm just starts to move and compress the valvespring. When you see this, you can be certain the intake valve is fully closed and ready for adjustment. Make your adjustment to the intake valve at this point.

Then continue bumping the engine over while watching the intake valve rocker arm. Bump the engine until the rocker arm opens the valve all the way and just starts to close the valve (valvespring compressed, but starting to rise). When you see this, adjust the exhaust valve. If you miss slightly while bumping the engine over, just go around again until you get it right. Adjusting each pair of valves in this manner ensures accuracy and is the quickest and easiest method of adjustment.

Check Box	Crank Position	Adjust This Valve
	TDC	#8 Exhaust
	TDC + 45°	#2 Intake
	TDC + 90°	#4 Exhaust
	TDC + 135°	#1 Intake
	BDC	#3 Exhaust
	BDC + 45°	#8 Intake
	BDC + 90°	#6 Exhaust
	BDC + 135°	#4 Intake
	TDC	#5 Exhaust
	TDC + 45°	#3 Intake
	TDC + 90°	#7 Exhaust
	TDC + 135°	#6 Intake
	BDC	#2 Exhaust
	BDC + 45°	#5 Intake
	BDC + 90°	#1 Exhaust
	BDC + 135°	#7 Intake

Rotate Another 45° To TDC

If you want a stiffer GM spring with the same diameter, you need to find the service package springs designed for the original off-road racing cam PN 3927140 (see valvespring chart). This spring is reddish brown in color with a flat wound damper (PN 3927142). Chevrolet does not recommend it for stock cams or specialty cams, but it has become a popular item for hot street engines with either hydraulic or solid lifters. The service spring installs at 1.70 inches with 110-psi seat pressure. It provides 190-psi open pressure at 0.450-inch lift and coil binds at slightly more than 0.500-inch lift or a spring height of 1.16 inches. When used with factory high-performance cams and proper valve adjustments, these springs put 7,000 rpm within reach.

Another factory valvespring was introduced in the mid 1970s. It was intended for use with the second-design, off-road racing cam PN 3965784. This spring is available as PN 330585. It is slightly larger in diameter and was intended for use on the late angle-plug heads with larger spring pockets. This dual-spring combination provides 140-psi seat pressure at 1.75 inches installed height and 290-psi open pressure at 0.500-inch valve lift. This is a good spring, but earlier heads require enlarging the spring pockets. You're probably better off finding a specialty spring that will do the job.

As far as aftermarket camshafts are concerned, it's good practice to use the spring recommended by the manufacturer, although virtually any cam with less than 0.500-inch lift will work well with the factory service spring PN 3927142. In all cases, it is important to check valvespring pressure and installed height to ensure optimum performance from these pieces.

The best retainer to use with the factory service spring is a stock steel piece PN 14003974 with an "A" stamping, but most all steel retainers are tough customers, so you needn't be afraid to use them for street applications. "A" retainers are recommended for valvesprings PN 3911068, PN 10134358, and PN 3927142. They are 1⅜-inch in diameter and are used on all ZZZ, ZZ1, and ZZ2 versions of the Chevrolet 350 HO V-8 and 300-hp 350s. Chevrolet's hardened high-performance valvespring keepers PN 3947770 are color-coded copper and should not be used with aluminum retainers because they are incompatible. If you use an aluminum retainer, run the keepers that came with them or use standard small-block keepers. The correct O-ring valvestem seal kit is PN 12511190. For extra seal protection, consider the special high-performance seals PN 4060483 used on the 350 HO engine.

Stock rocker arms are more than capable of living with any factory camshaft and spring combination. In cases where you're running more than 0.500-inch valve lift you may wish to consider the long-slot rocker arms available from Comp Cams, Moroso, Manley, Mr. Gasket, Crane, and other manufacturers. These rockers prevent rocker-arm-to-stud interference at high valve lifts. Regardless of the type of rocker arm you use, it should be teamed with specialty hardened, grooved rocker balls to ensure proper lubrication at high pressure points. Exhaust rockers tend to gall (because of the additional heat), so you should at least run grooved balls on them if not all of the rockers. Most factory small-block Chevy rocker arms have a 1.5:1 ratio. If you want to try a 1.6 or 1.65:1 rocker-arm ratio, you'll have to obtain a specialty roller rocker. The 1989-and-later engines use 1.5:1 ratio, self-aligning rocker arms, PN

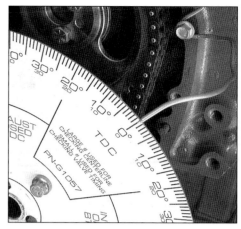

Establishing TDC with a degree wheel is the first step in properly degreeing your camshaft.

10089648, with built-in alignment rails to keep them properly positioned on the valvestems. They use pivot balls PN 3744340 and nuts PN 3744341. These rockers can be used on earlier engines.

Degreeing the Cam

Degreeing the cam ensures that it is installed in the correct position relative to the crankshaft and gives you a base from which to determine valve-to-piston clearance. Although rather rare, out-of-the-box cam phasing can be off for any number of reasons, including an improperly placed dowel pin or a misplaced keyhole in the cam gear. This can affect performance and reliability unless it is observed and corrected before the engine is started.

There are several ways to degree a cam, but the simplest method may be the one we describe here from Comp Cams called the "Lobe Center Line" method *(Note: this method works only with cams that have symmetric lobes; asymmetric profile cams must be degreed using the cam grinder's 0.050-inch lift figures)*. Regardless of the method you select, the first step is always to accurately locate TDC on the number one piston (front piston on the left, driver-side bank).

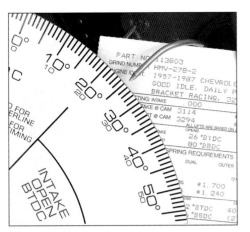

Checking the cam against the manufacturer's cam card will ensure proper cam timing. Remember, if you're degreeing a cam with asymmetrical lobes, you cannot use the "lobe centerline" method. After precisely setting the degree wheel to TDC as indicated in the text, mark the 0.050-inch timing figures on your degree wheel and verify them with your cam card.

Flat-tappet cams should be liberally coated with cam lube during installation. This heavy-duty lube helps the cam lobes survive those first critical moments during initial startup.

Affix a piston stop over number one cylinder, and then adjust and lock the stop bolt so the piston will be stopped about ½ inch from the top of the bore. Attach a degree wheel to the snout of the crank and firmly fasten a wire pointer to the block so that it points to the degree marks on the wheel. Start off by positioning and locking the degree wheel with pointer on BDC when the number seven piston appears to be at TDC (just eyeball it for now). Rotate the engine until number one piston contacts the stop, and mark the reading on the degree wheel.

Then, rotate the engine in the opposite direction until the piston once again contacts the stop. Note this second reading on the wheel. Now that you have a reading on either side of TDC, add them together and divide by two (finds the average). For example, if you read 18 degrees on one side and 21 degrees on the other, the average would be 19½

degrees. This means that true TDC is located exactly 19½ degrees from both of the marks on the degree wheel. Remove the piston stop and rotate the engine until the pointer indicates 19½ degrees between each of your marks and the pointer. Double check your observations, rotate the degree wheel (not the crankshaft) so that the pointer indicates exactly TDC, and then lock everything down tight.

Now that TDC has been determined, we'll proceed with the Lobe-Centerline Method to degree-in the cam. (Remember, this method only works with symmetric lobe profiles.) First, we'll locate the point of maximum lift on the intake lobe. Place a dial indicator on the number one intake lifter, rotate the engine until the maximum-lift point is indicated, and zero your indicator dial. This will only be an approximation, and like finding TDC, you'll have to sneak up on it. Continue rotating the engine slowly until the lifter once again begins to climb the lobe.

This time stop when the indicator reaches 0.050 inch before max lift and take your first reading. Rotate the engine further and when the indicator reaches 0.050 inch after observed max-lift point, take a second degree-wheel reading. The point exactly halfway between these readings is the true max-lift point and the intake lobe centerline.

Now all you have to do is observe where the centerline resides in relation to TDC. Count the number of degrees from this point to TDC and compare it to the number on the timing card that came with the cam. If it indicates that the cam should be installed at 110 degrees, the centerline should be 110 degrees from TDC. If you find that it is only 108 degrees from TDC, the cam is retarded and you will need a 2-degree bushing in the cam gear to advance it to 110 degrees. This can also be accomplished with an offset crank key or one of several other methods.

Prior to startup, lube the rocker and valvestem tips and verify that the rocker arms are properly aligned on the valvestems.

Preoil the engine until oil is freely flowing from every rocker arm to ensure full lubrication when the engine is first started.

When setting valve lash, make sure the feeler gauge is inserted straight into the lash gap. Make the adjustment so that a reasonably firm drag is felt when inserting and removing the feeler gauge.

With the cam degreed as designed by the manufacturer, you can check other critical valvetrain clearances, including valve-to-piston clearance. Keep in mind that if you alter cam timing or even valve lash, it can have a substantial effect on valve-to-piston clearance, particularly if you have an engine with tight valve-to-piston clearances. When you advance the cam, it will reduce valve-to-piston clearance on the intake valves. Retarding the cam moves the exhaust valves closer to the pistons.

Next to the cylinder heads, the camshaft and valvetrain represent one of the most important controls you have over engine output. There are remarkable power gains to be had from the right cam profile, if it is well matched to other engine components. By combining the correct cam timing with well-integrated intake and exhaust systems, it is possible to achieve truly startling torque and horsepower. But remember, nothing does a better job of fouling up your engine's performance potential as a mismatched camshaft.

Camshaft Prep Checklist

1. Inspect the camshaft for obvious defects such as chipped lobes or journals, damaged timing gears, a missing dowel pin, or other defects.
2. Lightly deburr distributor gear with a wire brush.
3. Check cam gear fit and alignment. Make sure the sprocket or chain does not rub against the block or chain cover.
4. Degree camshaft in engine prior to initial fire-up. Record all information for future reference.
5. Check valvesprings for correct installed height and seat pressure. Shim if required.
6. Check retainer-to-valveguide and/or seal clearance; increase if less than 0.050 inch.
7. Examine rocker arm relationship with stud, valvespring, and valvestem. Check for rocker slot clearance at the stud, rocker arm, interference at the edge of the retainer, and verify proper rocker arm-to-valve tip geometry.
8. Verify lifter installation. If using roller lifters, make certain retaining clips or other hardware does not rub against the lifter bore or block.
9. Check push rods for correct seating in the lifters and rockers, clearance at the cylinder head, and proper guide plate alignment and clearance. Adjust guide plate position if necessary.
10. Clean valvetrain components with solvent and blow-dry with compressed air. Check lifters, pushrods, and rocker arms for defects and store for assembly.

CYLINDER HEADS

Choosing a cylinder head for your small-block can be a challenging task because of the shear number of heads available. Since the mid-1980s and the introduction of factory designed Bow Tie heads, Pontiac-designed small-block heads, and numerous performance aftermarket heads, picking the right head has become more or less a matter of choosing the best casting for your specific application. While earlier editions of this book defined and illustrated the original Chevy performance head castings, they are becoming difficult to locate. Engine builders are now turning to currently available factory heads or aftermarket replacement heads that incorporate the improvements Chevrolet and engine builders have discovered over the years. If you don't already have a good set of original castings and you don't absolutely need them for restoration purposes, aftermarket or Bow Tie factory heads are a much better choice. We'll begin by examining currently available factory cylinder heads and then describe many of the aftermarket heads in detail.

In the mid-1990s, aftermarket aluminum cylinder heads gained dominance in the cylinder-head market. Manufacturers such as Airflow Research, Dart, Edelbrock, Brodix, Trick Flow, Canfield, World Products, and others all offer ready to run high-performance street cylinder heads in various configurations to fit your needs. These heads all include screw-in studs, guide plates, performance valvesprings and retainers, and ports designed for high-performance applications.

HO Aluminum Head

The current factory HO aluminum head PN 12556463 is very affordable and it comes completely assembled and ready to run. It includes valves, springs, retainers, ⅜-inch screw-in rocker studs, and guideplates. This cylinder head is used on high-performance HO engine assemblies, and it is based on the Corvette light alloy castings PN 10088113. It comes with heavy-duty valvesprings, PN 12551483. It also incorporates advanced design features such as D-shaped exhaust ports, high-velocity intake runners, and centrally located spark plugs for improved combustion efficiency. The combustion chambers measure 58 cc and valve sizes are 1.94 inch and 1.5 inch for the intake and exhaust. You should also be aware that this head has raised rocker cover rails with machined surfaces, so early style four-bolt rocker covers will not fit. Best of all, a pair of these heads will eliminate almost 50 pounds of dead weight from the front of your car.

GM Performance Cylinder Heads

These cylinder heads are the result of extensive development by Chevrolet and engine builders throughout the country. Even if you already have a good set of production castings, these factory heads are a much better choice for power and reliability.

Part Number	Description	Casting Number	Material	Spark Plugs	Heat Risers	Intake Runner Vol. (cc)	Combustion Chamber Vol. (cc)	Valve Diameter (in.) Intake/Exhaust	Notes
10125377	Service Head	1410183	Iron	Straight	Yes	–	64	1.94/ 1.50	Service head for 350 ci, 285 hp supplied with valves & springs
12356026	Service Head	14011083	Iron	Straight	Yes	–	64	1.94/ 1.50	Service head for 350 ci, 300 hp supplied with valves & springs.
10185086	Service Head	10088113	Aluminum	Angled	No	163	58	1.94/ 150	Service head for Corvette design 350 HO, 300 hp. Supplied with valves & springs.
3987376	Service Head	3991492	Iron	Straight	Yes	157	64	202/ 1.60	Service head supplied with valves & spring, screw-in studs, pushrod guideplates.
464045	Service Head	462624	Iron	Straight	Yes	161	76	202/ 1.60	Service head supplied with screw-in studs, pushrod guideplates.
10134392	Bow Tie Head	14011034	Iron	Angled	No	190	64	2.02/ 1.60	For off-highway use only.
10051167	Phase 6 Bow Tie Head	14011049	Aluminum	Angled	No	180	55	2.02/ 1.60	For off-highway use only. Standard port location. Includes valve seat and guide.
14011049	Phase 6	14011049 Bow Tie Head	Aluminum	Angled	No	180	55	NA	For off-highway use only. Bare without seats, guides, pushrod holes.
10051101	Raised Runner Bow Tie Head	10051101	Aluminum	Angled	No	196	55	NA	For off-highway use only. Intake ports are 0.200-inch higher than standard location; no seats, guides, and pushrod holes.
10134352	Bow Tie Low-Port Head	10134352	Aluminum	Angled	No	200	45	NA	For off-highway use only. 18° valve angle; no seats, guides.
10134363	Bow Tie High-Port Head	10134363	Aluminum	Angled	No	215	45	NA	For off-highway use only. 18° valve angle; no seats, guides.
10134364	Bow Tie High-Port Head	10134363	Aluminum	Angled	No	215	45	NA	For off-highway use only. 18° valve angle; no seats, guides.
10033867	Bow Tie High-Port Head	10134363	Aluminum	Angled	No	215	45	NA	For off-highway use only. 18° valve angle; no seats, guides.
10033867	Pontiac Motorsports Head	10033867	Aluminum	Angled	No	196	62	2.100/ 1.625	For off-highway use only. Guides supplied but not installed to aid porting.
10185040	Splayed Valve Head	10185040	Aluminum	Angled	No	263	45	NA	For off-highway use only. Splayed-valve design.

Most modern aluminum cylinder heads will include the accessory mounting holes as shown here on a factory iron cylinder head.

Many earlier heads have hidden cracks and other defects that are costly to repair and not worth the effort when you consider the performance gains offered by replacement heads.

Fel Pro and other manufacturers make high-performance gaskets suitable for both iron and aluminum heads. Fel Pro has taken the lead in developing gaskets for specific applications. Its PN 1003 is widely used on iron head applications and PN 1010 is a standard for aluminum heads.

Below: These Corvette-derived aluminum cylinder heads (PN 10185086) are completely assembled with 1.94/1.50-inch intake/exhaust valves, heavy-duty chrome silicon springs, retainers, screw-in studs, and guide plates. They have 58-cc combustion chambers and the intake runners measure 153 cc. These cylinder heads have angled spark plugs, which may not fit some exhaust manifolds and headers. These heads are plentiful and cheap for those working with a budget.

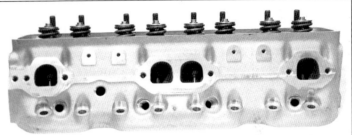

Splayed-Valve Cylinder Heads

Chevrolet's special maximum-performance splayed-valve aluminum cylinder heads PN 24502517 have 240-cc intake runners capable of flowing more air than the high-port 18-degree head with inline valves. These heads were developed for the limited IMSA GTP racing program in the early 1990s. The intake valves on these heads are tilted 16 degrees to the deck surfaces and splayed 4 degrees away from the bore center. The exhaust valves are angled 11 degrees and splayed 4 degrees. The intake and exhaust ports are symmetrical and the 45-cc combustion chambers can accommodate 2.200-inch intake valves and 1.625-inch exhaust valves. Valveguides and seats are not included, and no factory intake manifold is available, but the following compo-

nents are available for installing these heads: rocker arm stands (PN 1018041), valve covers (PN 1018045), intake gaskets (PN 1018042), and valve cover gaskets (PN 1018043). Splayed-valve heads currently require custom fabricated intake manifolds and exhaust headers.

Splayed valve heads are also racing oriented. They were originally developed in the 1990s for IMSA racing and eventually found their way into drag racing in the Pro/Stock Truck category. They have 240-cc runners, 45-cc chambers, and basically come semimachined to accept whatever valves are required.

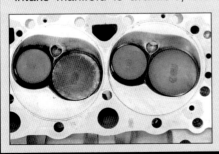

Combustion chambers measure 45-cc and will accommodate 2.200-inch intake valves and 1.625-inch exhaust valves.

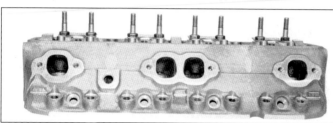

The HO or L98 cylinder head's angled spark plugs are aimed at the exhaust valves and positioned closer to the roof of the chamber. The practice of placing the plug in the path of maximum turbulence to promote efficient flame travel was initiated by Chevrolet in their early high-performance heads; most modern aftermarket aluminum head manufacturers have followed.

Chevrolet's basic cast-iron performance cylinder head is derived from the 3991492 casting that has been around for decades. It has 2.02/1.60-inch intake/exhaust valves and straight spark plugs.

If you decide to use this cylinder head, you may need to make some additional modifications. Because the exhaust ports exit approximately 0.100 inch higher than the stock, headers and exhaust manifolds may require some minor modifications. In addition, make sure there is adequate clearance around the angled park plugs. AC FR5LS ¾-inch reach spark plugs with ⅝-inch hex heads are recommended, and late-model rail type rocker arms are required (PN 10089648). These heads are machined on both ends to accept standard accessory mounts, and they should be installed with composition head gaskets having stainless steel fire rings to prevent a galvanic reaction (a form of corrosion) between the aluminum head and cast-iron block.

Cast-Iron Performance Heads

You have four basic choices if you prefer to use a cast-iron head. The first was originally used on the factory 285-hp 350-ci engines (PN 12353641). Available under PN 10125377, this head has the 1987 and later intake manifold bolt pattern having a 72-degree angle on the two center bolts. It uses 1.94-inch/1.5-inch diameter valves, 64-cc chambers, and PN 3901068 valvesprings.

Your second choice is the service head PN 12356026 used on the 300-hp 350SP engine (PN 12355345). It also uses 1.94-inch/1.5-inch diameter valves, 64-cc chambers, and requires late model, center-bolt valve covers. The primary difference between this and other cast-iron heads is that this head uses the standard pre-1987 bolt angle on the intake manifold's center bolts.

A large valve, high-performance head is offered under PN 12480092 . This head was used on the 1960 Corvette 283, as well as later Z28 302s and 350-ci LT1 V-8s. It features 2.02-inch/1.6-inch diameter valves and 64-cc chambers. A large chamber version is available under PN 464045. It was designed for low compression small-blocks, and its large 76-cc chambers are perfect for today's low-octane environment. It delivers 9:1 compression with the flat-top pistons used in LT1, Z28, and L82 (1971–1979) engines. The head has 2.02-inch/1.6-inch valves, heat-riser passages, screw-in studs, and pushrod guide-plates. The valve seats are heat treated for use with unleaded gasoline, and the straight spark plugs will clear all manifolds and most headers.

Bow Tie Racing Heads

Phase 2 Cast-Iron Bow Tie Head

The Phase 2, Cast-Iron Bow Tie head, PN 12480053, is Chevrolet's top-of-the-line cast-iron cylinder head. This casting was designed for competition use in applications where aluminum heads are prohibited. This head offers several advantages over the Phase 1 head it replaces. The exhaust heat risers are deleted, and hardened exhaust valve seats are included. Phase 1 and Phase 2 Bow Tie heads are easily distinguished from one another. While Phase 1 heads have a thin raised parting line between the exhaust manifold flanges, Phase 2 heads have a much wider machined bar, and the water temperature sensor pad is also machined flat.

Phase 2 heads have 64-cc combustion chambers and the quench area beneath the spark plugs is filled

Chevrolet's 3991492 casting comes in two versions. PN 3987376 has small 64-cc chambers with nonhardened valve seats, and PN 46045 as shown here has larger 76-cc chambers with induction-hardened seats. It is ideal for iron head applications using 9.0:1 compression ratio and unleaded fuel.

Phase 6 Bow Tie heads are some of the best-performing factory heads with standard intake port locations. These bare castings are available under PN 14011049. The valveguides and seats are not included and the pushrod holes are undrilled to permit extensive porting (PN 10051167 includes seats and guides). The valvespring pads are raised 0.200-inch to accommodate the installation of 0.100-inch longer valves.

to provide increased compression in competition engines. All Phase 2 heads have 2.02-inch/1.6-inch diameter valves with hardened seats for the exhaust valves. Phase 2 heads have the same ports as the earlier Phase 1 heads, including the 190-cc intake ports. They are the highest-flowing cast-iron production heads currently available from Chevrolet. The valvespring pockets will accept 1.5-inch diameter springs. Phase 2 heads are machined and tapped for screw-in studs (PN 3973416 for ⅜-inch studs or PN 3921912 for ⁷⁄₁₆-inch studs) and guideplates (PN 3973418), which must be purchased separately. Phase 2 heads require ⅝-inch hex-head spark plugs with tapered seats and a ⅜-inch reach.

Raised-Runner Aluminum Bow Tie Head

Raised-runner aluminum Bow Tie heads, PN 10051101, have intake runners that are 0.200-inch higher than the stock small-block port location to improve the line-of-sight delivery to the valves. These feature 0.240-inch minimum port wall thickness to suit all porting requirements. Deck surfaces are 0.600-inch thick, and the 55-cc combustion chambers are designed to increase compression without promoting detonation. The rocker covers are raised 0.300 inch and the intake manifold flange is stepped for improved gasket sealing. Use ¾-inch-reach plugs with either gaskets or tapered seats. Raised runner heads do not have pushrod clearance holes, so the pushrods can be positioned with optimum porting in mind. Valveguides and seats are not included, and you must purchase the separate guideplates PN 14011051. Longer than stock (0.100-inch) aftermarket valves are required, but stock length valves can be used if you remachine the spring pockets. A special raised-runner, single 4-barrel intake manifold (PN 10051103) is recommended.

18-Degree High-Port Aluminum Bow Tie Heads

These high-port 18-degree heads (10134364) have all the same performance features as the low-port version, but the intake runner floors are raised 1.220 inch above the deck surface. PN 10134363 is designed for fuel-injected applications with larger bore sizes of 4.060 to 4.125 inch. Smaller bore engines from 4.00 to 4.060 inch should use the alternate 18-degree head (PN 10134364), which has ideal valve positions for smaller bores. The former NASCAR Winston Cup version of the 18-degree head is offered under PN 24502482. It's identical to PN 10134364 except that the ports are CNC machined and the valveguides and seats are included.

Pontiac Motorsports Aluminum Head

This cylinder head (PN 10033867) was originally developed by Pontiac Motorsports and offers strong performance potential while retaining the standard intake port location. It comes with ductile iron valve seats installed for standard length 2.100-inch intake valves and 1.625-inch exhaust valves. Phosphorus bronze guides are included, but not installed, as a convenience for the head porter. These heads have 62-cc combustion chambers and use ¾-inch reach, gasketed, 14-mm spark plugs.

Aftermarket Performance Heads

Some of the best horsepower-per-buck values are found in the current offering of aftermarket performance cylinder heads. With only a few exceptions, they are aluminum alloy and have been carefully developed to meet the broad range of specialized requirements found in modern small-block

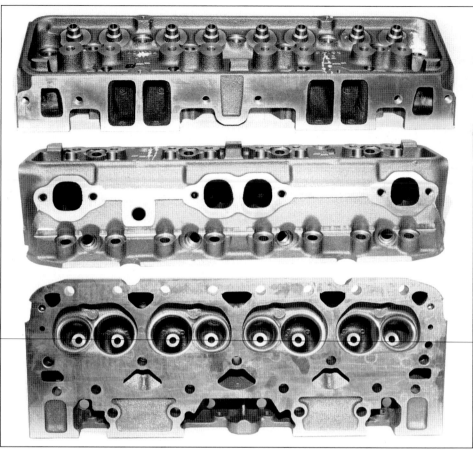

Phase 2 cast-iron Bow Tie heads are the best performing factory small-block iron heads. They are revised 2.02/1.60-inch large valve castings designed for competition use in applications where aluminum heads are prohibited. The chambers have a true volume of 64 cc and the intake runners measure 190 cc. Exhaust heat risers are deleted in these heads, and they are equipped with hardened exhaust valve seats.

engine applications. Leaders in the aftermarket cylinder head market include Airflow Research, Brodix, Dart Machinery, Edelbrock, Trick Flow, and World Products. Some, like Airflow Research, Brodix, and Dart also offer top echelon heads for all-out racing, as well as performance street heads. For specifics about these racing castings you'll want to contact the manufacturer for their latest offerings.

Airflow Research Heads

Airflow Research has been a long respected name in the cylinder head business, and they hold the distinction of being the first company to win a California exemption number for

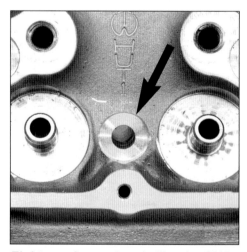

Eighteen-degree heads like the CNC ported models require smaller 3/8-inch-diameter head bolts between the intake ports.

their late-model aluminum street head. Available with either 180- or 195-cc intake runners, and 68-cc closed chambers or 74-cc open chambers, these heads use 2.02-inch-diameter intake valves and 1.60-inch exhaust valves, hardened seats, and 0.750-inch-thick deck surfaces for reliable street performance. They are available in several configurations, including a standard street design with 74-cc chambers, as well as various smog-legal versions. AFR also offers raised-port and racing heads with 210-, 215-, and 220-cc intake runners, plus a variety of special-application racing heads built to suit specific customer needs. They also revisit their designs periodically to make sure they stay current with the latest advances.

Brodix Aluminum Heads

Beginning at the top of the order (just below their all-out racing heads), the Brodix Track 1 is a top-line street/race aluminum head with 221-cc intake runners, 67-cc combustion chambers, 2.08-inch intake valves, 1.60-inch exhaust valves, blended valve bowls, a three-angle competition valve job, roller rockers, screw-in studs, guide-plates, springs, retainers, and 10-degree locks. Spark plugs are angled and the exhaust ports require headers with 1⅜-inch or larger primary tubes.

If your engine size or application dictates a smaller intake-runner volume, the Brodix Race-Rite series fits the bill. These heads are available with 180- or 200-cc intake runners, 67-cc chambers, and 2.02-/1.60-inch intake/exhaust valves in a quality street/race casting.

Dart Machinery Heads

Dart Machinery offers a variety of different cylinder heads from iron street heads to full-blown aluminum race heads. Since we're focusing on

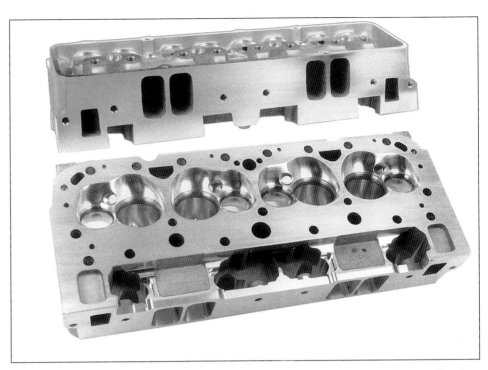

PN 10134352 is an older 18-degree low-port cylinder head with 223-cc intake runners and angled plugs. It was supplied without guides and seats and is still a good head if you can get a set.

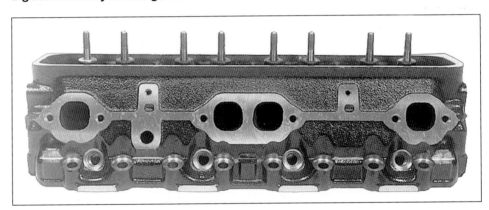

PN 10125377 is a basic cast-iron factory head with 1.94/1.50-inch intake/exhaust valves, 64-cc chambers, straight spark plugs, and a heat riser. It was used on the 285-hp 350 as a service head, and comes complete with springs and valves. A similar head, PN 10159552, was used on the 300-hp 350.

street heads, let's take a look at the Dart's Iron Eagle heads. These cast-iron heads are available with 165-, 180-, 200-, or 215-cc intake ports. You can also choose between straight or angled plugs and 64- or 72-cc combustion chambers. While the 165-cc head has 1.94/1.50-inch valves, the 180-cc and larger heads come with 2.02/1.60 or

larger heads, depending on the model. These heads are great for a stealthy look, or in classes where iron heads are required.

If you have your mind made up on aluminum, Dart's Pro 1 heads will fit the bill. These 180-, 200-, 215-cc or larger heads offer great performance out of the box. You'll have to choose between

Aftermarket Performance Heads

Some of the best horsepower-per-buck values are found in this table. Most of these heads are aluminum alloy, and all have been developed to meet the broad range of specialized requirements found in modern small-block engines. These manufacturers produce the best heads the aftermarket has to offer. Contact the manufacturers directly for the most up-to-date info on their high-end racing heads.

Popular Aftermarket Cylinder Heads

Manufacturer and Model	Material	Spark Plugs	Intake Volume (cc)	Combustion Chamber Volume (cc)	Valve Diameter Intake/ Exhaust (inches)	CARB Legal
Airflow Research 180	Aluminum	Either	180	68 or 74	2.02/1.60	Yes
Airflow Research 195	Aluminum	Either	195	68 or 74	2.02/1.60	Yes
Airflow Research 210 CNC	Aluminum	Either	210	76	2.08/1.60	No
Brodix Race Rite 180	Aluminum	Either	180	67	2.02/1.60	No
Brodix Race Rite 200	Aluminum	Either	200	67	2.055/1.60	No
Brodix Track 1	Aluminum	Angled	221	67	2.08/1.60	No
Dart Iron Eagle SS	Iron	Straight	165	72	1.94/1.50	No
Dart Iron Eagle 180	Iron	Either	180	64 or 72	2.02/1.60	No
Dart Iron Eagle 200	Iron	Either	200	64 or 72	2.05/1.60	No
Dart Iron Eagle 215	Iron	Either	215	64 or 72	2.08/1.60	No
Dart Pro 1	Aluminum	Either	180	64 or 72	2.02/1.60	No
Dart Pro 1	Aluminum	Either	200	64 or 72	2.05/1.60	No
Dart Pro 1	Aluminum	Either	215	64 or 72	2.08/1.60	No
Edelbrock Performer	Aluminum	Straight	170	64 or 70	2.02/1.60	Yes
Edelbrock Performer Centerbolt	Aluminum	Straight	165	60	2.02/1.60	Yes
Edelbrock Performer RPM	Aluminum	Either	170	64 or 70	2.02/1.60	No
Edelbrock E-Tec 170	Aluminum	Repositioned	170	64	1.94/1.55	Yes
Edelbrock E-Tec 200	Aluminum	Repositioned	200	64	1.94/1.55	No
Edelbrock Victor Jr. 23°	Aluminum	Angled	215	64 or 70	2.08/1.60	No
Trick Flow Kenny Duttweiler	Aluminum		195	64 or 72	2.02/1.60	Yes
Trick Flow R-Series	Aluminum		215	67	2.08/1.60	No
World Products S/R	Iron	Straight	Stock	67 or 76	1.94/1.50	Yes
World Products S/R Torquer	Iron	Straight	170	67 or 76	2.02/1.60	Yes
World Products Sportsman II	Iron or Aluminum	Either	200	64 or 72	2.02/1.60	Yes
World Motown 220	Iron or Aluminum	Either	220	64	2.08/1.60	No

64- or 72-cc combustion chambers, and angled or straight plugs. Valve sizes range between 2.02/1.60- and 2.08/1.60-inch, depending on the model. Dart also offers a number of racing heads with even wilder specs.

Edelbrock Aluminum Heads

Edelbrock's Performer aluminum heads are designed to complement their intake manifolds and camshafts to provide a total performance package. Edelbrock Performer heads are designed for street operation with 165- to 170-cc intake runners, 2.02-/1.60-inch valves, and 60-, 64-, 70-cc combustion chambers. The Performer RPM heads have 170-cc runners, 64- or 70-cc chambers, 2.02-/1.60-inch valves, and either straight or angled spark plugs. Performer heads are also available for late-model small-blocks with center-bolt valve covers, as well as 1987–1991 Corvettes.

Edelbrock utilizes a multi-million dollar, computer-controlled machining network that constantly measures tooling wear and makes automatic adjustments to their massive machining centers. This advanced system allows Edelbrock to produce hundreds of components with dimensions held to very high preci-

The 18-degree high-port head (PN 10134364) features 210-cc runners with 44-cc combustion chambers. It is designed for 4.00- to 4.060-inch bores.

Equalizing chamber volumes is a common blueprinting technique used to promote an equal amount of work from each cylinder.

sion. The network, one of the most advanced in the industry, should virtually guarantee the quality of all Edelbrock cylinder heads.

Trick Flow Specialties Heads

The Trick Flow Kenny Duttweiler Signature Series 23-degree aluminum head is a bolt-on street performance piece designed for good low-speed torque and top-end power. These heads come completely assembled with 2.02-/1.60-inch valves and accept all stock-type rockers, headers, factory-type intake manifolds, and accessories. Trick Flow also offers 18-degree heads, as well as heads for the LT1.

World Products Heads

Performance enthusiasts looking for reliable and power-producing cast-iron small-block heads can make good use of World Products complete line of Stock Replacement, S/R Torquer, Sportsman II, and Motown cast-iron heads. Their Stock Replacement iron heads are designed to replace the dwindling supply of 1962-to-present castings with a feature-laden design.

Four part numbers cover the full range, with 67- or 76-cc chambers, 1.94-/1.50-inch valves, and all accessory bolt holes. Four additional part numbers cover the same heads with late model 1986-and-later angled intake faces. All heads feature hardened valve seats to prevent recession from unleaded fuel.

S/R Torquer heads are a low-cost, big-valve power builder. They have 170-cc runners, 67- or 76-cc chambers, 2.02-/1.60-inch valves, screw-in studs, and hardened seats for unleaded fuel compatibility. These heads all feature straight spark plugs to eliminate plug wire problems associated with many header designs. You can buy these heads completely assembled or as fully machined bare castings. Small-bore 305 Torquer heads are available for 305-ci and other small-bore engines. These heads allow the use of larger 1.94-inch intake valves with small bores. They come with 171-cc runners, 58-cc chambers, and screw-in studs. Like the S/R Torquer, they are available completely assembled with valves and springs or as fully machined bare castings.

Dart II Sportsman heads have 200-cc runners with heart shaped 64- or 72-cc chambers, 2.02-/1.60-inch valves, angled or straight spark plug bosses, and hardened seats. Like the other World Products heads, they come completely assembled with a three-angle valve job, or can be purchased as fully machined bare castings. World's Motown and Motown Lite (aluminum) heads are great for big-inch small-blocks, with 220-cc intake ports and 2.08-inch intake valves.

Head Porting

Regardless of which heads you choose, a good valve job is the first requirement, but before this can be accomplished the cylinder head must be properly prepared. Head preparation should include minor porting to eliminate obstructions and smooth port contours. Many recognized cylinder-head shops perform street porting work that can substantially increase engine performance. Most of the new high-performance cylinder heads are already cast and machined for high-performance work, requiring only minor additional touches. If your budget can handle it, and you want a bit more performance, you might consider having one of the reputable shops work over your heads.

On the other hand, you can do a pretty fair job yourself if you work

Bolts, Studs, and Torquing Tips

Unless you're building a turbocharged or super-charged engine that will see extended periods of severe service in a racecar or a boat, there is little reason to use cylinder-head studs. Studs are needed to ensure even gasket crush and promote proper sealing in engines with very high cylinder pressures. However, the BMEP (brake mean effective pressure) in the average street engine rarely approaches the point where gasket integrity is threatened. Blown head gaskets are normally the result of improperly torqued bolts, detonation, or improperly faced surfaces on the head or block.

For street and bracket racing applications, it is usually safe to use stock Chevy head bolts. Factory fasteners have the proper elasticity to provide effective clamping at the recommended torque specs. Aftermarket bolts like those available from ARP, Manley,

Milodon, and others perform very well. If you angle-cut the heads to gain compression, be certain to have the machinist spot face all the head bolt seats to make them parallel to the deck surface. Remember also that the bosses along the outside of the head for the short bolts can get very thin after angle milling. It's possible to break or crack the head in this area if care is not exercised when torquing the bolts.

Another good move is to install the head and gasket on the bare block and observe their relationship through the empty cylinders. In this manner you can determine if any part of the gasket or combustion chamber are overhanging the bore. This problem can be remedied by using the correct head gasket for your bore size and by lightly blending the edges of the combustion chambers to match the bore size.

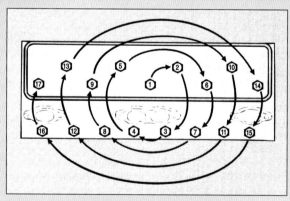

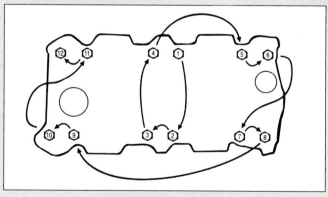

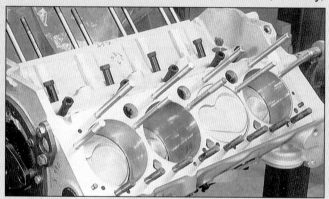

Follow the helical tightening sequence illustrated here for cylinder head bolts. First, torque all bolts to 25 ft-lbs. Then repeat the process in 20-ft-lb steps until you reach the full torque recommended for your fastener (typically 65 ft-lbs for factory bolts).

Here's the torque sequence for the intake manifold. Tighten the bolts in 5-ft-lb steps to a final torque of 30 to 35 ft-lbs. As the gaskets compress, the bolts will loosen slightly. Continue retorquing fasteners until they stay tight.

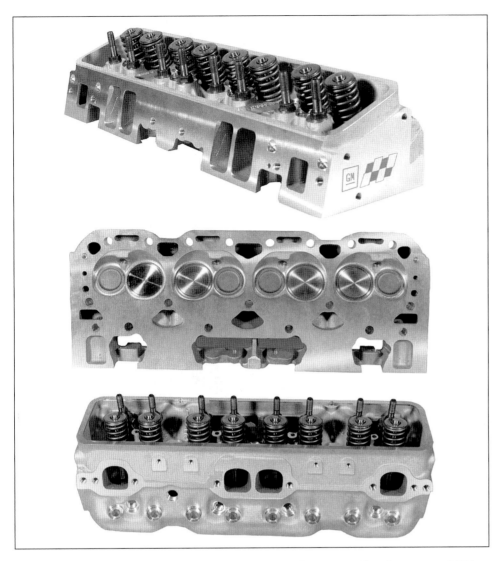

Chevrolet's Fast Burn aluminum head fits all 23-degree applications except LT1, LT4, and LS1. This head incorporates Chevy's Fast Burn technology designed to create exceptional burn characteristics with flat-top pistons. It's CNC machined, and Chevrolet recommends that it be installed without modifications. It has taller rocker rails for valvetrain clearance and improved sealing.

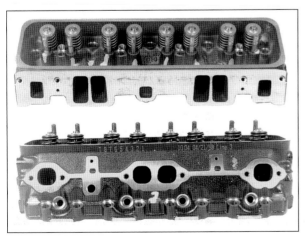

PN 12558060 is the L31 service head with valves and springs. It is a cast-iron replacement head with 170 cc/64 cc runners and chambers, 1.94/1.50-inch intake/exhaust valves, straight spark plugs, and Vortec ports. It's a replacement head for truck engines and makes a good starting point for Vortec-headed combos.

carefully and exercise restraint. A simple job of matching the ports to the gaskets will help. You can also smooth the radius on the short side of the port floor, where it turns into the combustion chamber. This critical shape has a pronounced effect on flow, so don't flatten the radius. Just smooth the contours. In addition, between the valve seat and port runner, the entire port necks down in the bowl area just below the valve seat. You can improve flow by removing excess material in this area, but make sure you maintain a slight radius between the valve seat and port bowl. The most important thing to remember here is to not get carried away. Think about what you want to accomplish and don't do it if you have any doubts. You can do more harm than good if you're careless.

Race-type porting is simply too specialized for most enthusiasts to handle themselves. It is extremely easy to ruin a set of heads as the result of inexperience and overzealous grinder work. Many publications attempt to illustrate various porting techniques, but the benefits are questionable, since many enthusiasts do not have the experience to precisely reshape the ports. The result can be a set of heads considerably less efficient than the stock castings and totally unmatched to the engine requirements. If serious porting work is what you have in mind, the first thing you should do is take your heads to a reputable cylinder head shop and let them perform the work. This is admittedly expensive, but you benefit from the expertise of someone who has been through it all before. Headwork is never cheap. Another, perhaps better, alternative is to purchase a set of ready-to-run ported heads like those offered by most aftermarket suppliers.

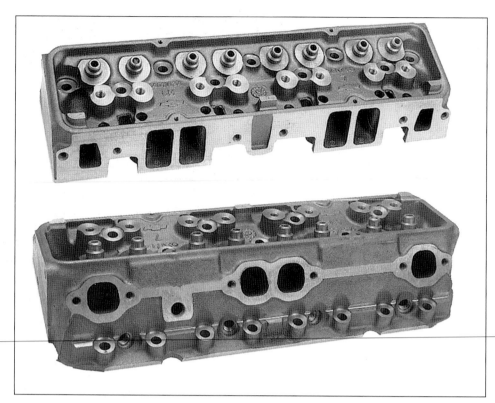

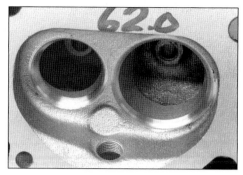

Chamber size and shape dictates the majority of an engine's combustion and performance characteristics. This early iron head chamber is very pretty, but not nearly as efficient as most of the modern factory and aftermarket chambers.

The Phase 3 Bow Tie head, PN 12480034, is cast iron with 184/64-cc intake/exhaust runners and chambers, respectively, 2.02/1.60-inch valves, angled plugs, and no heat risers. It is a very good cast-iron head for performance work.

Valveguides and Seats

Small-block Chevy engines require tight valveguide-to-stem clearances in order to provide good oil control and accurate valve seating. There are a number of ways to achieve this, depending on the final application of your cylinder heads. A street engine should have 0.0015- to 0.0025-inch valvestem clearance with stock valves. If the clearance exceeds this amount, the guides will have to be reconditioned. There are several options: valveguides can be sleeved or threaded to accept cast-iron or bronze inserts; the guides can be reamed and used with oversize valvestems; the old guides can be machined out and new cast-iron or bronze guides pressed in place; or existing guides can be knurled to regain proper valve fit.

All of these procedures produce acceptable results, except knurling. This quick-fix method will only last a few hundred miles, after which the valves will be rattling around as bad as if the guides were never knurled at all. So, for all practical purposes your choices boil down to using bronze or cast-iron sleeves or replacement valves and guides. There is little consensus on what guide material works best; some machine shops prefer cast iron, others recommend bronze. However, many experts believe that guide life is directly linked to the type of valve seals used to control guide oiling (along with several other factors, including the types of lifters, pushrods, rocker arms, valvesprings, retainers, and even oil and frequency of oil changes). It's not so much a job of selecting a specific guide and a specific valve seal; it's using a combi-

nation of guides and seals that are known by your machine shop to provide good results.

If your machine shop doesn't have any suggestions, consider these combinations recommended by engine expert Jay Steel from Taylor Engines in Whittier, California.

Stock Engines: Use replacement, press-in, cast-iron guides with stock O-ring seals on the valvestems. In addition, use guide-mounted seals on the intake valves only (use black rubber seals with a thin white stem scraper). If possible, also use the stock valvespring-mounted splash shields.

High-Performance: Use cast-iron or bronze-wall guides with rubber guide mounted seals on both the intake and exhaust valves. Eliminate valvespring mounted splash shields (heavy-duty springs can cut the splash shields in half!) but continue to use the stock O-ring seals on the valvestems, provided the valves are machined for them.

Racing Engines: Eliminate the O-ring seals on the valvestems, particularly when using needle-bearing rocker arms or restricted top-end oil-

Continued on page 101

Small-Block Spark Plug Tech

Production: Prior to 1970, all small-block Chevy cylinder heads were machined to accept 14-mm, ⅜-inch reach, flat-seat spark plugs with sealing washers. These plugs have 1¾6-inch hex heads. In 1970, Chevy continued using 14-mm threads, but switched to ⅝-inch-reach, tapered-seat plugs. These later plugs all have ⅝-inch hex heads.

High-Performance: The Corvette aluminum head uses a ¾-inch reach gasketed plug with ⅝-inch hex heads (e.g., AC FR5LS). Cast iron Bow Tie heads use ⅝-inch-reach, tapered-seat plugs with ⅝-inch hex heads. Several high-performance Bow Tie iron and aluminum heads, like the Phase 6, are machined to accommodate both gasketed plugs and tapered seat plugs. Tapered seat plugs are a better choice when indexing the plug electrodes with the piston domes (tapered-seat washers of varying thickness are available to make the job easier). If galling becomes a problem with tapered-seat plugs, use antiseize compound on the threads.

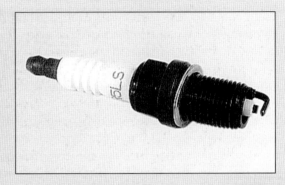

Maximum Effort: Raised runner aluminum Bow Tie heads and CNC Ported Bow Tie heads are machined for small-diameter 0.708-inch reach, tapered-seat plugs with ⅝-inch hex heads (the Champion S series). These plugs are designed to provide easier access with large-tube racing headers. The equivalent gasket-style plug has a ¾-inch reach and a ⅝-inch hex head. (Champion C series). Pontiac-designed small-block heads only accept 14-mm, ¾-inch reach, gasket-style plugs (e.g., the Champion C57C racing plug).

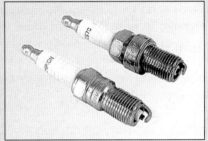

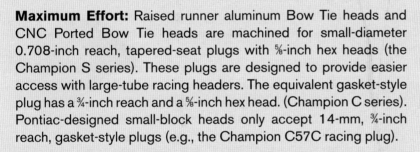

Thermocouple Plugs: Champion developed a special series of thermocouple spark plugs that monitor tip temperatures. These plugs are currently only available to top racing teams, but in the near future they may become generally available. If so, they could become a valuable tuning aid for the average enthusiast, since combustion temperature is a relatively accurate measure of air/fuel ratio, mixture distribution, etc.

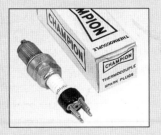

Projected Tip: Projected-tip plugs were designed for applications where cylinder contamination from leaking valveguides and piston ring blow-by require a hotter plug tip to prevent fouling. Most late-model engines are equipped with powerful high-energy ignition systems that reduce the need for projected tips. A good rule of thumb is to use the factory recommended plug and heat range unless you have a definite fouling problem that requires a hotter plug or a projected tip.

Small-Block Head-Gasket Tech

Gasket Basics: Before you select a head gasket make certain that it fits the cylinder bore (no overhang within the cylinder). Avoid universal gaskets that do not precisely fit the bore. Since gasket thickness varies, and the piston-to-head clearance on small-blocks is critical, you must know your engine's requirements before you can make a selection. Minimum clearance is 0.035-inch for engines with steel connecting rods and generally 0.057 to 0.065 inch for engines with aluminum rods. Pick a gasket that will give close to the minimum clearance, since this will usually optimize combustion chamber quench and flame travel.

Gasket Material: Composition head gaskets (made of layers of material) are suitable for both iron and aluminum heads, while steel-shim (single sheet of steel) gaskets have raised sealing beads around the critical openings and should only be used on cast-iron heads. Shim and composition type head gaskets are available from Chevrolet and several aftermarket sources such as Fel Pro, McCord, Victor, and Detroit Gasket. The best composition gaskets for aluminum heads on high-performance engines have preflattened steel wire "fire rings" to optimize combustion pressure sealing while minimizing brinneling (marking the aluminum head surface). The best steel-shim gaskets for iron heads are precoated with a silicone-like material to prevent water leaks.

Recommendations: Many production 4.000-inch bore small-block Chevys use steel-shim gaskets; these 0.026-inch thick gaskets are available as PN 3830711. The composition head gasket for the same bore size is PN 10105117 and is 0.028-inch thick. This gasket is recommended for stock and moderately modified street and marine engines. PN 14088948 is a 0.051-inch thick composition gasket for the Corvette and HO aluminum cylinder heads. It can be used on both iron and aluminum heads. A 0.039-inch composition-style gasket with a stainless steel jacketing is available for small-blocks as PN 10159455. This is a good choice for high-performance street/strip combinations. Heavy-duty competition gaskets from Fel Pro are a Teflon-coated, composition design with solid fire rings. Available under PN 10185.054, they are 0.040-inch thick and fit 4.00- to 4.125-inch bores. For 18-degree aluminum heads with 4.166-inch bores, use PN 10185054 (also available as Fel Pro number 1003); for 4.200-inch bores, use Fel Pro PN 1034. Steam holes between bores must be drilled when used on 400-ci engines. No retorquing is required on gaskets from GM and Fel Pro.

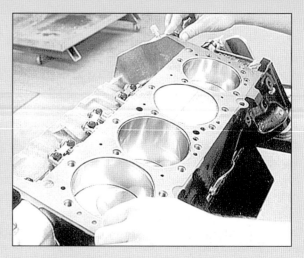

Make sure the gasket bore is large enough so that it does not protrude in the cylinder. If it does, it will be eroded by combustion and fail quickly.

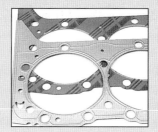

Composition gaskets are made of layers of material (back) and are suitable for both iron and aluminum heads. Steel-shim gaskets (front) have raised sealing beads around the critical openings and should only be used on cast-iron heads.

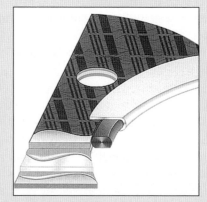

The latest composition gaskets for aluminum heads on high-performance engines have preflattened steel wire fire rings to optimize combustion pressure sealing without damaging the head surface. They are available from Fel Pro and GM.

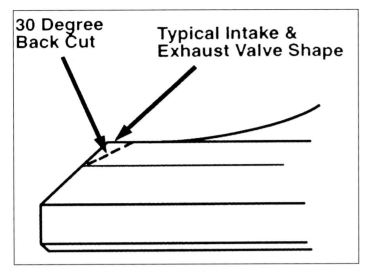

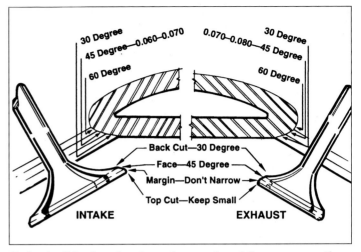

While it's considered questionable by some builders, grinding a 30-degree back cut on the intake and exhaust valves just under the seat contact ring is often claimed to slightly improve flow.

Refer to this drawing for valve seat and face preparation specifications. If you don't have the tools required to perform your own valve job, you can use these specs to check the work done by your machine shop.

Cylinder Head Prep Checklist

1. Degrease and perform a careful visual inspection. Look for any signs of damage.
2. Magnaflux and pressure test all used heads to locate cracks.
3. Inspect valves and guides for wear. Inspect seats for cracks, erosion.
4. Recondition or replace valveguides if required.
5. Machine for screw-in studs if required.
6. Cut spring seats for large diameter springs if necessary. Note: Some heads have very little material between the spring seat and the water jackets—proceed with caution.
7. Machine the tops of the guides for press-on seals if used.
8. Enlarge pushrod guide holes if additional pushrod clearance is required.
9. Match intake ports to heads and exhaust ports to manifolds or headers.
10. Smooth port contours, especially in the bowl areas (pocket porting) as desired.
11. Perform a quality three-angle valve job with proper seat widths and angles.
12. Install valvesprings to proper height and check spring pressures.
13. Check for adequate spring, retainer to guide and seal, and rocker clearances.
14. Check for uniform valvestem height.
15. Measure and equalize combustion chamber volumes.
16. Install studs and guideplates if required.
17. Thoroughly clean heads with soap and water, blow dry with compressed air, and store in plastic bags until ready for assembly.

How to CC Combustion Chambers

For maximum performance, combustion chambers should all be of equal volume. This allows each cylinder to perform the same amount of work by standardizing the compression ratio. The individual chamber volumes should be checked by filling each chamber with a measured amount of liquid. The heads need not be assembled for this check, but the valves must be installed with a light coating of grease on the seats. The heads should be supported in stands that allow them to be tipped slightly so the chambers are not quite level. This makes it easier to fill the chambers and remove stubborn bubbles. You can even bolt a cylinder head to your engine stand and rotate it to just the right position. To seal the chamber surface you'll need a 6x6-inch Plexiglas plate with a small hole located near one edge. A coating of light grease is smeared around the edges of the chamber, and the Plexiglas plate is pressed down on the head surface with the hole located near the edge at the highest point. Take care that none of the grease squeezes into the chamber; it will affect the accuracy of your measurements. Finish sealing the head by installing the spark plugs in the chambers.

To make accurate measurements you'll need a chemist's burette graduated in tenths of a cubic centimeter (cc), although you can obtain good results with a graduated flask. A convenient fluid to use is plain water or isopropyl alcohol with a bit of food coloring added to improve visibility. Fill the burette to the top line carefully. Capillary action will cause the fluid to climb the walls of the tubing slightly, so make sure you measure to the same point (usually the top or bottom) of the indicated level. Open the petcock and allow fluid to begin filling the chamber. Don't let it fill too quickly or the fluid wilt splatter out through the hole and change the reading. Since the head is tilted, you will see the fluid reach the Plexiglas and start working its way up toward the filling hole. When it gets close to the hole, slow the flow and work up slowly until the chamber is full. Watch the edges of the chamber to make sure that none of the fluid leaks past the grease seal.

Read and record the volume of each chamber. When you have measured each chamber, determine the best method for equalizing them. A common approach is to mill the head with the largest chamber so that it matches the volume of the largest chamber on the other head. Then the remaining chambers are lightly worked over until they are all equal in volume. Just remember that you should never sink a valve to increase chamber volume. If your heads are being used for class racing where no grinding is allowed, you are pretty well stuck with a simple mill cut, but heads for other uses (including street engines) can be dialed in with minor grinding in the chambers.

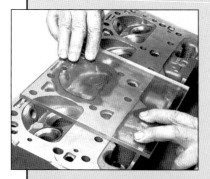

After installing the spark plugs, smear a light coat of grease on the valve seats and around the chambers. Then install the valves and place a Plexiglas plate on the head. Position the plate so the small fill hole is located near the upper edge of the chamber.

Carefully open the petcock and begin filling the chamber. When the chamber gets close to full, slow the flow and work slowly until the chamber is full.

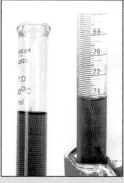

Read either the top or bottom of the fluid level. First set the level to zero, then directly read chamber volume when it is full (this one is at 74.6 cc).

After the chamber is full, watch the fluid level for a few seconds. If it drops, there is a leak at the valve, spark plug, or the glass plate. With even the slightest leak, you should redo the measurement to verify accuracy.

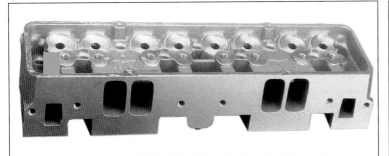

PN 24502615 is an aluminum Bow Tie head with 210-cc runners, shallow 35-cc chambers, and a 15-degree valve angle. It comes without guides and seats, so your porter can do the work. It is intended for small-displacement drag racing engines.

The aluminum CNC High Port Bow Tie head is available under PN 24502582. It has 245-cc intake runners, 65-cc chambers, 2.150/1.620-inch intake/exhaust valves, and angled spark plugs. It is intended for 9:1 compression engines.

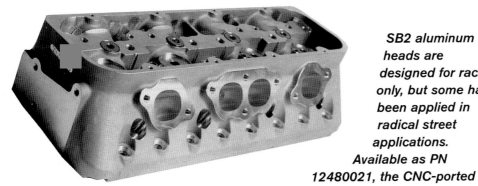

SB2 aluminum heads are designed for racing only, but some have been applied in radical street applications. Available as PN 12480021, the CNC-ported SB2 has 287-cc runners, 54-cc chambers, 2.150/1.625-inch intake/exhaust valves, and angled plugs, and it comes with seats and guides.

ing. Unless there is no other choice (e.g., using dual valvesprings), never use all-white Teflon/wire-spring type seals; they restrict guide oiling too much. When you must use Teflon seals, consider using bronze-wall guides, as they seem to survive better with less oil.

After the guides are reconditioned, your machinist can turn his attention to the valve seats. For any application requiring long life on unleaded gasoline, like virtually every street buildup, press-in hard inserts should replace the stock exhaust seats in the cylinder heads. They aren't inexpensive, but they can add 50,000-plus miles of additional service. Some cylinder heads have induction-hardened seats from the factory and may not require

hard-seat inserts; discuss these options with your machinist.

Considering the cost of new valves (about $80 per set), many engine builders opt for new instead of reconditioned valves. Speed-Pro, TRW, and other manufacturers offer valves with hardened tips that can reduce wear with high spring pressures and mechanical (solid-lifter) cams. However, if you're building a street engine and your valves are in good condition (showing little face, tip, or stem wear), regrinding the faces and stem tips is an acceptable option.

A quality three-angle valve job should always be performed, using a 30-degree top cut, a 45-degree seat, and a 60-degree bottom cut. Seat widths should be about 0.065 inch (to 0.010 inch) for the intake and

0.075 inch (to 0.010-inch) for the exhaust. Seats should be held near the lower tolerance limit for performance use, and widened to near the upper tolerance limit for street longevity. To optimize performance, grind only the minimum amount necessary to clean the seats. The more the valves are sunk into the seats, the less efficiently the ports will flow. If the seats require a lot of grinding, consider installing hard-seat inserts in both the intake and exhaust sides or look for replacement head castings.

The final steps in basic head preparation include installing the valvesprings so that they provide the cam manufacturer's recommended seat pressure. This involves measuring the compressed spring height at which the desired pressure is produced, then adding the appropriate valvespring shims so the recommended pressure is applied to the valve. If guide-type press-on seals are used, the top of the valveguides must be machined so that the outer diameter is concentric with the inner diameter. If this is not done, the seals will not wipe the valvestem uniformly and excess oil may be drawn down the guides, increasing oil consumption and possibly detonation.

INDUCTION SYSTEM

There are probably more induction systems available for the small-block Chevy than any other engine in existence, and with the advent of electronic engine management and electronic fuel injection, the selection becomes broader every day. Race and street manifolds are designed differently for their different applications, and as we have stressed with other engine components, the intake system must be selected to complement the engine package and application.

New generation electronic fuel injection (EFI) inductions have given the induction system a whole new look. The most commonly recognized factory EFI is the tuned port injection (TPI) system used since 1985 on high-performance Camaros, Corvettes, and Firebirds. The less-sophisticated, but highly reliable, GM Throttle Body Injection (TBI) induction is also widely used, especially on trucks.

The main difference between these two systems is the fuel delivery point. Port injection intake manifolds, like the TPI, are effectively "dry-flow" systems that only move air. The fuel injectors are located near the cylinder head ports and aimed toward

A single 4-barrel Holley carburetor on a dual-plane intake has been the default performance induction system for most hot-rodders since the late 1960s.

the valves. As a result, the manifold runners never contend with liquid or fuel particles. Throttle body injection and carbureted systems, on the other hand, are "wet-flow" systems. The fuel is injected into the incoming airstream at about the same location as a standard carburetor. The manifold runners must carry both fuel and air and still have many of the problems associated with carbureted systems. Later in this chapter we'll discuss the various fuel injection options available for the small-block and see how the difference between port injection and throttle body injection can affect performance. Before we get to this,

we'll take a look at the latest designs in conventional carbureted inductions.

Dual-Plane Manifolds

Most factory manifolds are of the dual-plane, 180-degree configuration. With this arrangement, you have what amounts to two separate air chambers that feed the fuel mixture to the engine. Each chamber supplies four alternate cylinders in the firing order. Since the small-block firing order is 1-8-4-3-6-5-7-2, one chamber feeds cylinders 1-4-6-7 and the other feeds cylinders 8-3-5-2. The "180-degree" designation comes from the

More modern applications make use of a variety of high-performance induction systems like this Demon SixShooter 3-2-barrel arrangement on a 434-ci Shafiroff small-block.

Twin Holleys like these on an original 1969 302-ci Z28 are highly prized for restoration purposes, but equal or better performance is now available in a variety of single, dual, and triple carburetor systems from major induction system manufacturers such as Barry Grant (Demon), Edelbrock, Holley, and a host of smaller companies.

fact that the engine draws alternately from each chamber every 90 degrees of crankshaft rotation and from each individual chamber every 180 degrees.

Most theorists believe a dual-plane configuration makes an ideal street manifold because of the even mixture distribution often attributed to this design. Since each chamber feeds only four cylinders, there is a smaller volume of air to be excited during each inlet sequence. This tends to transmit stronger signals to the carburetor and consequently, dual-plane manifolds are able to utilize carburetors with greater flow capacity. No one has really addressed the subject directly, but some indication of manifold design vs. carburetor size may be drawn from an examination of factory carburetion. Typically, factory high-performance engines were outfitted with larger carburetors than those recommended by specialty sources. The 302-ci Z28 engine was equipped with a 780-cfm carburetor, and even with moderate rear-end

gearing, it was still a very driveable combination. The 350-ci engine received an 800-cfm carburetor and it was also very tractable under part-throttle street conditions. In large measure, Chevrolet was able to use these high-flow carburetors because the efficient GM aluminum dual-plane manifolds maintained strong induction pulses to the carburetor. An added benefit provided by the large carburetor was that it helped overcome the slightly restrictive nature of the manifold at higher engine speeds.

The common hot-rod practice at that time was to cut down the center divider in these manifolds in an attempt to make the manifold more efficient at high RPM. This modification, in effect, makes the manifold similar to a single-plane design (discussed next) because each cylinder is exposed to a common plenum. By sharing the mixture resources, each cylinder is afforded an opportunity to draw from a larger volume of fuel mixture. The idea is well conceived, but in practice it is only partially suc-

cessful because (1) the induction signal was presented to all carburetor venturis, reducing its strength and the ability of the carburetor to respond crisply at low engine speeds, and (2) the basic dual-plane design virtually requires unequal length runners—another source of induction inefficiency.

In any wet manifold, the primary mission of the runner is to direct mixture flow toward the intake valve with minimal loss of velocity and minimal fuel drop out. If the runners are not equal length, the longer runners will deliver a leaner mixture since more fuel may drop out of suspension during the longer trip to the valve. This phenomenon is directly related to engine speed. As speed increases, this drop out problem becomes more acute, and distribution efficiency of a dual-plane design—which may be very good in low- and mid-RPM ranges—will often deteriorate and decrease overall efficiency at high RPM (generally above 6,000 rpm). On the other hand, the low-RPM and

Complete kits such as the Performer series from Edelbrock are designed to offer an integrated system for your small-block engine. The intake manifold and carburetor are dyno-matched to the camshaft selection to ensure maximum compatibility and performance. These packages are tested and proven on all popular sized small-block Chevys.

Edelbrock offers brand new Quadrajet carburetors for replacement applications and for performance use by those who appreciate the performance potential of a well-built Q-jet. They are available in 750- and 795-cfm versions.

The Speed Demon from Barry Grant has become one of the most popular carburetors on the market. It features advanced styling and incorporates all the features you could want in a performance carburetor, including mechanical or vacuum secondaries, billet construction, contoured venturi openings, clear float level gauges, and a range of sizes from 575 to 850 cfm. Speed Demons are designed for engines with cam profiles between 220 and 240 degrees duration at 0.050 inch of lift.

midrange qualities of a good dual-plane manifold, like factory designs, will usually produce improved acceleration in heavier cars with relatively high gearing. Current air-gap-style dual-plane intakes produce far fatter torque curves while nearly matching single-plane intakes at engine speeds of 6,000 rpm and above. Depending on the engine configuration, they may hang on even longer, perhaps even approaching 7,000 rpm in some cases.

Single-Plane Manifolds

In a high-speed performance engine, a single-plane manifold holds all the cards. The runners are nearly equal in length and they draw from a common plenum or mixing chamber. The even mixture supplied by this approach does positive things for horsepower. From a power standpoint, many engine modifications are directed at achieving equal work from each cylinder of the engine, and achieving uniform mixture distribution is one of the essential goals of this approach. A side benefit is often a reduction in emissions from equaliz-

A nice feature of the Holley EGR manifold is the hidden EGR valve. The valve is out of the way behind the carburetor, so it doesn't interfere with the air cleaner or valve covers.

ing thermal and combustion efficiency across the engine.

Manifold designers know that the size and shape of the plenum chamber can have a significant effect on induction system efficiency. As mentioned earlier, a larger plenum displays a weaker signal to the carburetor. This reinforces the notion that single-plane

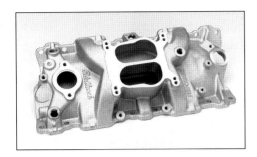

Edelbrock's Performer has become the basic single 4-barrel intake manifold of choice for mild-mannered small-blocks. It accepts Holley, Carter, and Q-jet-style carb flanges so that all popular carbs can be used on it.

Performer RPM intake and the more recent Performer RPM Air Gap intakes are dual-plane intake that feature constant cross sectional area runners for optimum performance. These manifolds have proven to be the best performing and most desirable street manifolds ever offered for high-performance street cars.

manifolds generally perform better with smaller carburetors than those typically used on dual-plane manifolds. The smaller carburetors maintain a higher mixture velocity, which offsets the velocity loss these manifolds incur at lower engine speeds. Yet the nearly straight, nearly equal-length runners are capable of delivering a greater mixture volume at high engine speeds.

Single-plane manifolds are not entirely without fault, however, and some consideration should be given to their limitations. Reversion is more pronounced in a single-plane manifold. There are two types of reversion. First, the closing of the intake valve is thought to cause a backward flow (pulse) through the manifold runners toward the plenum and carburetor. This condition is not considered as critical as the second type: exhaust pulse reversion. Exhaust reversion occurs when exhaust gas pulses, created inside the exhaust system, enter the intake runner during valve overlap. In a dual-plane manifold, this condition dissipates in one plenum/plane while the other plenum/plane is supplying fuel, but an open-plenum manifold is subjected to continuous reversion pulses as each cylinder draws mixture from the common plenum.

It is felt that a larger plenum volume helps absorb the pulses and reduces the reversion effect on carburetion. The now-common use of relatively tall carburetor spacers is evidence of this approach in the reversion battle. They have the effect of enlarging the plenum chamber and weakening the booster signal at the carburetor. In addition, spacers force the reversion pulses to travel a longer distance, and often make more of a turn, before they reach the carburetor. This implies that spacers normally work best when combined with larger carburetors and plenty of RPM. At slower engine speeds, the increased velocity of a smaller carburetor and the sharp booster signals produced by a smaller plenum provide crisp throttle response and good driveability. So spacers offer only small gains on street engines, but it's entirely possible that larger engines could benefit from a slightly increased plenum volume.

Factory Intake Manifolds

It's nice to have specific guidelines to follow, and when it comes to selecting small-block induction systems, there is still one overriding rule of thumb for 99 percent of all carbureted applications: Use a single 4-barrel carburetor. Multiple carburetion induction is capable of outperforming a single 4-barrel setup, but only when applied to a race motor that is designed to make use of the extreme-RPM flow capability of a tunnel-ram manifold and twin 4-barrels. Enthusiasts who desire the competition look for their street machines find exotic intake systems an irresistible lure, and they sometimes work tolerably well—after some hard work getting them at least somewhat dialed in. So the real question is: Which one is the best choice and why?

Obviously, the first place to look is the factory, where you will find the choices are considerably better than they used to be.

Quadrajet Manifolds

For general use, the standard cast-iron Quadrajet manifold has provided excellent service since 1965. There are zillions of them around and they can generally be obtained at the wrecking yard for something between 15 and 25 bucks. This dual-plane manifold was used in a number of semiperformance applications and it works better than most people care to believe. The current iteration of this intake manifold is available in lightweight aluminum as PN 14007377. It features all the necessary emission provisions and makes a good street performance manifold for Quadrajet or spread-bore-equipped cars.

Cast-Iron High-Rise Manifold

This cast-iron high-rise manifold (PN 14096011) is identical in design to the aluminum Z28 manifold (PN 10185024). It is less expensive than the aluminum version and is offered primarily for racing categories that require a cast-iron manifold. The

Factory Small-Block Intake Manifolds

GM has a wide variety of manifolds for the small-block. Each is the result of substantial dyno and on-track testing. You'll find street, off-road, marine, drag race, and circle-track configurations among this group of single-4-barrel designs.

Part Number	Material/Type	Carburetor Bolt Pattern	Description	Application	Notes
14007377	Aluminum Dual plane	Quadrajet or Spreadbore Holley	Production Manifold	Street Performance	Low profile, excellent hood clearance, EGR, heat riser and choke stove mount
10185024	Aluminum Dual Plane	Holley	High-Rise ZZ2 HO 350	Street Performance, Bracket Racing, Oval Track, Off-road	Former Z28/LT-1 intake, revised version of earlier manifold, 4.5 inches tall
10185063	Aluminum Dual Plane	Quadrajet or Spreadbore Holley	Low-Profile ZZ3 HO 350	Street Performance Bracket Racing, Oval Track, Off-road	Lower profile offers 1/2-inch more hood clearance. Same power as PN 10185054
14096011	Cast Iron Dual Plane	Quadrajet or Spreadbore Holley	High-Rise	Street Performance, restricted racing classes, marine	Cast iron version of Z28 intake PN 10185024
14096241	Cast Iron Dual Plane	Quadrajet or Spreadbore Holley	High-Rise	Street Performance, restricted racing classes, marine	Cast iron version of Z28 intake PN 10185024, center bolts drilled at 73° for '87 & later heads
10051102	Aluminum Single Plane	Holley	Standard-Runner Bow Tie	Limited Competition	For Bow Tie heads PNs 14011049, 10051167, and 10134392. Air gap runners, no heat riser
10051103	Aluminum Single Plane	Holley	Raised-Runner Bow Tie	Full Competition	Runners raised 0.200-inch for high port head PN 10051101, will fit low port 18° head PN 10134352 by port matching intake flanges to 5° angle
10185053	Aluminum Single Plane	Holley	High-Port 18° Bow Tie	Full Competition, high RPM	High port 18° heads PNs 10134364 and 24502482, 6.75-inches tall
10185053	Aluminum Single Plane	Holley	High-Port 18° Bow Tie	Full Competition, high RPM	High port 18° CNC ported heads PN 24502482
24502487	Aluminum Single Plane	Holley	High-Port 18° Bow Tie	Full Competition, high RPM	High port 18° heads PNs 10134363 and 24502482, "Line of sight" ports
24502481	Aluminum Single Plane	Holley	High-Port 18° Bow Tie	Full Competition, road racing and short oval track	High port 18° heads PNs 10134363 and 24502482, smaller runners for better mid-range torque
10093374	Pontiac Aluminum Single Plane	Holley	Pontiac High-Rise	Full Competition, road racing and short oval track	Pontiac Std. Port head PN 10033867
10093389	Pontiac Aluminum Single Plane	Holley	Pontiac High-Rise	Full Competition, road racing and short oval track	Pontiac "rolled deck" high port head PN 10093328
12341415	Chevy/Pontiac TPI 1985-1988	Electronic Fuel Injection	SLP/GM Parts Replacement EFI System	Hot Street Performance	Siamesed Runner High Flow Tuned Port Injection
12341416	Chevy/Pontiac TPI 1989-1993	Electronic Fuel Injection	SLP/GM Parts Replacement EFI System	Hot Street Performance	Siamesed Runner High Flow Tuned Port Injection

carburetor flange is machined to accept both standard flange and spread-bore carburetors. Because of its performance configuration, this manifold is particularly suitable for marine applications, where cast iron exhibits better corrosion resistance than aluminum.

Aluminum High-Rise Manifold

The aluminum high-rise intake manifold (PN 10185024) used on the 5.7-liter HO engine assembly is very close to the original Z28/LT1 intake manifold, but it has a few significant changes for late-model applications. There is no oil filler tube, and while there is a cast provision for a choke stove, the holes are left undrilled and untapped. This manifold only accepts standard Holley carburetor flanges, and because it is intended for late-model applications, the upper edges of the gasket sealing flanges are machined to fit the raised rocker cover rails of the Corvette aluminum cylinder heads (PN 10185086).

Aluminum Low-Rise Manifold

This manifold (PN 10185063) is similar to the high-rise HO intake manifold (PN 10185024) but is ¾-inch lower to provide improved hood clearance. It has a dual-pattern flange that will accept standard Holley or spread-bore Quadrajet carburetors. It provides all the necessary provisions for EGR, hot-air choke, and late-model accessory brackets. This manifold comes stock on ZZ3 and ZZ4 350-ci HO engine assemblies and fits all small-blocks through 1986.

Cast-Iron High-Rise Manifold

This late-model manifold (PN 14096241) is machined to fit 1987 and later 305 and 350 small-blocks with iron heads. This high-rise intake manifold has the center two bolt-holes on both sides spot faced for the 72-degree bolt angles used on late-model

The Performer RPM Q-jet is basically a Performer RPM intake specifically configured for Q-jet and Holley spread-bore carburetors. It is superseded by the more recent Performer RPM Air Gap intakes.

The factory aluminum dual-plane intake PN 14007377 features all the necessary emission provisions and makes a good street performance manifold for Quadrajet or spread-bore Holley-equipped cars.

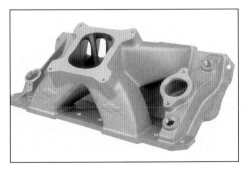

This factory intake PN 10051102 is a Bow Tie, standard runner single plane similar to the raised runner intake PN 10051103. Both manifolds have the air-gap configuration and are designed for use with Fel Pro 1205 and 1206 intake gaskets. GM recommends two-inch spacer with these intakes if hood clearance is available.

The cast-iron high-rise version of the aluminum Z28 intake is a budget-oriented manifold for low-buck builds. This manifold, PN 14096011, is identified by orange paint on the Bow Tie.

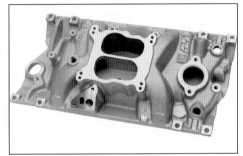

This is the Vortec intake manifold designed for max power and torque when used with Vortec heads. Available under PN 12496820, it is an aluminum intake designed for Holley or spread-bore carburetors. The manifold is EGR equipped and requires special intake gaskets PN 12529094 and special bolts PN 12550027.

cylinder heads. It's the same height as the aluminum high-rise PN 10185024.

Bow Tie Intake Manifold

This single-plane aluminum manifold (PN 10051102) is designed to fit all small-blocks with Bow Tie cylinder heads. It has the correct alignment for standard runners, but the consumer must port match the head and manifold for best results. It is recommended for use with the following Bow Tie cylinder heads (PN 14011049,

PN 10051167, and PN 10134392). Chevrolet recommends locating the gasket to the top of the intake port, and removing material from the bottom of the port opening to gain a proper match.

Raised-Runner Bow Tie Intake Manifold

This manifold (PN 10051103) features intake runners that have been raised 0.200 inch to match the raised runners on high-port Bow Tie heads (PN 10051101). It works best with a 2-inch-tall carburetor spacer and features an air gap beneath the inlet runners to help cool the mixture. There are no heat riser passages. The carburetor flange pad is drilled for standard Holley carburetors only.

18-Degree Manifold

This aluminum high-rise intake (PN 10185053) is designed specifically for the high-port, 18-degree Bow Tie

Barry Grant also offers their SixShooter 3-2-barrel intake manifold in a Vortec version for Vortec-head engines.

cylinder head (PN 10134363). It is similar to the raised runner Bow Tie intake manifold (PN 10051103).

Pontiac Standard Port Manifold

This aluminum intake manifold (PN 10093375) was designed specifically for the Pontiac-designed aluminum small-block head (PN 10031103). It's a single-plane, single 4-barrel intake with a standard Holley flange.

Aftermarket Intake Manifolds

Many enthusiasts look to specialty performance manufacturers for their manifold needs, and it's here that special-application designs abound. Dual-plane, high-rise manifolds are still available, but the field is generally covered with single-plane, open-plenum manifolds. Dual-plane units like the Edelbrock Performer and Performer RPM are still a top selection for moderate street performance in medium-to-heavy cars with automatic transmissions. Remember that these low-speed, torque-efficient manifolds were designed for exactly

that purpose. They give excellent service with standard gearing, and they really help that "kick in the pants" feel when combined with moderate rear-end gears.

When you move into the realm of bracket-race engines, you surpass the capabilities of most dual-plane and average street, single-plane designs. These manifolds can still be used effectively on heavier cars in the lower brackets, but the light, fast cars in the upper brackets need high-RPM manifolds and carburetion to match. Most current class-legal drag cars are equipped with plenty of gearing, loose torque converters, and a short block capable of well over 6,000 rpm. These engines routinely operate in the 8,000-rpm range and they need an induction system that's up to the task.

Recent developments have brought about the introduction of highly sophisticated single 4-barrel manifolds that are capable of matching the low-end performance of the earlier manifolds while far surpassing them at high speeds. One of the most successful of these manifolds is the

Edelbrock Victor Jr. series. It is very efficient at engine speeds up to 7,000 rpm, and the low-end and midrange characteristics are equally strong. The reasons for this are many, but the major strong point is very even cylinder-to-cylinder mixture distribution. This is characteristic of most single-plane manifolds, but you can really see it come around on the dyno.

There are, of course, other makes on the market, and many of them are excellent choices for street or bracket use. Holley and Weiand both offer good street manifolds for the small-block Chevy.

Port Matching

Simple port matching is a procedure that anyone can master with a little patience and attention to detail. The best procedure is the bolt-centerline method. This involves taking very specific measurements from lines scribed using the manifold bolt holes as a guide. The first step is to make sure the manifold bolt holes line up with the bolt holes in the head. Place the gaskets and manifold on the

Tuning single 4-barrel carbs is pretty straightforward in most applications. The mixture screws (both 2- and 4-corner idle) are adjusted for the highest vacuum reading of the highest RPM reading. Then the idle is adjusted and the mixture screws are revisited for a finer tune.

Quality gasket selection is critical with most intake installations. The gasket must match the intake and the head without leaks or poorly matched mating surfaces that will disrupt airflow. Fel Pro gaskets are the most popular choice.

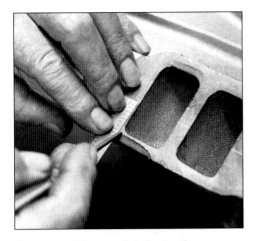

Port matching an intake to the cylinder head is a good idea. Unless the mismatch is really bad, port matching generally won't gain you more than three to five horsepower, but it is a fun procedure to perform and it is certainly worth doing on any performance engine.

Standard low-buck number-1850-style Holleys are the most basic carbs offered. They have inexpensive side-hung floats and no secondary metering block, but they can still deliver reasonable performance when tuned properly.

This view down the throttle bores of a Barry Grant engine running at full throttle reveals a well-defined and fully atomized fuel cone coming off the bottom of the boosters in this Race Demon carburetor. Fuel delivery is very even in each throttle bore.

This cutaway shows a typical Demon carburetor with down leg boosters. Note the path of idle fuel to the base plate and the fuel path through the main well to the boosters. Fuel is fully emulsified in the main well before moving to the booster.

block, mocked up with the cylinder heads and gaskets (the heads don't need to be torqued in place). Use a flashlight and make sure the holes line up. A slight mismatch where the manifold holes are slightly high is acceptable (the manifold will be drawn down as it's tightened. In any case, you should be able to get the bolts started without undue force. If the holes do not line up, you'll need to have the manifold or heads machined. Take the mocked-up engine to your machine shop and have them verify the mismatch and suggest a solution. If the bolt holes line up, the next step is to apply machinist's bluing to the port area of each cylinder head. Use a straight-edge to scribe a thin, well-defined line between the centerline of the holes. A small straightedge is then used to scribe the perimeter of each port.

The mating surface of the manifold is also treated with machinist's bluing and similar lines are scribed through the bolt centerlines. Use the small scale to measure the height and width of each head port opening so that the port shape and location can be transferred to the manifold. All measurements are taken relative to the centerline of the nearest bolt center. After you have measured each port and transferred the shape to the intake manifold, you can grind the ports to shape, forming a smooth transition between the head port and the manifold port. This method works particularly well on open-plenum manifolds, where it is possible to peer down the port and double check for any mismatch.

Another method, perhaps even easier, involves using a set of intake gaskets as grinding templates. Apply a strong contact cement (like weather-strip adhesive) to both the intake manifold and cylinder head port surfaces. Then install an inexpensive set of gaskets and bolt the manifold in place. After sufficient time for the cement to set up (a least an hour), pry the manifold off. Take your time so you don't damage the manifold surfaces. The gasket will tear, usually right down the middle, leaving a grinding template on both the heads and manifolds. The only hard part is scrapping the gaskets off when you're done grinding.

Manifold Installation Tips

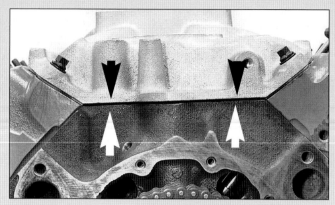

Before you begin manifold installation, set the manifold on the block with the runner gaskets in place. Make sure the bolt holes line up. Also make sure there is 0.060 to 0.120 inch of clearance between the manifold's bottom rails and the upper block rails as shown by the arrows.

Check the relationship of the angle between the manifold flange and the cylinder head. If the angles are too mismatched, the gasket may not seal well.

Numerous factory and aftermarket gaskets have been devised to seal the manifold/block end rails. No method is as good as the simple ¼-inch bead of high-temperature RTV silicone sealer laid across the end rails. Add a little dab in each corner to fill the gap and coat the area around the water passage openings for extra insurance against water leaks.

To ensure an effective seal, be careful not to move the manifold around as it contacts the silicone. When you tighten the bolts, the silicone squeezes out from the gap, forming a seal. Install the intake bolts and torque to 30 to 35 ft-lbs, using a circular sequence that starts in the center. If your engine has Vortec heads, the gaskets have rubber sealing rings and all of this is unnecessary.

Always use a fresh base gasket for the carburetor and don't overtighten the carburetor studs or bolts; firmly snugging them is all that is necessary.

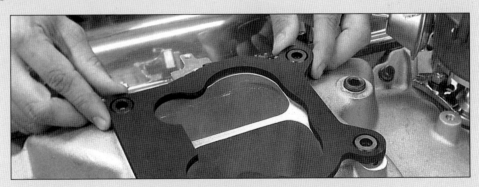

Small-Block Intake Manifold Gasket Guide

Part Number	Description
10147994	Production heads and standard runner performance heads
10185042	For splayed valve heads PN 10185040
10185007	For high-port 18° heads PN 10134363, PN 10134364 & PN 24502482
FEL-PRO 1205, 1206 or Mr. Gasket 102	For standard runner Bow Tie manifold PN 10051102

Fuel System Requirements

High-performance fuel systems are essential for any application with increased fuel demands. Modern high-performance electric pumps like the BG unit shown here are capable of delivering all the fuel you need. Their windings are designed for continuous duty, and they are available in a variety of sizes to suit your needs. EFI fuel pumps with higher pressures are also available from BG, Holley, and other manufacturers.

Clean fuel is important to ensure long pump life and proper fuel delivery. A high-quality in-line or remote fuel filter should be a part of every fuel system.

In this typical application, fuel is drawn from the bottom of the fuel tank, through the fuel filter and pump, and on to the engine. A built-in bypass on this BG pump can be seen routing return fuel back to the tank.

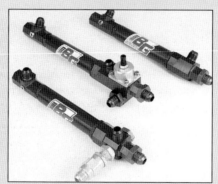

Here are three fuel log strategies for different applications. The lower unit is a pill-style bypass fuel log, while the center one features a diaphragm-style bypass. The upper one is a straight dual-outlet fuel log.

Three basic fuel regulators: a two-port bypass regulator (upper left), a four-port racing regulator (upper right), and an EFI regulator (right). The bypass regulator constantly bypasses unused fuel back to the tank so that the regulator has an easier time of maintaining a steady pressure. The four-port regulator is typically used for racing applications with dual carburetors, and of course, the EFI regulator is capable of controlling the higher pressures required for electronic fuel injectors.

This is your most basic regulator setup. The fuel line comes in and the outlet line goes to the carburetor. If there is no bypass at the pump, this pressure gauge will probably flicker with the pulsations of the pump. The unused port on this regulator could be used to make a bypass by installing a line with a fixed jet in it. Some experimentation would be necessary to determine the jet size, but something on the order of a number-60 jet would be a good starting point.

The King Demon RS has a removable base plate, which allows butterfly size to be changed without machining.

This view shows the boosters of a King Demon carburetor. On the left is a annular booster and on the right is a straight booster. The annular boosters typically provide finer mixture quality at lower engine speeds.

Carb Spacers

Inexpensive bolt-on carburetor spacers are probably the best-kept high-performance secret. They are almost always worth a modest power increase. As mentioned earlier, spacers work best on single-plane intake manifolds. The increased plenum volume provided by spacers improves the quality of mixture distribution and fuel atomization and provides a greater immediate volume of air/fuel mixture for each runner/cylinder to draw from at high engine speeds. The catch is loss of booster signal quality and a reduction in booster and throttle response.

Unfortunately, spacer selection is an inexact science and there is no way to know how a given combination will react until you try it. In all cases, the final result is quite dependent on the specific intake design. As a rule of thumb, the bigger the cam and the higher the engine speed, the taller the spacer needs to be, up to about two inches for single-plane manifolds. Dual-plane manifolds are more responsive to shorter spacers, but you

The King Demon RS model features removable venturi sleeves that allow you to adjust the size of the carburetor by changing the sleeves. All of these carburetors are three-circuit carbs with billet base plates, large capacity bowels, fuel level sight glasses, adjustable air bleeds, emulsion bleeds, and idle feed restrictors.

have to be careful because any spacer tends to bleed off low-speed torque. Dual-plane intakes generally like a spacer somewhere between ⅜ and 1½ inches tall.

Single-hole open spacers are usually less sensitive to various manifold and carburetor combinations and are easier to tune. Spacers with four individual holes maintain greater signal strength, but will tend to magnify any specific problems inherent in the manifold design. In some cases, however, four-hole spacers can signifi-

The position of the butterfly in relation to the transfer slot in the base plate determines how smoothly the carburetor will transition from the idle circuit to the main circuit.

cantly aid top-end power because they help maintain carburetor metering accuracy.

Clearance above the carburetor is always an issue with any spacer installation, so make certain you know how much room you have under the hood before getting too excited about spacers. You don't want to increase plenum volume and provide a smoother air path into the manifold, only to have incoming airflow choked off because the carburetor is jammed up tight against the lid of a low-profile (i.e., low-performance) air cleaner.

Fortunately, spacers are relatively inexpensive, so trial-and-error tuning shouldn't kill your wallet. You can also trade and swap spacers among your friends to find the best combo.

Carb Selection

When using any factory production manifold or a low-speed specialty manifold, every effort should be made to keep carburetor size to a minimum. Single-plane manifolds in particular rely on increased mixture velocity to improve efficiency and large carburetors wholly defeat their

All metering blocks on Demon carbs are machined from billet aluminum to prevent porosity and resultant variations in the metering circuits.

purpose. When these manifolds are used on any engine, no matter what the displacement, carburetor sizes should be kept under 750 cfm. In most cases a 600-cfm carburetor will substantially improve the engine response and overall performance. For smaller engines in the 283–327-ci range, a small carburetor will really shine on the street. Many people are having great success using a Road Demon or Road Demon Jr. on these engines. This is particularly true of cars with automatic transmissions. In these instances, the small carburetor provides crisp throttle response and

Idle-Eze is Barry Grant's patented idle-air compensation valve. It eliminates the need to drill holes in the carburetor butterflies to obtain proper idle speed and transition. It is adjusted with a screwdriver inserted through the air cleaner stud hole. It provides additional idle air for engines with large camshafts and poor booster signals.

This formidable inline setup is based on a pair of Road Demon Jr. carbs. Their short overall length makes them an ideal choice for tunnel ram applications. They are available in 525-, 625-, and 725-cfm versions with vacuum secondaries, two-corner idle, and a manual choke.

Selecting Holley Carburetors

Holley 4-barrels are some of the most versatile carburetors available for high-performance work. They are available in a broad range of CFM ratings, configured for stock, high-performance, and racing applications. A Holley 4-bbl on top of your engine is still a universal sign that you mean business.

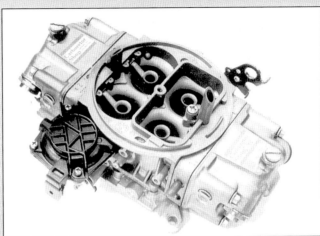

Holley's 3310 vacuum-secondary 4-bbl is by far the most desirable Holley carb for street performance, trucks, and some circle-track racing. The 3310's vacuum secondaries make for an excellent transition from a well-tuned primary circuit. It can be tailored to suit the unique requirements of nearly any application. If you want excellent driveability and throttle response from a street carb, the 780-cfm 3310 is a great choice.

For racing applications and outer-limits street machines, the Holley Double Pumper is the leading contender. Available in sizes ranging from 600 to 850 cfm, the Double Pumper features an accelerator pump on both the primary and secondary metering circuits. Double Pumpers can be configured with adjustable four-corner idle circuits for precise tuning, and they are easily modified to suit any gasoline or alcohol race engine.

Holley Dominators are pure race carbs designed to flow massive amounts of air. Most of them feature an intermediate idle circuit in addition to the tow standard metering circuits, and they're quite tunable. The 750-cfm Street Dominators can be modified for strong street performance or racing.

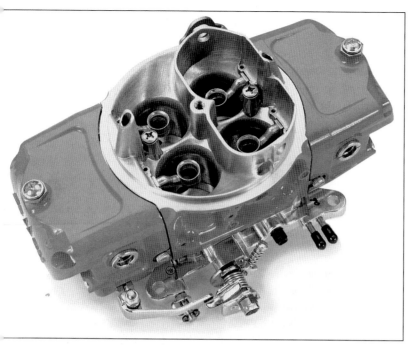

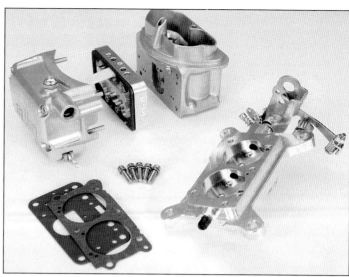

Here's a breakdown of the 250-cfm Demon 2-barrel used on the Barry Grant SixShooter system. It uses the same billet components found in other Demon carburetors and its design and function make it an ideal choice for old school street rodders looking to add a little modern touch to their engines.

Speed Demons are also available in both mechanical and vacuum secondary versions. The basic Speed Demon comes without a choke, but a choke kit is available for those who feel the need.

remarkably brisk acceleration. Then again, in many applications, you should take care not to overlook the advantages offered by retaining the stock carburetor.

A new or remanufactured Quadrajet from Edelbrock often eliminates an expensive carburetor change. The Q-jet was offered as standard equipment on many Detroit medium-performance engines and it makes a good performance carburetor, especially in applications where low-speed efficiency and throttle response are an important consideration.

The key consideration is venturi diameter. You will note that carburetors with smaller maximum flow ratings have small primary venturis, producing increased mixture velocity and throttle response. If you're going to use a high-performance carburetor, you may wish to use venturi diameter as a basis for comparison. Once again, the goal is to optimize carburetor

selection for your individual car and engine combination. Bear in mind right from the start that a *carburetor that is too large will hurt performance far more than one that is too small.* If you use a carburetor that is too small, you will be able to feel the engine "go away" when the RPM surpasses the carburetor delivery capacity. The engine will still run fine, but it will feel flat at the very top end. On the other hand, a carburetor that is too large will not send an effective signal to the metering circuits, reducing overall performance and fuel economy. If it's greatly oversized, the low-speed acceleration will practically disappear. Severe cases even suffer from reduced power in the midrange. This is far more difficult to detect since the engine may still feel responsive—it just doesn't pull as hard as it should when the car is accelerating.

Fine Tuning

Carburetors nearly always work well in out-of-the-box form, but their efficiency can usually be improved with minor jet changes, idle adjustments, power-valve alterations, and other adjustments that can dial-in the combination. This fine-tuning process must be performed with careful consideration of other engine and drivetrain components, e.g., gearing, transmission type, tire diameter, camshaft profile, and the like. Careful evaluation is the name of the game. The engine will reveal what it does and doesn't like, but it's up to you to recognize and interpret the signals. It's beyond the scope of this publication to delve deeply into the science of carburetor tuning. (The books *Holley— Rebuilding & Modifying, Super Tuning and Modifying Holley Carburetors, How To Tune and Win With Demon Carburetion, Super Tuning and Modifying Carter Carburetors,* and *How To Build Horse-*

Here's your basic Mighty Demon, which features a main body (without a choke housing), adjustable air bleeds, Race Demon metering blocks, Idle-Eze, and all the other basic features of all Demon carbs. The Mighty Demon is an affordably priced race-style carburetor available in 650-, 750-, 825-, and 850-cfm versions, plus an 850-cfm with annular boosters.

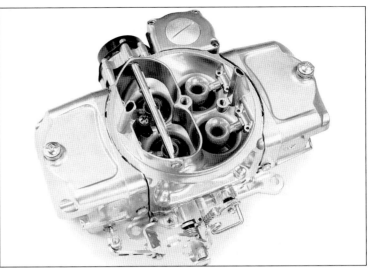

Here's a vacuum secondary 625-cfm Road Demon with down-leg boosters in the primaries and annular boosters in the secondaries. The 525-cfm Road Demon uses annular boosters in all four throttle bores. These carbs target stock-type engines. The 525-cfm is for V-6 and small V-8 engines, the 625-cfm is for 302- to 400-ci engines, and the 725-cfm is designed for 350- to 500-ci engines.

power, Volume 2, available from CarTech Books, cover this topic.) You can generally depend on factory calibration to be pretty close for most day-to-day applications. If you want to experiment some, set your sights on good off-idle response and crisp reaction in the midrange, but don't over compensate for problems that may be related to improper gearing or a lazy spark advance.

On all reasonable street applications, you will have better luck with a carburetor that utilizes vacuum secondaries or some sort of vacuum air-valve and secondary-lockout system. Mechanical secondary Speed Demons and Holley double-pumper carburetors are great carburetors, but they work most effectively in relatively light cars with very low gears and in racing conditions where the carb is constantly transitioning into the secondary throttles. In a true racing setup, the mechanical-secondary double pumper is nearly impossible to beat, but for the street, stick with vacuum secon-

daries. Demon and Holley both offer high-performance vacuum-secondary carbs. A careful workbench mechanic can tune a vacuum carb for outstanding day-to-day performance, but you must write down every tuning change and what specific (hopefully, measured) effect it has on performance. If you're in doubt about any change, make a careful back-to-back test to see if the alteration actually improves performance and/or economy. Be methodical and take your time.

Electronic Fuel Injection

Today's electronic fuel injection systems are very sophisticated, but they operate on simple principles. There are two types of electronic control: speed density and mass airflow. Mass airflow systems use an airflow sensor (called MAF for Mass AirFlow) to measure the amount of air entering the engine. This is often accomplished with a heated wire inside the sensor tube. The electronics continu-

ally adjust the current flow through the wire to keep it at a constant temperature. The varying current is directly proportional to the air mass passing through the tube. This information is then used to assist the ECM in selecting the appropriate fuel metering.

Speed-density systems don't use a mass airflow sensor. They calculate the fuel requirement primarily based on engine load, as measured by manifold vacuum and the throttle position sensor (TPS). A manifold absolute pressure sensor (MAP) sends pressure readings to the computer, which also reads manifold air temperature and engine speed, to calculate fuel metering. Mass airflow systems and speed density systems both use oxygen sensors to let them know how accurate the fuel metering is at any moment. The oxygen sensor's input fine-tunes the fuel delivery and helps maintain the air/fuel ratio near the stoichiometric 14.7:1 ratio. The computer calculates fuel delivery based on its

The PowerRodder carburetor is a two-piece carburetor available in 500-, 600-, and 700-cfm versions. It has no power valves and no metering rods, and it utilizes a central float design. It has oversized vacuum secondaries and an electric choke. Its target applications are stock-type engines or mild performance engines with stock or near stock idle characteristics.

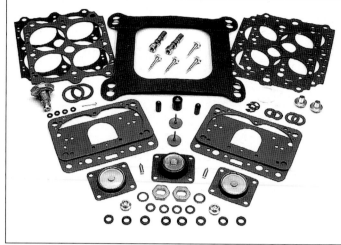

Most performance carburetors give very good service for a long time. When necessary, it's best to overhaul them with a complete kit from the manufacturer as shown here. This ensures the same top quality replacement parts to make to carburetor like new again.

This view shows the clean functional design of the SixShooter system from Barry Grant, Inc. What street rodder wouldn't want to have this awesome setup on his engine?

preprogrammed engine map, a digital encoding of specific fuel (and spark timing) requirements determined, or mapped, during extensive engine dynamometer and road testing. When all sensors are functioning, your engine will operate near maximum efficiency. The computer constantly monitors the sensors and will set a trouble code to alert you if any of them fail. If the failure is severe, the computer reverts to a "limp-home" program that will allow you to keep driving at reduced performance until the defect is repaired.

Adding electronic fuel injection to a small-block is straightforward,

but still expensive. Most suppliers offer complete systems that include an intake manifold, throttle-body air valve, high-pressure fuel pump, electronic control module, and all the necessary sensors. To keep the cost down, most systems use speed-density control. This eliminates the expensive MAF sensor, but also loses some accuracy, since airflow is calculated rather than measured. Engine maps for speed density systems are very high quality, and you generally won't notice the difference, but maximum accuracy is still obtained with a mass airflow sensor supplying precise information to the ECM.

Other sensors contributing to an EFI system include a throttle position sensor, coolant temperature sensor, and a block-mounted knock sensor that tells the computer to temporarily alter the timing to combat engine detonation. The throttle position sensor input assists the ECM in determining fuel delivery based on the throttle valve angle. It's the most direct input from the driver regarding engine power requirements. The coolant temperature sensor tells the computer when the engine is cold (at startup) so it can supply the appropriate fuel curve until the engine warms (most of the systems monitored by the ECM are affected in one way or another by the coolant temperature). The distributor also sends a reference signal to the ECM so it can keep track of engine speed and crank angle for accurate computation of fuel demand relative to ignition timing.

All EFI systems require high-pressure fuel pumps and high-quality fuel filters. This is much more critical than with a carburetor.

Clear sight glasses are a stock feature on all Demon carburetors. The actual glass window allows you to get a clear view of the float level while adjusting it according to the built-in level gauge on the side of the float bowl.

Injectors are easily plugged, and restricted fuel delivery will quickly cause a lean condition, which can lead to overheating and serious mechanical damage. For most street applications, the stock in-tank Camaro or Corvette pumps are adequate. When you begin to generate serious horsepower, you'll need a good Bosch fuel injection pump or one of the high-pressure units offered by SX Performance or other manufacturers.

At first glance, EFI systems may seem complicated, but they are not difficult to understand if you study the information available from specialty manufacturers and suppliers. CarTech Books even has a book to help you, called *Building & Tuning High-Performance Electronic Fuel Injection*, by Ben Strader. The benefits include crisper throttle response, better fuel economy, and a whole new high-performance look. There is plenty of evidence to suggest that a properly tuned carburetor can match the power output of injection, but it takes a lot of effort to make a carburetor match the injector's efficiency throughout the driving range.

Float-level adjustments are one of the most commonly misunderstood problems with carburetors. Raising the float creates a higher head pressure on the jets and generally richens the mixture ever so slightly. Lowering the float level reduces head pressure and may lean the mixture slightly. If the float level is too high, fuel can spill over during high-speed turns or violent drag race launches. This changes the fuel ratio and affects power. If the float level is too low, the carb may run out of fuel during periods of high demand.

Now that EFI has become popular and as more and more rodders are starting to understand how to program it, high-performance EFI kits like this Holley 950 Commander unit are proliferating rapidly. Base fuel maps are very well calibrated and most applications will run pretty well right out of the box.

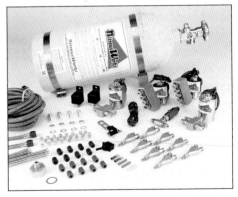

Nitrous oxide systems are still extremely popular and most nitrous kit manufacturers continue to upgrade the systems with new features. Kits are available to increase power by 100 to 500 hp and more, if you dare.

IGNITION SYSTEM

The ignition system may seem relatively uncomplicated. All you need is a power source and a means of distributing a high voltage (spark) to each cylinder at the proper time. In reality, the problem is far more complex. The wide range of possible operating conditions makes optimum ignition timing and spark delivery vital for overall engine efficiency, especially when emissions and economy are part of the picture.

Selecting an ignition system for your small-block Chevy requires the consideration of several important factors. Since timing is the basis of all engine functions, it is critical that, above all else, the ignition system maintain rock-solid integrity. This was easy enough in the early days when the primary mission of the ignition system was providing smooth engine operation, but now that it has been called upon to help control emissions and to compensate for other less-than-ideal conditions, the standard ignition system has become quite complex.

Chevrolet has offered a variety of Delco-Remy-built ignition components over the years, but two basic types have been used on the vast majority of production vehicles. Each of these systems is suitable for normal

From 1955 to 1975, all small-blocks used conventional Delco breaker-point ignition systems. When the points open (arrow) electrical flow to the coil was disrupted causing a field collapse and a burst of high voltage, which was routed to the appropriate spark plug via the distributor cap. Dual points added dwell time or the amount of time power is applied to the coil. Additional dwell time improved high-speed performance.

Dual points with high spring tension work well to about 7,000 rpm, but the increased rubbing block wear, eventually alters the desired point gap. This is the main drawback to a point system. When rubbing block wear occurs, the points corrode, changing the point gap and the dwell time.

high-performance use once they have been correctly tuned. With some minor modifications most of these Delco ignition systems are also suitable for semiprofessional racing.

Ignition Basics

Prior to 1975, all small-block Chevys used a conventional Delco breaker-points distributor with mechanical- and vacuum-advance systems. This setup used a single set of breaker points as a switching device to control the flow of electrical power to the primary windings of the ignition coil. When the points opened, electrical flow was disrupted and the electromagnetic field created around the primary windings collapsed. The collapse was assisted by a condenser (a storage device for electrical energy, like a small battery), which reduced arcing across the points and ensured the rapid collapse of the magnetic field in the coil. The field collapse generates a burst of high voltage in the secondary windings of the coil. This voltage is routed to the appropriate cylinder through the distributor and spark plug wires.

You can visualize voltage like electrical pressure. The more voltage you have, the more power you can push through a circuit. If your engine is operating under adverse conditions or

To minimize rubbing-block wear, early point-type distributors required periodic application of a suitable lubricant to the cam surface. But only a very small amount could be applied, since excess lubricant could be thrown off and contaminate the contact points. With lubrication, adjustments, and block wear, point-type ignitions now seem archaic compared to modern breakerless systems that never require adjustments.

the ignition system components are not in top shape, voltage requirements for effective ignition can easily double. On the other hand, a well-tuned engine running with an optimum air/fuel ratio may be able to begin ignition with only average secondary energy. In these situations, any additional voltage is unused. The

high voltage potential of a high-energy ignition system can be considered just that: potential. It is available to fire the plugs under adverse conditions such as lean mixtures, high speeds, and cold-start conditions.

The conventional breaker-point system can be reliable, but it requires maintenance. The common

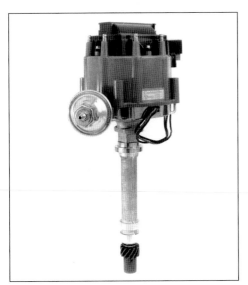

In 1975, GM introduced their High Energy Ignition system, or HEI. It has proven reliable under a wide range of operating conditions, and available performance enhancements have made it a solid performer even at higher engine speeds.

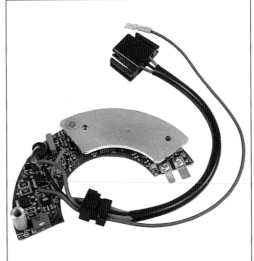

MSD's Digital HEI module PN 83645 works in conjunction with its performance coil PN 8225 to improve HEI performance. The module is a direct plug in and will produce up to 7.5 amps of current. The latest version includes a built-in rev limiter.

One of the biggest problems with early factory HEI units was rotor burn-through from the high-intensity spark. This would cause a failure-to-start problem. You can avoid it by installing a high-quality cap and rotor assembly from MSD.

Understanding Spark Advance

Spark advance is the number of crankshaft degrees that the spark occurs before the basic (static or initial) spark timing. It has a great effect on how smoothly and efficiently your engine will run. In order to obtain the maximum pressure on the piston at the optimum position in the power stroke, ignition is often initiated well before the piston reaches the top of the compression stroke. However, as engine speed increases, there is less real time for the ignition process to be completed. Fortunately, flame speed increases nearly proportionally with engine speed primarily due to the increase in combustion-space turbulence. This means that for most of the RPM range, the crank angle through which combustion takes place can remain relatively constant. It is fortunate that flame speed is linked to engine speed. If this relationship did not exist, it would be impossible for spark-ignition engines to operate at high speeds, because there would be insufficient time for efficient combustion to take place.

The job of the various advance-control mechanisms, whether they are located in an electronic black box or controlled by various mechanical systems in a distributor, is to ensure that the spark is delivered to each cylinder at the correct time to gain maximum work (horsepower) from combustion. This should occur at all speeds from idle up to the rev limit. Timing advance is expressed as the number of crankshaft degrees before TDC that the spark is delivered to the plug. A spark triggered after TDC is said to be retarded. Simply stated, the purpose of spark advance is to harness optimum power from the combustion process regardless of engine speed and load.

Initial Advance

Initial advance is the amount of fixed advance supplied to the engine during the start-up period. When the distributor is installed into the engine block and tightened in place, initial timing is fixed. Within the distributor, the rotating breaker-point cam or reluctor is mounted on the centershaft. By loosening the hold-down bracket and adjusting the position of the distributor housing in the block, it's possible to change the relative position between the breaker plate and the centershaft, changing the initial timing at which the spark occurs relative to the crankshaft. Once set, the distributor clamp is tightened, locking the housing (and initial timing) in place.

Mechanical Advance

While flame propagation speed increases with engine speed, this relationship is not directly proportional below about 3,000 rpm, especially in low-compression engines with low combustion-chamber turbulence. From idle to 2,500–3,000 rpm, the combustion rate increases much more slowly, and the centrifugal (mechanical) advance mechanism compensates by advancing ignition timing as engine speed comes up from idle. However, as speed continues to climb, turbulence in the charge begins to speed flame propagation and reduce combustion time. This faster combustion rate offsets the need for further ignition advance. To match these variations in combustion time, most centrifugal mechanisms rapidly advance ignition timing in the lower RPM ranges, but as the engine speed builds, timing is held constant or advances very slightly. If engine speed and best centrifugal advance are plotted on a graph, the curve usually resembles a steep slope up to about 2,500 rpm, followed by a flat plateau at higher speeds. To accomplish this, most small-block distributors are equipped with bob weights and springs that move the breaker-point cam or reluctor relative to the distributor centershaft, advancing the ignition point as engine speed increases.

downfall of a breaker-point system is rubbing-block wear and dwell-angle variation. The points are opened and closed by a cam on the distributor shaft. It works against a rubbing block located on the breaker points. When this rubbing block eventually wears, ignition characteristics change because the point gap is altered, changing the amount of time the points are open or closed (called dwell time).

HEI

In the 1970s, electronic ignition systems and ignition controls were developed to eliminate breaker-point problems altogether and to provide a much hotter spark to work with lean, emissions-calibrated mixtures. To this end, the GM High Energy Ignition (HEI) has been used in all General Motors cars since 1975, and it has proven highly reliable under a wide range of operating conditions. HEI is the logical extension of earlier electronic systems and features a number of improvements and a drawback or two. The major difference in the HEI

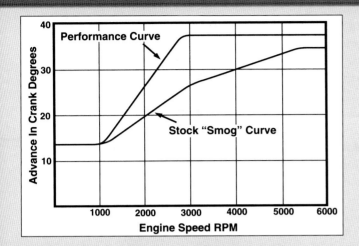

Set the initial timing about 12 to 16 degrees advanced. Then adjust the advance curve to start about 1,000 rpm. Have the curve add about 20 to 24 crank degrees by about 3,000 rpm. The exact timing requirements will vary depending on the cylinder heads, transmission type, fuel octane, and other factors.

Vacuum Advance

The other major factor affecting ignition timing is the variation in combustion time as the density of the air/fuel mixture changes. Since mixture density is much lower when the throttle is partially closed, cylinder pressure, turbulence, and flame speed are reduced. As a result, more time, in the form of additional ignition advance, is needed to burn the mixture. Since charge density and flame speed are directly related to manifold vacuum, a vacuum-sensitive mechanism is commonly used to increase or decrease advance independently of the centrifugal mechanism.

Virtually all small-block Chevy vacuum-advance mechanisms use a spring-loaded diaphragm connected to the contact-breaker or magnetic-pickup plate with a linkage arm. At high vacuum levels, the diaphragm is retracted against the spring. This moves the breaker-plate in a direction opposite to that of the distributor centershaft, triggering the points or magnetic pickup sooner, advancing ignition timing. As the throttle is opened, vacuum decreases and the spring in the diaphragm assembly returns the breaker plate to its standard position, eliminating the additional timing advance that could otherwise cause ping or detonation at higher engine loads.

It is helpful to view the vacuum-advance system as a load-sensitive ignition control. Since the vacuum advance is progressively activated as power demands are reduced, e.g., during cruise, this system is the single most important ignition factor affecting fuel economy during normal street driving. If economy is at all important, the engine should be equipped with a fully functional vacuum advance.

Total Advance

Total advance at any RPM is the amount of timing lead supplied to the engine when all of the variable-advance systems have corrected spark timing. This includes initial advance put in by basic adjustment of the distributor housing, centrifugal advance supplied by the springs and weights in the distributor, and vacuum advance supplied by the vacuum canister.

is the relocation of the coil and control electronics to within the main distributor housing. HEI is designed as a self-contained system, optimized to fire lean fuel mixtures at slow and moderate engine speeds. It's just the ticket for late-model emissions-calibrated engines, as it requires virtually no maintenance, provides accurate ignition timing, and greatly extends

spark plug life. Many knowledgeable ignition people feel that a properly set-up HEI is all the ignition needed for 95 percent of all high-performance applications.

HEI upgrades are available from specialists such as Performance Distributors, and MSD. MSD, in particular, offers a wide variety of specialized components, including a billet HEI dis-

tributor (also available from Chevrolet) that provides the best features of an HEI along with the performance and reliability of MSD racing technology.

Aftermarket Ignitions

There are so many types and brands of specialty ignitions available it becomes nearly impossible to sort

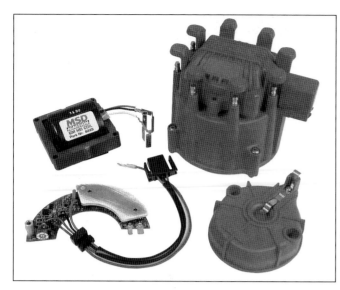

The Ultimate HEI kit from MSD combines the digital module and performance coil with a high-performance distributor cap, rotor, and coil cover to make converting your stock HEI into a powerhouse ignition a quick do-it-yourself job.

MSD's Pro Billet HEI is a complete billet distributor with all of MSD's high-performance technology built in. Three sets of springs and four stop bushings allow you to custom tailor your advance curve and there is a vacuum advance unit to ensure maximum economy.

A peek inside the Pro Billet HEI reveals its high-quality components, including a digital module, built-in rev-limiter, ball-bearing construction with heavy-duty shaft, nylon weight bushings, vacuum advance unit, and precision weights. This is the top-of-the-line HEI package designed to meet all your HEI ignition needs and more.

the good from the also-rans. Almost as soon as there were ignition systems, somebody began figuring out ways to improve them or to make money by claiming new and improved designs. Every ignition system advertisement sings the praises of high energy, and they all claim to have more than the next guy. Unfortunately, there is a lot of junk floating around and much of it will do you little good.

For early model cars, a stock breaker-point ignition provides good performance when it is well maintained. If you decide to add a hot coil and a multispark ignition module, like the potent boxes from MSD, you're in great shape for a street machine. Still, many people are attracted by the low maintenance requirements of an all-electronic ignition. And now that these systems are available with a broad range of performance capabilities for reasonable cost, electronic ignitions have become a virtual necessity.

This inexorable drive for electronic ignition power and reliability began in the mid 1960s, when the capacitor-discharge system, or CD, came into vogue. They were originally designed to augment a breaker-point system, but eventually they were combined with breakerless distributors. CDs featured a control box that boosted battery voltage to about 300 volts. This higher voltage was applied to the primary side of the coil when the points opened and that really shocked the coil into producing 30,000 or more volts on the secondary side. This high-energy spark, along with a fast rise time, made these units suitable for racing, provided the distributor and breaker points were able to operate at the desired RPM limit. They had a lot of spark energy, but the spark duration was very short. Normal and rich mixtures were easily lit with a CD, but lean mixtures were another story. There was a chance that no combustable mixture would be near the plug at the precise moment the spark was delivered, and the almost instantaneous nature of the spark limited the possibility for reliable ignition.

The first truly breakerless ignition developed was a magnetic-impulse system. It used a constant magnetic field passing through a pickup coil. A toothed wheel, called the reluctor, moved past the pickup coil and the changes in the magnetic field sent a small electrical impulse through the pickup coil to the switching electronics that fired the spark plugs. Many of

Ignition Coil Basics

It all happens in the ignition coil. The coil is composed of two separate wire windings (the primary and secondary) over a common iron core. It's basically a transformer that uses a magnetic field generated by the primary winding to produce a higher voltage in the secondary winding. The voltage increase is dictated by the ratio of turns in the primary versus the secondary windings.

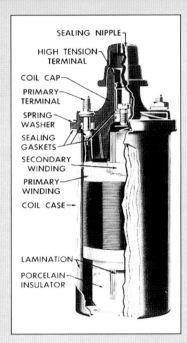

Many performance coils have a winding ratio of 30,000 turns/150 turns, or about 200 to 1. But this turns ratio would only increase battery voltage (12 volts) to about 2,400 volts. Since ignition coils generate up to 60,000 volts, there must be other factors involved . . . read on.

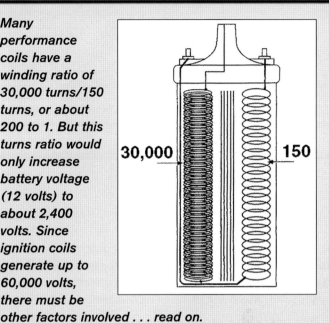

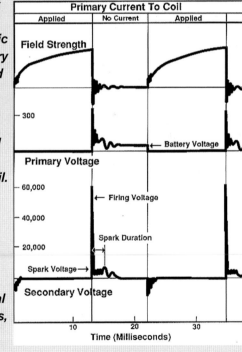

Voltage is generated in proportion to how fast the magnetic field builds or collapses. If the field collapses quickly (in less than one millisecond) it will cause about 250 to 300 volts to be generated in the primary winding. This primary spike, multiplied by the 200 to 1 turns ratio of the coil, produces up to 60,000 volts to fire the spark plugs.

This is what happens to the magnetic field, primary voltage, and secondary voltage as power is applied and removed from the coil. When 12 volts is applied to the coil, the magnetic field builds. After several milliseconds, the primary power is abruptly removed and the magnetic field collapses. This rapid change in the field generates nearly 300 volts in the primary and up to 60,000 volts in the secondary, firing the spark plug.

The pin moving inside the slot (arrow) determines the total mount of centrifugal advance in a mechanical advance mechanism. For some performance applications, there is too much movement. A larger-diameter bushing can be slipped over the pin to limit the amount of movement. Limiting distributor advance to about 10 degrees gives you a total of 20 degrees of centrifugal advance (since it rotates at one-half engine speed). This permits as much as 12 to 14 degrees initial timing for improved low-end performance (providing that you have good gas in the tank).

Fine-tuning the vacuum advance is much easier if you use an adjustable vacuum diaphragm such as these from Crane and Mr. Gasket. These units have a screw adjustment that controls the vacuum level at which the advance begins. They can be tuned to accommodate most requirements.

Changing the mechanical advance curve rate and starting and stopping points in the RPM range involves swapping advance springs (arrows) and bob weights. This work was previously done most accurately with a distributor machine. Newer electronic distributors use the same method, and the very latest allow you to electronically adjust advance rates.

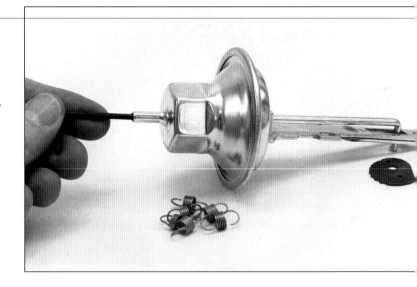

these early system designs worked well, but some were rate sensitive. In other words, the output to the plugs was directly tied to the speed of the reluctor. So at low engine speed, spark energy was quite weak; in some cases it was too weak to start the engine. However, high-RPM spark energy was very good, making them desirable for racing where engine speed was almost always high. They had no point bounce and a good immunity to dirt and grease. They were unaffected by wear and required virtually no maintenance.

The MSD 6A multiple spark discharge control box is the center point of a wide range of add-on electronics. This reasonably priced unit produces a killer spark that can improve cold starting as well as low- and high-speed operation. Many users also note an improvement in fuel economy. The MSD 6AL unit is an enhanced version that incorporates a soft touch rev control adjustable in 100-rpm increments. It also permits the addition of a Two Step Rev Control, which allows you to set two rev limits: one for starting-line RPM and the other for over-rev protection.

A distributor machine has always been an essential tool for checking and adjusting a mechanical advance curve. Additionally, it can verify every function of the distributor. Experienced operators of the Sun distributor machine can guarantee your distributor will work perfectly while developing maximum performance for your car/engine/gearing combination.

Adjustable timing control units allow you to alter ignition timing via a simple dash-mounted knob. Up to 15 degrees can be added to or subtracted from total timing to compensate for temperature, fuel quality, and other road conditions.

Variations of magnetic systems included various triggering devices, three of which remain available. The least common uses a distributor with the old breaker-point cam lobes to trigger a proximity sensor mounted near the cam. An electronic control module fires the spark plugs when the lobe tips come close to the sensor. Interestingly, in this system the original breaker points may be left in place so that the system can be converted back to a stock ignition by flipping a switch in the event of an electronics failure.

The second, and perhaps the most common, design uses a separate trigger wheel either mounted over or in place of the stock distributor cam. The sensor detects the teeth of the trigger wheel as they rotate past, signaling the control box to fire the coil. These units work effectively, but worn bushings can degrade their accuracy. Both types of these breakerless systems are currently used in many specialty and factory ignitions.

The third type is an LED (light emitting diode) system that makes use of light-sensing circuitry. The LED is mounted on the breaker plate and positioned so that a shutter wheel, mounted to the distributor shaft, can alternately cover and uncover the light beam. This alternates power to the primary circuit and fires the spark plugs.

Optical systems are quite reliable and provide stable timing. They are insensitive to most ignition problems, but some systems can be affected by dust and grease. A variation of these three systems combines the construction of the optical and magnetic systems. It is called the Hall-Effect ignition, and it uses a magnetic field and a chopper wheel similar to those used in an optical system. Each arm of the chopper wheel is a small magnet.

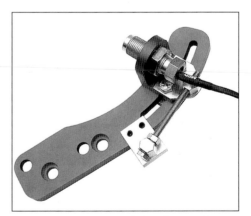

Crank-trigger ignition is used to positively time the spark. MSD's flying magnet system uses four precision located magnets to precisely time the spark according to crank location. The system is designed to prevent false triggers, and is available in all popular balancer sizes. The strong rare-earth magnets are riveted in place. The new crank-trigger EZ-Adjust is designed to permit small and precise adjustments by turning a bolt rather than loosening the entire assembly.

Advanced Ignition Electronics

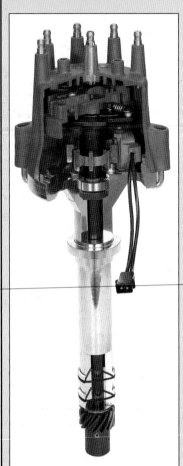

MSD's Pro Billet series of electronic distributors offer the versatility needed to accommodate ignition requirement. Pro Billet distributors offer proven adjustable mechanical advance featu high-output magnetic pickups, sealed ball bearings, CNC machined T6 aluminum housings, MSD's unique cap and rotor combinations for optimum performance.

Pro Billet distributors are made for almost every application. The Pro Billet Ready-To-Run distributor is an entry-level uni with its own stand-alone internal ignition module. The Pro Billet Chevrolet V-8 distributor is fully featured and can be use with MSD 6, 7, 8, 9, and 10 Series ignition systems. The Pro Billet EFI Ready-To-Run unit is fully configured for plug-and play use on EFI-equipped cars. Street Pro Billet distributors are available with vacuum advance and a Pro Billet Small Diameter distributor is available for street rods and other applications that may have space limitations. Pro Billet distributors are available with adjustable slip collars for adjusting distributor gear depth, and you can also get them with the advance locked out and a cam sync connection for aftermarket fuel injection systems.

The Digital E-Curve distributor is a digitally controlled stand-alone ignition system. Springs and advance weights are eliminated. The digital module allows you to select from nearly 100 different advance curves, including vacuum advance. Timing curves and rev limit adjustments are made with the rotary dials located underneath the rotor. You can adjust mechanical and vacuum advance curves electronically. A 3/16-inch vacuum port is located on the bottom of the billet base so it doesn't interfere with mounting or wiring the distributor.

The sensor, called a Hall Cell, is located on the contact plate. This electronic chip senses the magnetic field generated by each arm of the chopper wheel. The associated electronics reacts to the Hall Cell signals and switches the primary current to the coil. Like optical systems, the Hall-Effect ignition is relatively insensitive to environmental conditions and does not require close operating tolerances.

In recent years, the development of both multi-firing and extended-spark (sometimes called extended-burn) ignitions have added unique capabilities to both high-performance and conventional ignition systems. Instead of producing a single short spark for ignition, these systems either produce multiple high-voltage sparks or one long-duration spark. In multispark systems, the number of sparks per ignition cycle at idle can be as high as six, when time between power strokes is the greatest. As engine speed increases, the number of sparks decreases to about two at high RPM. In extended-spark ignitions, a single, long-duration spark jumps the plug gap during the time a multiple-spark system would generate several sparks at the plug.

Potential horsepower increases from multiple-spark or long-duration systems depend on the flame propagation characteristics of the combustion chambers. Cylinder heads with larger chamber volumes can benefit most from these ignitions, and although it's impossible to predict the benefits on any single engine, gains may vary from negligible to as much as five percent. Small-blocks with small-volume chambers usually show little or no improvement from multi-firing ignitions. However, multiple-spark or long-duration ignitions almost universally help smooth out a rough idle and minimize plug fouling that can hurt engine performance during the first critical seconds after leaving the starting line. For the street, these high-tech ignitions can make stubborn starting a thing of the past, and improvements in gas mileage are not unusual.

There are other types of systems found mainly on racing engines. These include magnetos, crank-trigger systems, and more complex forms of MSD systems, including high-power multiple coil ignitions with electronic advance curves, high-speed retards, and other exotica. Magnetos have been popular racing pieces for many years. The faster they spin, the hotter the spark they produce. They are

Understanding GM Computers

Inside the Black Box Modern electronic engine management systems are seemingly complex, but once you understand their basic function, they reveal themselves as relatively simple feedback control systems. In a nutshell, they monitor engine operation and make constant adjustments to ensure optimum efficiency under all operating conditions. The heart of this system is the electronic control module (ECM). It's a compact, self-contained microprocessor that receives sensor inputs and sends control signals to the fuel injection and ignition systems according to established instructions to perform these operations are contained in a programmable read only memory chip or PROM. GM calls the PROM unit a Mem-Cal, or memory and calibration unit. It contains the basic microprocessor instructions for normal operation and special backup instructions, called the Cal-Pak, that tell the computer how to handle the fuel and spark curves during a failure or limp home mode.

The ECM contains a buffered 5- and 12-volt power supply that feeds the microprocessor, associated electronics, and various engine-monitoring sensors. Each sensor returns a voltage signal to the ECM, scaled in proportion to the event it is measuring. The ECM understands these signals and responds by adjusting the ignition and fuel curves accordingly.

A Memory For Each Task To accomplish its various tasks, the ECM contains three distinct types of memory circuits. The read only memory (ROM) chip contains the control-logic instructions that tell the microprocessor how to do the most basic tasks like read this sensor or send that pulse to that injector, etc. ROM is nonvolatile memory. It cannot be changed or erased, and it does not require battery or backup power to retain its instructions. The second type of memory is called RAM or random access memory. The ECM uses RAM as a work area or scratch pad during calculations. This memory is volatile, meaning it is erased when power is lost. Finally, the third memory used in the ECM is called PROM, or programmable read only memory. As mentioned, it contains engine-calibration instructions for a specific vehicle based on year, model, and emissions commitment.

Altering PROM instructions is the only method by which the ignition and fuel curves can be changed (short

of installing devices to trick the computer by returning altered sensor voltage readings). Various high-performance PROMS are available that alter the calibration curves. But before you plug one into your ECM, you really need to know a bit more about how the factory programs its PROMs.

What's Wrong With Factory Programming? The most important thing to understand is that wide-open throttle (WOT) operation has virtually no restrictions by the federal government or state agencies. Because of this, factory engineers make the ignition and fuel curves for WOT as aggressive as possible, with engine reliability the only constraint. However, part-throttle operation is closely managed to control emissions, and it is in this area where performance chips usually optimize engine calibration. In other words, there is almost nothing to be gained during WOT operation, so any changes that are normally felt occur during part throttle use. The PROM alterations often remap the entire fuel and spark curves to improve part-throttle response. The overall result is usually an increase in emissions, reduced fuel economy, and virtually no improvement in full-throttle power (sometimes even a reduction in WOT power is noted). Because the computer has the ability to learn and store information about these changes, it adjusts itself to accommodate some alterations, but with the new PROM programming, it will never gain optimum efficiency unless the exact engine and vehicle combination is thoroughly mapped on an engine dyno and loaded into the PROM.

PROM Experimentation Trying various performance chips can be expensive, but if you decide to give it a try, make sure you compare the different chips under carefully controlled conditions. Fuel and ignition curve modifications may promote moderate power gains, but often at the expense of fuel efficiency. If an aftermarket chip has a CARB exemption order, it has been found to maintain acceptable emission qualities. If it delivers measurably more power, you have a winner. If not, the original factory calibration will probably serve you well, since factory PROM instructions work best with the learning and adjusting capability of the ECM, optimizing calibration for economy, emissions, and performance.

really a simple generator that operates without outside power. The instant a magneto begins to turn, it starts generating electrical power. If you have ever been the victim of the popular racer's prank of spinning a magneto while holding the lead you know how much kick they can produce. At low RPM, they barely have the energy to fire the plugs, so they are usually reserved for high-RPM, race-only applications.

Crank-trigger systems were developed for drag racing to combat ignition problems due to camshaft twist, timing chain flex, and distributor wear. They are basically magnetic-impulse systems, except that the timing wheel (reluctor) is much larger and mounted next to the harmonic balancer at the front of the engine. There are four magnets embedded in the wheel, and a pickup/sensor positioned near the wheel senses the passing magnets, sending ignition pulses to the control box. The distributor is still used to channel the secondary voltage to each cylinder, but primary timing is handled entirely by the magnetic pickup (where it is unaffected by camshaft twist and other problems).

Secondary Considerations

The parts of your ignition system between the output on your coil and your combustion chambers are often referred to as the secondary side of the system. These parts carry the high voltage from the coil to the spark plugs in the combustion chambers. Spark plugs in your small-block should be the proper heat range, and they must be gapped to match the ignition system's requirements. Greater secondary voltage often permits the use of a slightly colder plug. Dyno tests sometimes indicate that plugs one or two heat ranges colder

than stock can produce an increase in power, although this may not occur in every case. In addition, a higher secondary voltage has more energy to jump across an air gap, so increasing spark plug gap by 0.010 to 0.020 inch may provide a fatter spark that will more reliably ignite the air/fuel charge. This can be of particular help with lean mixtures or high compression ratios (but don't go over 0.050-inch gap, since secondary voltages may go high enough to damage ignition components, and electrical emissions also dramatically increase). More reliable ignition can, in turn, increase the speed of flame-front propagation, and this may require slightly less total ignition advance to reestablish optimum power. If the ignition timing is not optimized when the flame propagation times are altered, the result can be a reduction in power. Usually, just a small change is all that's needed, assuming the ignition advance was right-on prior to modifications.

Platinum-tipped plugs offer measurable advantages in both long life and reliable ignition under adverse conditions. Platinum-tip designs are widely available in auto-part outlets and are very reasonably priced. They are certainly worth your consideration. Other new spark plug designs seem to offer even more power-producing potential. Split-Fire plugs are one of these unusual variants. They have shown reasonably reliable power increases in some dyno tests. The patented plugs have a unique construction that helps expose the air/fuel charge to the electrical discharge between the center electrode and the ground strap. Other experimental plugs of which we are aware may produce even more power in some applications. If manufacturing and legal issues are settled, they may be available within the next year. Stay tuned!

The potent output of modern ignition systems often permits the use of slightly colder spark plugs and wider plug gaps. Dyno tests indicate that increasing the spark plug gap by 0.010 to 0.020 inch will sometimes show a slight power increase. Don't go any farther than 0.050 inch because the excessive secondary voltage needed to jump the wider gaps can damage ignition components.

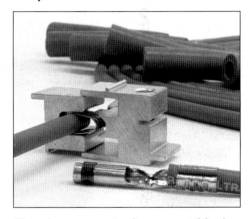

The plug connector is a very critical area. Make certain the connectors are installed on the wires tightly and with a solid connection to the core. You don't want to be accidentally pulling wires out of their connectors later because of a poor wiring job.

Spark plug wires used with modern electronic ignition systems must withstand higher voltage levels and prevent spillover into vehicle electronics, including engine-control computers. High-quality, high-temperature silicone-jacketed wires are available with solid cores for racing (where interference-causing emissions are not a consideration) or with a carbon-fiber or

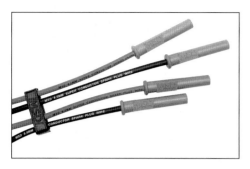

Leading ignition companies like MSD offer 8- and 8.5-mm performance wires with very low resistance, and the ability to suppress electro magnetic interference (EMI). These MSD Super Conductor wires have less than 50 ohms of resistance per foot, which allows more energy to make it to the spark plug.

helical-wound cores for street or racing applications where interference suppression is important. MSD, Mallory, Moroso, and others make excellent 8-mm heat-resistant cable that does an excellent job of electrical emissions containment. These wire sets are substantially superior to the carbon-impregnated, string-core stuff that is supplied as standard equipment by many auto manufacturers. You can add additional protection to your secondary wires by jacketing them in tubing made of glass cloth that is highly resistant to heat, the most common cause of premature wire failure. MSD offers glass-cloth tubing and a self-vulcanizing silicone rubber tape that can be wrapped around the wires to secure the cloth tubing or to add additional heat protection at critical points, especially around header tubing. High engine compartment temperatures will bond the tape permanently to the ignition wires, improving their insulation resistance to both heat and high voltage.

Many speed shops sell a variety of great looking colored plug wires. Some of these wires are much better suited for performance use than others. Carefully examine the core and

the insulation before you buy. If they have a carbon-string core, put them down or make your mind up to replace them every year or so. If you have headers, make sure the plug wires are insulated with temperature-resistant silicone rubber. Keep in mind that wire manufacturers can claim they use silicone insulation as long as the jacket material is composed of only some silicone rubber. These cheaper wire sets will not withstand the heat radiated from headers. If you want the best, stick with top-of-the-line wires from ACCEL, MSD, Mallory, Moroso, or others designed for serious racing applications.

Setting Ignition Timing

There are numerous backyard methods to test and adjust ignition timing on a breaker-point system. Some of these can be accomplished without any fancy equipment. However, all of these methods are questionable in accuracy, and since most modern ignitions use magnetic or other breakerless pickups that make it virtually impossible to visually determine the distributor position that will trigger the coil, it's best to forget old-fashioned techniques and only set timing with a strobe-type timing light. If you don't have a top-quality timing light, it's worth investing in one. Watch out for cheap units that have low light output; these strobes make it impossible to read the timing mark unless you're in complete darkness (and that's a great way to get your fingers chopped up in the fan blades). The best timing lights use an inductive pickup that quickly clamps on the outside of the ignition wire. Top-quality lights will provide a stable indication of timing from idle to over 8,000 rpm.

Checking initial timing with a strobe light is a relatively straightfor-

ward process. Connect the timing light to the number 1 spark plug terminal or wire according to the instructions provided with the light. Disconnect the manifold vacuum hose leading to the vacuum advance canister. Leave the hose connected to the manifold and plug the open end to prevent a vacuum leak. Start the engine and make certain the idle is below the point at which the centrifugal advance starts to activate. On most engines centrifugal advance may begin as low as 800 to 1,000 rpm. Point the timing light at the timing plate on the front of the engine. The flashing light will illuminate a timing mark on the spinning crankshaft damper and the stationary marks on the timing plate. If you have trouble seeing the marks, try enhancing them with a narrow stripe of white paint. The relative position of these marks will indicate the amount of initial ignition advance. In all but the crank-trigger systems, timing is adjusted by rotating the distributor housing (the pickup must be adjusted on the crank trigger system to vary timing). Loosen the clamp securing the distributor and advance or retard (rotate) the distributor slightly until the timing light indicates the correct number of degrees (move the distributor counterclockwise to advance timing on the small-block). Once this is set, the distributor clamp should be firmly tightened.

This procedure is fine if you already know what the initial ignition timing should be for optimum performance. On a modified engine, the stock timing figure may no longer be applicable. Information presented in this chapter will help you find the best initial advance for your engine, but if you're just looking for a place to start, try setting initially at about 5 to 10 degrees advanced.

A timing light can also help troubleshoot the vacuum and centrifugal

Setting Rotor-to-Cap Alignment

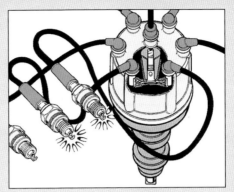

If the rotor is not pointed precisely at the proper terminal when the spark energy is released, the wrong plug or two plugs at once may be fired. This problem is called incorrect rotor phasing and it means lost horsepower.

When the coil is triggered, a high-voltage discharge is routed to the center of the distributor cap. This energy moves along the rotor to a single terminal on the distributor cap, and then on to the appropriate spark plug . . . or does it? If the rotor is pointed directly at the correct terminal, everything works fine, but if the rotor is pointed somewhere between two terminals, spark energy may find its way to the wrong plug, or to two plugs at once. These problems are due to incorrect rotor-to-cap alignment, or what is commonly referred to as improper rotor phasing. Whatever you call it, it means lost horsepower and premature wear for the rotor, cap, and sometimes the ignition coil.

In the days of breaker point ignition, one could rotate the distributor shaft and make a careful estimate when the points would just open, indicating the moment of spark discharge. Then, holding the distributor shaft steady, it was possible to examine where the rotor was pointing in the distributor cap. This method was not the most accurate, but it did not require any special equipment. Now, most distributors use magnetic or other breakerless pickups that make it nearly impossible to visually determine at what distributor shaft position the coil will be triggered. So another method of measuring rotor-to-cap alignment must be used, preferably one that is accurate for all types of systems. Use a clear plastic distributor cap, or in the absence of a clear cap, drill large holes in the side of a conventional cap for use as observation ports. A timing light directed at the cap will reveal that exact rotor position at the time of spark discharge.

The question is: Where should the rotor be pointing? The most obvious answer: directly at the center of one of the distributor cap terminals is usually correct, except when the distributor is equipped with vacuum advance. In this case, the rotor-to-cap alignment does not remain fixed, since as manifold vacuum increases the advance canister moves the breaker plate to advance ignition timing, and moving the plate relative to the fixed distributor cap alters rotor-to-cap alignment.

Distributors with vacuum advance must have the rotor alignment set off-center or "late" in the direction of rotation when no vacuum is applied to the canister. This will ensure that when the vacuum advance is acti-

vated, rotor alignment will move past center to the same position on the opposite, "early" side of the terminal. Distributors that do not have vacuum advance canisters should have the rotor-to-cap alignment set dead on, since the breaker plate does not move. (It better not move!)

Correcting rotor-to-cap alignment can be difficult on some distributors and easy on others. On standard point or breakerless distributors, the breaker plate or pickup coil must be moved or rotated within the distributor housing to alter rotor alignment. This sometimes involves drilling and tapping new holes for plate or pickup mounting. It's also possible to cut the metal blade on the rotor and solder it back pointing in a new direction. However, the easiest way is to use an MSD adjustable rotor. By loosening the two screws, turning the rotor, and then retightening the screws, rotor misalignment can be corrected.

Using MSD's Cap-A-Dapt with adjustable rotor allows you to correct rotor phasing quickly and easily. Simply loosen the two screws, twist the rotor, retighten the screws, and recheck alignment with a timing light. You will still need a spare cap with observation ports drilled in it to observe the rotor alignment.

Ignition Curve Requirements

If you make a significant change to your small-block on which you have already established optimum mechanical and vacuum advance curves, the recommendations in this chart will help you establish a new ignition curve to regain peak power.

Modification	Vacuum Advance	Mechanical Advance
Increase compression ratio	Retard overall curve (increase spring tension)	Less overall advance, especially at peak-torque (heavier springs and reduce advance weight movement)
Add a high-flow induction system	Remains unchanged	Less advance throughout RPM range (heavier springs and reduce advance weight movement)
Add headers	May need to either advance or retard, depending on charge temperature and exhaust contamination	If charge contamination is reduced, charge temperatures are usually lower. This often requires a slight increase in advance throughout the RPM range (lighter springs and more advance weight movement)
Longer duration cam	Reduce spring tension in the diaphragm to bring the curve in faster	Initial advance needs to be faster and, to a lesser extent, total advance should occur at a lower RPM (both accomplished with lighter springs)
Supercharger	Needs special vacuum advance mechanism with pressure retard	Total advance should be reduced and the curve should come on slower (stiffer springs and less advance weight movement)
Turbocharger	Needs special vacuum advance mechanism with pressure retard	Reduce total advance with quicker initial part of the curve. Slow curve when turbo boost builds. (use a combination of light and stiff springs, plus reduce advance weight movement
Ported cast-iron heads	Remains unchanged	Slow high end of curve (add one heavy spring)
Aluminum heads	Reduced surface temperatures call for slightly more advance (increase advance amount and slightly reduce spring tension)	Often needs less total advance due to better cylinder filling, but faster initial advance due to lower port velocities and swirl (lighter springs and slightly reduce advance movement)
Switch to unleaded gas (same octane)*	Reduce overall advance (increase spring tension and amount of advance)	Reduce overall advance (increase spring tension and reduce advance weight movement)

*Note: Removing the lead in gasoline reduces the ignition delay time and requires reduced advance. Leaded fuels burn slower and require more advance.

ignition advance mechanisms. By reattaching the vacuum hose to the advance canister while viewing the timing marks (make sure the vacuum hose is connected to manifold vacuum not a ported source on the carburetor), it's easy to confirm vacuum advance function. The timing mark on the vibration damper should move substantially ahead of the stationary TDC mark. In a similar fashion, the mechanical advance can be tested by simply increasing engine speed above idle (make sure the vacuum advance is disconnected for this test).

Finally, a quality timing light can help you determine how accurately the ignition system functions at high engine speed. Slowly increasing engine speed to near peak RPM while observing variations in the timing mark can reveal spark scatter, high-speed retard, or other mechanical or electronic abnormalities. For safety reasons, never stand in line with the fan or fan belts or remove the belts when checking high-speed ignition timing.

A performance ignition system should generate a rock-solid timing mark at all engine speeds; there should be no visible signs of widening, spreading, or jumping. If any of these problems are indicated, they can usually be traced to several mechanical and/or electronic sources, but the most common causes are a loose timing chain, worn distributor bushings, or a sticking mechanical advance. In addition, since the oil pump is driven off of the bottom of the distributor, spark scatter can often be traced to pressure pulses generated by the oil pump, especially when high oil pressure is used; refer to the oiling chapter for possible cures.

Spark plug wire heat protection is another important concern with hotter-than-ever underhood temperatures. In addition to shrink sleeving and self-vulcanizing tape, MSD offers specially woven glass-quartz fiber sleeves to protect both the wires and the spark plug boots.

High-voltage ignition coils are one of the cheapest paths to greater spark energy. These coils provide greater output than a factory coil, but you must make certain they are compatible with your ignition system. Some coils have very low primary resistance and can damage electronic control boxes. MSD's Blaster series and the HVC II series are among the hottest coils available.

The Zero-Cross distributor offers a means to adjust cylinder-to-cylinder timing using adjustable magnet tabs. The position of each reluctor tab can be adjusted up to six degrees to produce a custom timing event for each cylinder. This allows you to correct for other cylinder deficiencies such as a bad runner or cylinder head port, localized cylinder head heating, improper header length, and other problems that often occur in engines where compromises are required.

Ignition System Prep Checklist

1. Before the engine is assembled, lightly deburr the distributor drive gear on the camshaft and the mating gear on the distributor with a wire brush or wheel.
2. Check the oil pump intermediate driveshaft for burrs on the distributor drive end. Repair as necessary. Make certain the shaft mates easily with the distributor drive and is the proper length.
3. Examine the distributor housing for signs of damage including cracks, worn bushings, and missing parts. Repair as required.
4. Have a reputable shop set up the desired spark advance curve. If you're using points, ask them to check for dwell fluctuation at high speed.
5. Check rotor-to-cap alignment.
6. Depending on the type of distributor you have, install new hardware, including distributor cap, rotor, points, and condenser.
7. If you suspect a problem with an electronic distributor, have it checked at an ignition shop.
8. When installing the distributor in the engine, check to see that the distributor driveshaft doesn't bottom against the oil pump driveshaft. This occurs occasionally on engines with excessive decking and manifold milling.
9. If you're running a billet steel camshaft, make certain you use a special bronze distributor drive gear to prevent excessive wear.
10. When installing the ignition system in the car, verify tight connections and proper routing for all wires.
11. Install new secondary ignition cables and route them away from hot engine components.
12. Adjust timing and dwell to recommended specs, depending on the type of ignition and the advance curve you are using.
13. Install new spark plugs of the correct heat range for your engine.

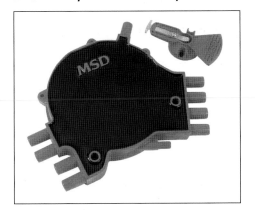

MSD's LT1 distributor cap and rotor kit replaces the factory system with high-performance components. The injection-molded parts are designed to resist breakdown and resulting misfires.

OILING SYSTEM

In most applications, small-block Chevy oiling systems are probably the simplest and most reliable arrangement ever offered. While oiling problems may still be encountered, they are almost always the result of some other problem. Common sense preparation is all that's required for basic high-performance small-blocks.

Small-blocks require very clean oil and regular filter changes. A steady, nonfluctuating oil supply between 150 and 270 degrees at 60 to 80 psi is recommended. This recommendation is intended primarily for racing applications and is probably a little excessive for a street-driven motor. Most street engines operate just fine with 35–50 psi of hot-oil pressure. Some drag racers are comfortable running 30–40 psi at 8,500 rpm. We don't necessarily recommend this, but it's a good indication of how well the small-block oils. Modern competition oiling systems often include dry-sump scavenging and a variety of minor refinements, many of which have been designed into the recent Bow Tie blocks.

Perhaps the best recommendation for a street engine is moderation. Keep oiling system modifications to a minimum. Your main concern should be with keeping the pickup covered with oil at all times. There are basic blueprint specs to be followed and we will offer some tips regarding oil temperature and oil control. But first we need to take an overall look at the small-block's oil delivery system to get a feel for just how it lubricates every internal moving part.

Production-Block Oiling

The main oil gallery runs parallel to the camshaft and directly above it. The lifter galleries run directly through the lifter bores on either side of the main gallery. In the bottom end, each pair of cylinders is

As we've said throughout the book, the performance and reliability of your engine will be determined by the sum of every part you put in the mix. The combination of oiling components shown here has both advantages and disadvantages. The big-block oil pump offers more volume, and the larger number of gear teeth used in the pump reduce ignition fluctuations. However, the pump also causes substantial additional drag. The curved factory windage tray helps maintain good oil control, but doesn't improve power.

A standard small-block oil pump delivers between 35 and 55 pounds of hot oil pressure depending on a number of factors, including, but not limited to, bearing clearance, rod side clearance, engine oil viscosity, and engine speed.

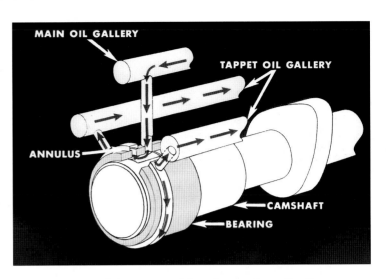

The small-block oiling system is a full-pressure lubrication system that is one of the simplest and most reliable in use today. The main gallery intersects the annulus passage that feed the lifter galleries. The mains are oiled last, but that hasn't been a problem in most applications. Some later-model Chevy small-blocks were built with priority main oiling for racing purposes.

separated by a main bulkhead with a vertical oiling hole connecting the main gallery to the camshaft journals and then to the main bearing journals. Although the engine oils the cam journals "before" it oils the main bearings, this has not been found to have any adverse side effects in street and moderate high-performance applications. Some recent Bow Tie blocks are designed to provide "priority main" oiling that feeds oil to the main bearings directly from the oil gallery.

These blocks also feature a front inlet to the main oil gallery to simplify dry sump plumbing. Most racing mechanics favor restricting the valvetrain oiling so that more oil is available for the lower end, but this should be considered a racing modification only. Solid or roller lifters and roller rocker arms that don't require a large amount of oil must be used when oil flow to the valvetrain is limited.

The oil pump is attached directly to the rear main cap. A passage intersecting the main feed from the pump provides direct oiling to the rear main bearing. Oil from the pump continues its flow through the oil filter and up to the center main gallery where it oils the cam and main journals and fills the lifter galleries. Oil in the lifter galleries lubricates the lifters and is fed up the pushrods to the rocker arms and valvestems. Upper engine oil returns via holes in the valley that drain oil back into the sump. This system works fine for street applications, but at high speeds, power is lost when oil draining back contacts the spinning crankshaft. The small-block is often modified to redirect return oil to the front or rear of the block, where large drain-back passages route oil directly to the sump.

When you look at factory oil-flow diagrams, you also notice that the oiling holes in the crankshaft lead the TDC position by 60 degrees so that upper-shell rod bearing oiling is accomplished just prior to the point of highest loading. When you consider the system as a whole, it is not surprising that so many Chevrolet racecars manage to finish the race and run strong even with a stock oiling system. As long as you keep the pickup covered with oil, lubrication problems will be few and far between.

Oil Pumps

The best place to start examining the small-block oiling system is at the oil pump. The factory now offers only one oil pump for production small-blocks: the Z28 pump PN 3848907. This bulletproof pump has 1.20-inch tall gears and is standard equipment on all small-block engines. Chevrolet also offers a high-volume, high-pressure pump with 1.50-inch tall gears (PN 14044872). These pumps are supplied without a pickup unit because of the wide variations in oil pan design. It is always advisable to braze or TIG weld the pickup tube in place, but this should only be done after the relief valve and spring have been removed from the pump cover. Many backyard mechanics have ruined the relief mechanism by overheating while welding. Then they are puzzled when the engine loses oil pressure.

If you feel that your system needs more pressure, you can install the stiffer Chevrolet relief spring PN 3848911. Make sure the spring you get has a white stripe painted on it. Some engine builders like to modify the pumps by drilling lubricating

Block Oiling Preparation Tips

Make sure the main feed passages (arrows) are full size from end to end. Occasionally, factory core drills (some are stepped) do not travel to the bottom of the passage, leaving a restriction in the oil passage. Enlarge the passages or remove any restrictions using long drills (three flute core drills, sometimes available from surplus stores, drill without grabbing).

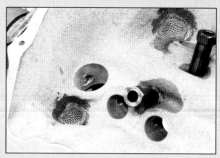

Installing plugs in the oil-drain passages to redirect oil flow to the front and rear of the block will keep some oil out of the spinning crank assembly. Breather-type stand-off tubes as shown here accomplish the same thing. Screens can be added to front and rear drain passages to prevent metal particles (like failed roller trunnions in rocker arms) from entering the sump.

Some engine builders like to plug the rear drain-back holes to prevent oil from draining on the large rear crank throw. This approach seals off the valley and forces all oil to drain at the front, via the timing cover.

Don't forget the "forgotten" plug. If you don't remove it before the block is cleaned, debris can hide in the main oil passages. And if you forget to reinstall it before the rear main cap is bolted on, oil will not be directed through the oil filter!

Drill a 0.030-inch hole in the cam gear thrust face to improve oiling and prevent galling. For race engines, drill a second 0.030-inch hole in the center main oil gallery plug. That will allow air to bleed off and reduce the chance of oil starvation immediately after engine start-up.

When tapping the front center oil gallery for a screw-in plug, make certain to sneak up on the tap depth so that the seated plug will not sit so deep that it covers the oil feed hole to the front main bearing.

The oil filter adapter contains a fiber-disk and spring bypass valve. Make sure everything is clean and that the valve is positioned correctly in the housing (arrow).

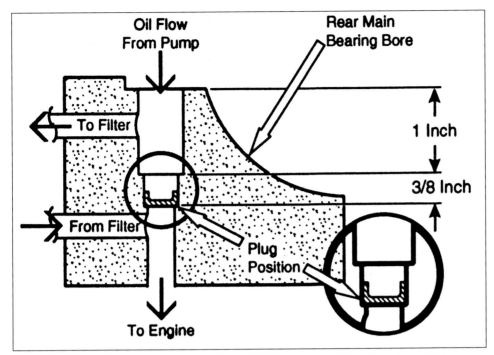

On later-model factory engines, the hidden plug was changed out in favor of a ball bearing driven into the space. In either case, the plug is located above the rear main cap (or under it, if you are working on the engine stand).

This cutaway shows the location of the hidden plug in the oil gallery. This plug must be removed to thoroughly clean the galleries. If it is not replaced, oil pressure will be erratic and oil will not flow through the oil filter.

holes through the idler gear and milling antichatter grooves in the pump cover and the pump housing. This equalizes the pressure on the gears and prevents oil cavitation at high engine speeds. Big-block oil pumps were originally used in small-blocks for just this purpose. Big-block pumps also have additional gear teeth allowing them to operate more smoothly. However, the small-block pump is still up to the task when properly modified, and it has a lot less drag than the big-block high-volume pump.

To finish preparing the pump, you should gently deburr all edges with emery cloth and then wash the pieces in clean solvent and blow them dry (also see the sidebar *Oil Pump Tech Tips* for more pump preparation tips). A basic step in assembling oil pumps is to treat them to a liberal coating of assembly lube on the gears, gear shafts, and the inner housing. The pump cover bolts should be sparkling clean and treated with Loctite to

ensure that they stay secure.

Before you clean engine components for final assembly, take some time to gently relieve and radius the cavity in the top of the rear main cap. If you look down through the oil passage, you'll see that it makes a slight jog about two-thirds of the way down. A long shank carbide cutter can be used to radius the hump and provide a straight, free-flowing path for the oil to follow.

To install a small-block oil pump correctly you should preassemble the pump and pump driveshaft before you insert it into the block. The intermediate driveshaft snaps onto the oil pump with a plastic retaining sleeve PN 3764554. See the sidebar *Oil Pump Driveshaft Tech* for tips on ensuring that your driveshaft has the proper end clearance. There is usually plenty of room, but in some cases where the intake manifold has been milled or the incorrect pump shaft is used, the shaft, pump, and distributor gear can stack solid. You should also be aware

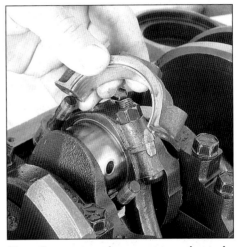

The oil pump makes pressure based on engine speed, bearing clearances, oil viscosity, and so on. Pressurized oil escapes back to the crankcase by squeezing out through the space between the rods and the crank throws, as shown here. The oil pressure feed oil is seen in the center of the crank journal.

that the 400-ci engine requires an intermediate shaft with a machined relief to clear the larger main bearing bores. For cheap insurance, aftermarket sources can supply steel intermediate shafts with bulletproof steel retaining sleeves.

Oil Pump Tech Tips

Inspecting and/or replacing the oil pump is a wise investment in almost every engine build-up. To determine the condition of the pump, disassemble and clean the components in solvent. When dry, visually inspect the spur gears. Look for pits or wear on the teeth. The inside of the pump housing should have virtually no detectable wear. Install the gears in the pump housing and measure the end clearance with a depth micrometer or feeler gauge. Normal clearance is between 0.002 and 0.006 inch. Inspect the pump cover for wear; there should be only light surface marks from gear contact. Remove the roll pin holding the pressure-relief spring in the pump cover. The relief valve should move freely.

If your oil pump passes this inspection, it is almost certainly reusable. If the only thing wrong is excessive (or insufficient) end clearance—and this should be checked on even brand new oil pumps—have the housing or pump gears machined (some builders sand them on a flat surface with 400-grit wet/dry paper) until you have 0.003 to .0005 inch. On the other hand, if there are signs of wear or particulate damage (pits, scratches, etc.), buy a new pump. And before you install a new pump, take it apart and perform the same inspections.

The pickup should be tack brazed or welded to the pump cover to prevent it from moving during engine operation. However, brazing/welding should only be done when the cover is removed from the pump and the pressure-relief valve and spring are removed from the cover. After welding, check the cover for flatness, clean oxidation from the relief valve bore, and make sure the valve moves freely.

Before reassembly, deburr all edges with emery cloth. Then thoroughly wash all components with clean solvent and blow dry. Prelube the gears, gear shafts, and pressure-relief valve during assembly with assembly lube or engine oil. When you install the cover, apply a drop of red Loctite to the threads of each bolt and torque to 10 ft-lbs.

Oil Pump Modifications

There are several modifications that can be performed to the pump, pickup, and pressure-relief sys-

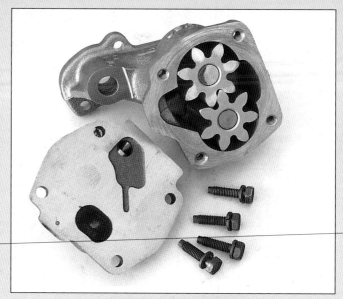

The internal pressurized oiling system of the small-block is considered by many engine builders to be just about bulletproof, and the oil pump is equally well designed. The oil pump is mounted on the rear main cap and contains a pair of 1.200-inch tall seven-tooth gears. They're driven via a connecting shaft from the bottom of the distributor, which in turn, is driven by the camshaft. The pump draws oil from the sump in the pan and directs pressurized oil to the main oil gallery by way of passages in the rear main cap and block.

tem for high-performance and racing applications, and some are illustrated in this chapter. Some enthusiasts replace the pump with high-volume units available from Milodon and other sources. This is an excellent option, since these pumps offer large free-flowing passages, close internal clearances, and a boost in oil pressure. Another common upgrade is the replacement of the stock pressure-relief spring with the Chevrolet "white stripe" spring for racing applications. Using the GM spring is preferable to shimming the existing spring, since shims limit the travel of the spring and valve assembly. This can cause a restriction in the bypass circuit and develop excessively high oil pressure, especially when the engine and oil are cold. In fact, the pressure can build up high enough to blow the oil filter to smithereens!

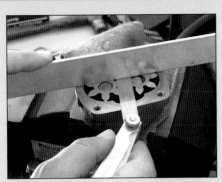

Check the inside of the housing. It should have virtually no detectable wear. Install the gears In the pump housing and measure the end clearance. Normal clearance is between 0.002 and 0.006 inch, but many racing pros prefer no more than 0.0035 inch.

The Milodon 18750 pump (right) is well built, uses ⅜-inch taller rotors, and delivers a solid 65 psi. This is an excellent choice for a high-performance street or bracket engine.

After the pickup is adjusted to provide proper pan clearance, it should be brazed or welded to prevent it from moving during engine operation. Welding should only be done when the pump is completely disassembled.

Dedicated engine builders like to radius the oil feed slots in the rear main bearing cap to ease the oil's journey to the bearings. While it is not known how much this helps, it is generally seen as a good idea and something cool to do while you're prepping parts.

The oil filter mounting pad is sometimes blueprinted by radiusing the entry holes, but it's most critical that the surfaces remain smooth and flat so the oil filter adapter will maintain pressure.

The oil filter adapter holds a fiber disc and a spring-loaded bypass valve. Some engine builders like to remove it and plug the bypass so that oil is forced through the filter. This is not good practice on most engines, because a plugged filter may starve the oiling system.

Small-block oil pumps almost never wear out as long as they are treated to good, clean oil. Nevertheless, they are frequently replaced because they are not very expensive. Their simple design allows for near-instant oil pressure when starting your small-block.

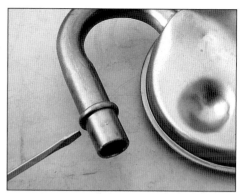

The factory pickup is mounted to the oil pump with an interference fit. A variety of tools have been used to drive the pickup into the pump using the raised bead on the pickup tube. Special tools are made for this task, but most one-timers used a large screwdriver blade or a box/open-end wrench and a hammer.

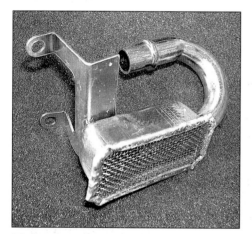

Most aftermarket pickup tubes are a looser fit. They are usually mounted with a brace and several bolts, like this Milodon unit.

The pickup tube is driven into the large opening on the side of the pump housing. A dab of lubricant or white grease is helpful here.

When the pump is bolted in place, the driveshaft engages the drive spud on the pump. The driveshaft shown here incorporates the steel connecting sleeve recommended on all high-performance applications.

Oil Pans and Screens

A good pan to use on early blocks is the high-performance Z28 piece PN 465220 along with the semicircular tray baffle PN 3927136. This pan must have the thick, late-style rubber end seals; it will leak oil if you use the thinner, early seals. Strict budgets may require the use of a stock oil pan. Keep in mind that some factory pans have internal baffling, and these should be used whenever possible. Look for the type having a flat baffle welded into the front of the pan. This baffle is somewhat helpful in controlling oil slosh. Engines built before 1980 have a left-hand (driver-side) dipstick location, while 1980 to 1985 blocks have dipsticks on the right-hand side and some have pan-mounted dipsticks. Cast-iron Bow Tie blocks have pads for both right- and left-hand dipsticks, but they are undrilled.

If you are building an engine with the 1986 and later one-piece rear main seal, you must use the single-piece oil pan gasket and the appropriate oil pan. Two choices are the Corvette 6-quart pan PN 10055765 or the 5-quart Camaro pan PN 10110837. If you require more capacity you can get custom late-style pans from CV Products in North Carolina. Early blocks that have been outfitted with the adapter to use the late one-piece rear seal must use the 1986 and later gasket set, except for aluminum Bow Tie blocks PN 24502501 and race-prepared Bow

Oil Pump Driveshaft Tech

The oil pump is driven by a short shaft that connects the stubby shaft on the oil pump to the bottom of the distributor gear. A plastic sleeve keeps the driveshaft aligned with the pump, preventing it from slipping to one side, wobbling, and possibly breaking. The plastic sleeve also locks the driveshaft to the pump, preventing the shaft from falling out of the engine when the block is turned upside-down (during assembly).

While the stock pump driveshaft and plastic collar are adequate, we strongly recommend replacing them with a high-performance part in all engine buildups, including street-stock engines. Replacement shafts are made of a stronger material and use a permanently attached metal sleeve instead of the plastic collar. This ensures that the shaft will stay aligned with the pump, reducing the chance of shaft failure and subsequent loss of oil pressure. Always use a high-performance driveshaft when you are using a high-volume or high-pressure pump. If you decide to use the stock pump driveshaft, make sure to use a new plastic attaching sleeve to keep the driveshaft securely aligned with the pump.

Checking Driveshaft Length

There are several different oil pump driveshaft lengths, but only one will fit properly in your engine. If you have replaced the shaft or added high-performance components, perform the following check to ensure that the pump shaft will not "stack solid" when the distributor is tightened down on the intake manifold. Mock up the engine with both heads, head gaskets (you don't need to torque down the head bolts, just run them up snug), and intake manifold (installed with port gaskets but without end-rail gaskets). Then install the distributor and tighten the hold-down clamp. Rotate the engine upside-down on the engine stand so you can install the oil pump. Lower the pump and driveshaft into the rear main cap and rotate it until it engages the distributor drive gear. Now seat the pump on the main cap and snug the attaching bolt. Try to move the pump shaft up and down. If the shaft length is correct, it should fully engage the drive tangs and have 0.010 to about 0.040 inch of free play. If it has substantially more or less than this, you are probably using the wrong length shaft. Insufficient clearance can also be caused from excessive deck, head, or intake manifold machining.

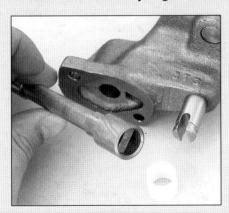

The oil pump is driven via a shaft from the bottom of the distributor gear. A plastic sleeve keeps the driveshaft aligned with the pump.

We strongly recommend replacing the stock shaft and collar with a high-performance part in all engine buildups, including street-stock engines.

With the heads and intake manifold in place, install the distributor and tighten the hold-down clamp. Rotate the engine upside down and install the pump and driveshaft. If the shaft length is correct, it should have 0.010 to about 0.040 inch of free play.

Tightening the oil pump mounting bolt to the proper torque spec is as critical as any other fastener on the engine. You don't want that pump falling off.

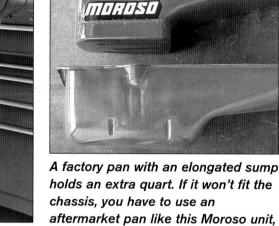

A factory pan with an elongated sump holds an extra quart. If it won't fit the chassis, you have to use an aftermarket pan like this Moroso unit, which holds an extra quart in the deeper sump.

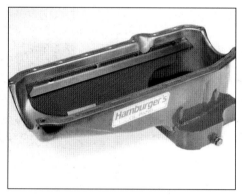

This extra capacity Hamburger wet-sump pan is a road-racing unit, but it has most of the same features you want in a good street pan. It has a deflector rail, which acts as a scraper, and a windage screen that helps to grab the oil and strip it off the crankshaft.

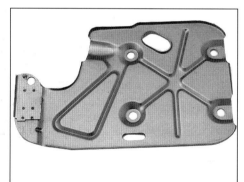

Standard factory-type windage trays are less elaborate and are probably useful at lower engine speeds. It is questionable whether they help at high speeds, because they tend to bounce the oil right back into the spinning melee.

Tie blocks PN 24502503 that are designed for pre-1986 oil pans.

There are several schools of thought when it comes to using custom or specialty oil pans and baffling. Most performance pans feature additional capacity. They hold additional oil that can make the difference between life and death for bearings at very high RPM, and they move the oil level away from the zone of turbulence beneath the crankshaft assem-bly. Engine oil tends to wrap itself around a high-speed crank assembly and act very much like taffy in a taffy-pulling machine. If the oil level is too close, whirling ropes of oil can be drawn from the sump and cause additional drag. Simply moving the oil level away from the spinning crank is enough to encourage additional oil to drop out of the rotating assembly. This is the idea behind the ultradeep pans used in many drag race engines.

Deep pans and dry-sump systems serve a common purpose: to move the oil to a location where it will not be affected by the spinning crank. But in reality they only address part of the problem; they do nothing to actually remove oil from the crank assembly.

When windage trays were first developed, the idea was to prevent oil aeration, but they only served to bounce more oil back into the problem area. Once this deficiency was recog-nized, they were replaced by screens that allowed some oil to filter through, while a crankshaft scraper removed oil from the crank. Power gains proved that this was the right idea, and further investigation produced wet-sump sys-tems that equal, and in some cases, out-power a dry-sump system. In rac-ing applications this becomes an important consideration since the wet-sump system is nearly always lighter than the dry-sump unit.

If you're building a specialized street machine, you may find it helpful to equip the engine with specialty oiling components. In many cases they will offer the versa-tility you are looking for. Cars in this category often make use of deep

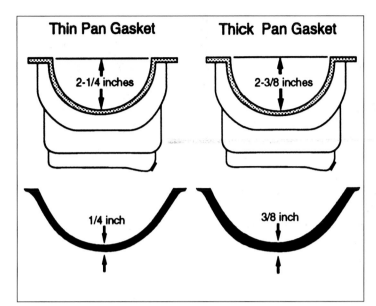

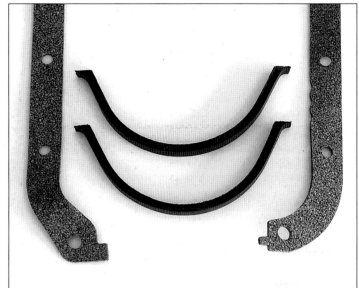

As shown in the illustration and accompanying photo, from 1955 to 1975 all small-blocks used 1/4-inch rubber-end gaskets on the pan. The 1976 and later engines use a ⅜-inch-thick rubber end gasket.

sump pans from Moroso and Milodon, but you should always verify ground clearance before ordering a new pan. If you are forced to use a low-profile pan, these same manufacturers offer special designs that are approximately the same depth as stock pans but have widened sump sections to accommodate a larger oil volume. If you plan on using a windage tray, it's advisable to purchase one compatible with the pan design to ensure easy installation. Try to avoid chrome oil pans in anything but a full-custom show car. The chrome tends to hold in the heat and partially defeats the purpose of your system. One final addition is the magnetic GM drain plug PN 23011420 that collects small metal particles and keeps them out of the bearings.

Oil Filters

There are several oiling system components that are often overlooked. Chief among them is the oil filtering system. The small-block is blessed with an excellent design in this area, but it's important to understand how the filtering process works so you don't inadvertently perform a modification that degrades lubricant quality.

The original 265-ci V-8 introduced in 1955 did not have a provision for an oil filter, but all engines produced since then have full-flow filtered oiling. Until 1968, small-blocks used a canister-style oil filter that contained a replaceable cartridge. This is an excellent filtering system and there is no reason to change it. All 1968 and later engines came with the more convenient screw-on filters. Early blocks can be updated with an adapter kit, but keep in mind that both filters are equally efficient, and the filter cartridges cost less. Some engine builders even prefer canister filters, and they take great pains to convert later blocks to the early configuration. This can be made easier with the use of Chevrolet's conversion kit PN 5574538.

Cooling, Plumbing, and Gauges

Any good performance oiling system should be equipped with a radiator-type oil cooler. There are about a

You can now get one-piece gaskets for early or late applications from Fel Pro.

zillion of them on the market these days and some of them are very effective. Look for the types where the oil flows from one end to the other. This often produces the least restriction. Another important consideration is mounting hardware. Some coolers have very flimsy mounting bosses and they may break loose on rough roads. The best choice is a cooler with large ½-inch passages and a stout, fit-

Oil Pump Pickup Positioning

Since most replacement pumps are supplied without the pickup installed, you'll have to perform this operation yourself. There is definitely a right and wrong way to do the job. Follow these steps and you'll put the pickup where you want it: submerged in oil about ¼ inch from the bottom of the oil pan.

First, install the oil pump on the rear main cap. Rotate the crank a few turns to make certain nothing contacts the pump or windage tray if used. Lubricate the end of the pickup tube and the oil pump counterbore with assembly lube and install the pickup using a quality tool. Set the oil pan on the block; it should fit flush without a gasket. If it is held off the block, rotate the crank to determine if the pan is hitting the rotating assembly or a stationary object like the oil pump/pickup or the windage tray.

If the pan fits properly, remove it and pivot the pump/pickup upward so it will contact the pan when you set the pan back on the block. Reinstall the pan and force it flat against the pan rails, pushing the pickup back down. Now remove the pan and carefully rotate the pickup down another ¼ inch and mark its position. Then remove the oil pump/pickup, disassemble the pump, and braze the pickup in place.

Install the pickup in the pump using a quality tool like this one from Goodson.

After you're sure the pan doesn't hit the rotating assembly or windage tray, rotate the pickup as shown.

Set the pan on the block and push it down against the pan rails, forcing the pickup down.

Then rotate the pickup an additional ¼-inch further down for additional clearance from the pan.

To install a standard gasket correctly, start by laying down a bead of sealer on the block pan rails.

At the end rails, place a small dab of sealer under the rubber end rail as shown here.

Press the end rail rubber gasket down over the dab of sealer until the rubber gasket blends into the pan rail gasket.

When the gaskets are in place, torque the oil-pan bolts to spec. Do yourself a favor and don't miss any – an oil leak is the last thing you want on your new performance engine.

ted brace around the circumference. This allows sturdy mounting and good cooling without restriction. Names like Earl's, Russell Performance, and Hayden will keep you on the right path.

A variety of specialty adapters are often needed when adding remote filters and coolers. Some adapters just screw-on like standard filters, and these require care to prevent leaks. Many of these quickie units also have restrictive passages that can cause a drop in oil pressure. Since there are so many on the market, make sure you check their design carefully before you lay out your cash. However, you won't be far off the mark if you stick

with proven pieces like those from Moroso, Trans-Dapt, and Traco. The Traco adapter is universally accepted, because it doesn't leak and the passages are large and free flowing. It is drilled for ½-inch pipe fittings.

Fittings with sharp 90-degree turns and restrictive adapters/couplers should be avoided. Manufacturers like Earl's, Russell, and others have special, high-flow fittings in all popular sizes and shapes. These fittings feature gentle bends, superior sealing, and they are compatible with standard hoses or braided steel lines. If you're going to the trouble of installing a remote oil filter and/or cooler, use quality hardware and you will avoid oil leaks and delivery problems.

Another important aspect of the oiling system is the provision for monitoring oil pressure and temperature. Always take oil pressure readings from the pressure takeoffs at either end of the block and determine oil temperature by direct measurement in the oil pan, if possible.

Consider using an oil pressure gauge with a warning light, like those from AutoMeter. For years you've been told that gauges are the only way to go and that idiot lights are for idiots. Well, some of those "idiots" include big-name race drivers who are too busy racing to check all the gauges as closely as they should. A

Always pre-oil a new engine prior to starting it. Install the oil filter and insert a commercially available pre-oiling tool into the distributor drive hole to engage the oil pump drive. Make up a simple pressure gauge that can be screwed into the rear oil gallery takeoff tap. Install a ⅛-inch plug in the front oil gallery takeoff. Attach an electric drill to the pre-oiler shaft and spin the pump to pressurize the system. Do this until oil flows from every rocker arm. It helps to rotate the engine by hand periodically while you are pre-oiling.

Setting Up a Dry-Sump System

A number of manufacturers offer dry-sump oiling systems for most popular competition engines. Moroso, Hamburger Oil Pans, Aviad Metal Products, Weaver Brothers, Milodon, and Peterson Fluid Systems are just a few. Their systems are all similar, but there are variations in terms of pump size, number of scavenge stages and pressure stages, tank capacity, and scavenge pickup locations.

Dry-sump oiling requires the elimination of the stock oil pump and the installation of a plug in the cylinder block passage on the rear main cap. Most systems use a nonbypassing in-and-out aluminum adapter on the oil filter pad. Experienced engine builders will drill out the stock 5/16-inch mounting bolt holes and retap them for 3/8-inch bolts installed with Loctite to make certain the adapter remains rigidly mounted. This is particularly important if a heavy oil filter is mounted on the adapter.

The best dry-sump pumps offer three scavenge stages and one pressure section. Two scavenge stages should always be connected to the oil pan; the exact location will vary depending on the application and the oil pan manufacturer. Some connect several sump drains into a separate log that is then scavenged by the pumps, but more often the pan is baffled into two separate sections with one scavenge line routed to the rear of each compartment.

A third scavenge line is often connected to the rear of the lifter valley or the rear of the valve cover to scavenge upper-engine oil. If the scavenge connection is made at the valve cover, it should be made on the predominant outboard side based on the type of racing and the number of left- and right-hand turns on the course.

Oil scavenge and pressure lines should be 3/4-inch, -12 hose with screen filters installed to catch errant metal particles. The preferred method is to route pressurized oil through a remote mounted oil filter and include an oil cooler in the line. A cooler can also be installed in the scavenge lines, but the primary oil filter should be the last thing the oil sees before entering the engine.

Oil pressure is adjusted externally on most dry-sump pumps. Most manufacturers recommend 10 psi per every 1,000 rpm (e.g., 70 psi at 7,000 rpm). Racing small-blocks should run a minimum of 60 to 70 psi. The engine crankcase should be vented to the atmosphere. Some racers vent the engine to the tank, and then vent the tank, but this opens the possibility that blow-by could contaminate the oil supply.

Dry-sump systems offer a lot of advantages, but they are also considerably more expensive, more complex, and require more time-consuming upkeep. Generally, the horsepower and durability gains outweigh the negatives, so if the rules in your racing class permit it, consider a dry sump as another essential part of a winning combination.

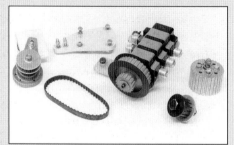

Multistage dry-sump pumps are the norm in all maximum-performance racing engines. It can be configured for any number of scavenge stages and is easily rebuildable, should any engine metal get into it after an engine failure.

This dry-sump pan is configured for dual-compartment scavenging with both pickups angled toward the front of the engine for easy plumbing. Note the screen windage tray, which is not standard equipment on most dry-sump pans.

Dry sump tanks should be as tall as possible with a tapered bottom to ensure that the bottom feed oil pickup is never uncovered, regardless of acceleration, side loading, or braking.

Oil System Prep Checklist

1. Always pre-oil your engine immediately before firing it up for the first time. Pre-oil it for sufficient time to ensure that oil is distributed to all components, including every rocker arm. This may take up to five minutes and may also require rotating the crank to make sure oil passages are aligned to feed oil through the entire engine.
2. Always verify oil pump clearances (see sidebar Oil Pump Tech Tips) and deburr the pump gears, even if the pump is brand new.
3. Once proper pickup position is determined, tack weld or braze in place, making sure to remove the bypass spring and valve before welding. Remove corrosion and make sure cover is flat before reinstalling.
4. Never use upper engine oiling restrictors with stock-type rocker arms or hydraulic lifters.
5. If you install screw-in front oil gallery plugs, make certain they do not screw in too far and restrict the oil feed hole to the front main bearing.
6. Make sure to reinstall the oil diverter plug in the oil feed passage below the rear main or oil will not flow through the filter.
7. Use only the highest quality filter and ash-less oil. Change oil after initial fire up and frequently thereafter.

Various adapters are available for external oil cooler and filter applications. Commercially available filter adapters are offered by most of the aftermarket performance equipment manufacturers. Any of them will get the job done.

Adding an oil cooler is one of the greatest favors you can do for your oiling system. Make sure the unit is plumbed with high-flow fittings and try to mount it where it will receive some degree of continuous airflow.

big winking red eye gets their attention every time, and that's what really matters. So unless you're a reliable gauge watcher, it's a good idea to back up the system with a light or pressure switch that cuts off the engine if pressure drops dangerously low. And, whatever you do, don't install an oil pressure gauge and leave the gauge light unwired. After all, you do drive the car at night, don't you?

Dry-Sump Oiling Systems

Dry-sump oiling systems are recommended for all severe-service applications where not prohibited by rules. The efficiency and reliability of dry-sump oiling systems has made them the leading choice for oiling systems in nearly all racing applications.

Wet-sump systems simply store the engine's lubricating oil in the oil pan with the pump and/or pickup submerged in the oil, while the more efficient dry-sump systems hold the oil in an external tank. In a wet-sump arrangement, the oil is poorly controlled. The forces of acceleration, braking, and cornering may cause the oil pickup to become uncovered, causing an interruption in the supply of lubrication. The oil may also cause a drag on the rapidly spinning crankshaft if a proper windage tray is not incorporated. This reduces horsepower and aerates the oil, which diminishes its lubricating capacity.

Dry-sump systems correct these problems and offer numerous advantages for high-performance applications. All of the oil is stored in a separate tank, thus removing it from the primary source of heat. An externally mounted dry-sump pump continuously scavenges the oil pan dry and routes all the oil to the external tank from which it is cooled, filtered, and returned to the engine under pressure. External tanks often hold 10 quarts of oil or more, thus ensuring a steady supply of engine oil under all operating conditions. Because no oil remains in the oil pan, the engine is unaffected by crankcase windage, and the oil pan can be made very shallow, which permits the engine to be mounted lower in the chassis to improve vehicle dynamics. Dry-sump systems also lessen the requirement for track cleanup after an engine failure, because there is no oil in the pan to foul the track surface.

EXHAUST SYSTEM

The small-block Chevy responds well to exhaust system modifications, but that doesn't necessarily mean tube headers are required. You may have heard it said that Chevrolet never made an efficient exhaust manifold for the small-block and that tubular headers are essential for optimum performance. That isn't entirely true and there are many applications where a factory style exhaust system is much more desirable. The fact is that small-blocks can run reasonably well with cast-iron exhaust manifolds. The trick is to have a well-designed and integrated system. If your application requires quiet efficiency and/or the need to fit into a cramped engine compartment, then cast-iron factory exhaust manifolds are your most affordable choice.

The most obvious application for cast-iron manifolds is a street machine that is being built on a strict budget. This is particularly true when the application involves an engine swap where a specific set of headers is just not available. In some cases, an existing header can be slightly modified or rebuilt to fit the engine/chassis combination, but it's more likely that one of the many types of factory manifolds will fit with very little difficulty. They are all

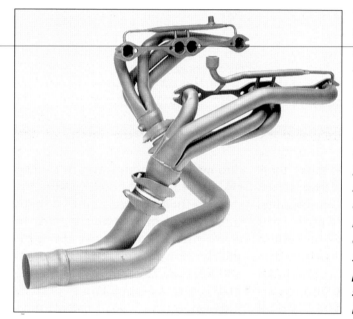

Tubular exhaust systems like this Edelbrock system for late-model cars and trucks are CARB certified and relatively easy to install with your existing catalytic converter. Like most headers, they are available with or without coatings. This nearly header-like configuration can substantially improve performance without sacrificing reliability or longevity.

designed to hug the side of the engine closely, and they have either center exit or rear exit head pipe flanges. For engine swappers who desire a clean, quiet installation, factory manifolds are the key. And in many cases, you can boost performance by using the old Corvette exhaust manifolds with larger 2½-inch openings. They are still available through GM (PN 3797901 left-hand w/generator mount on side; PN 3846563 left-hand w/generator mount on end; PN 3814970 right-hand w/generator mount on side) and some of the specialty Corvette restoration houses.

Today's performance applications can take advantage of emission certified tubular factory exhaust headers designed for the Corvette and for 1986 and later Camaros and Firebirds. Camaro/Firebird headers are manufactured by SLP Engineering and sold by the GM Performance Parts network. Complete exhaust systems are available for these F-body cars, and in many cases a talented fabricator could modify these headers to work in almost any swap. They are a good choice, because they are built from heavy-wall stainless steel.

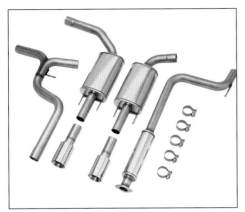

A 50-state legal cat-back exhaust system is a quick performance upgrade that works well on any car. All of the major exhaust manufacturers offer these kits for popular performance applications.

Aftermarket Headers

Standard tubular exhaust headers are a different story entirely, and it's worth taking a quick look at their development. Engineers have long understood that a major portion of an engine's energy passes out through the tailpipe in the form of heat. They also realized that while the most effective way of utilizing this energy is through turbocharging, other techniques can be employed to take advantage of the inertia of these spent gasses to help draw in the fresh intake charge. Much of the theory we discussed in the camshaft chapter can be put to good use with the addition of tube headers. The scavenging effect of a properly designed header can assist induction and boost power. The main thing to remember is that although headers do much more than simply reduce backpressure across the engine, there is no guarantee they will make more power. Since the primary tubes separate each of the engine's cylinders from the others, it offers the opportunity to let each cylinder help the others to draw in a

combustible mixture and exhaust spent gasses. During the early search for the benefits of this so-called scavenging effect, header designers discovered that the length, diameter, and shape of both the primary pipes and the collectors had a great deal to do with the header's ability to boost power. Typically there are two things happening inside a header when the engine is running. As each exhaust valve opens, a pressure wave is created that travels down the length of the primary pipe at approximately 1,700 feet per second. When the pressure wave reaches the end of the tube and exits into the collector, the sudden release of pressure creates a slight suction pulse that travels back up the header tube to the exhaust port where it actually helps to draw out residual gasses and draw in the incoming fuel charge. The suction pulse is further strengthened by the inertia of the exhaust gasses that are moving through the pipe away from the exhaust port at about 300 feet per second.

Naturally, it is difficult to get all of these elements timed exactly right, and that is the chief reason for making all the primary pipes equal in length. Interestingly, this important point is much lauded but seldom practiced. In most cases it just isn't practical to make the primary pipes precisely equal length. Some headers get really close, while others miss by a mile without even apologizing. As it turns out, the actual benefits are sometimes difficult to discern unless you have access to a dyno or lots of track testing time. In a race motor, optimum header tuning is extremely important because the engine was built with the intention of equalizing and optimizing power output from each cylinder. When a header system is designed and built with this in mind it can operate very effectively.

Installing and maintaining headers in a roadster chassis is much easier than in a conventional engine compartment. Block-hugger headers and custom exhaust headers are a necessity on most street-rod applications.

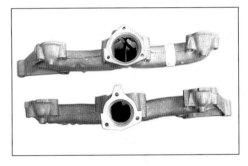

Early Corvette exhaust manifolds are highly prized for their extra large passages and full 2½-inch diameter outlets. These manifolds may make some small difference on a hot street engine, but not nearly as much as even a basic set of unequal length headers.

On the other hand, street motors must be built with many other considerations, like sound deadening and fuel economy, so much of the scavenging effect is lost. For that very reason it is less important to have equal length tubes on a street header.

In fact, it's pointless to look for a street header that has equal length tubes, especially if you're going to route them through some sort of muffled exhaust system. (What we find is that the reduction in back pressure increases engine efficiency without regard to header pipe length.) Regardless of the claims, it would prove difficult for one manufacturer to clearly demonstrate that his header design is superior to another in a street-oriented application. It is true that street header design is important in terms of pipe diameter and collector length and diameter, but most manufacturers are pretty well dialed in on this stuff and the important differences center more around quality of construction, ease of installation, spark plug access, and the useful life of the header.

This still doesn't mean that every header on the market is going to be a top performer. The major manufacturers all exercise pretty much the same approach. They know that a good street header is going to use small diameter primary pipes to help keep exhaust velocity high at slow engine speeds. The collectors will generally be longer than those on a race header since the longer collector helps to promote low-speed torque. The reasons for this are complicated, but it revolves around the header's ability to scavenge the cylinder despite the remainder of the exhaust system.

Race motors follow a completely different formula. While primary pipe size has decreased on street headers, race headers continue to get larger; at least that is the case with top running comp cars where the engines are putting out about 1,500 hp. When the engine is capable of making that much horsepower, it can effectively use the 2⅛- and 2¼-inch headers that some of the pros are running. But you have to remember that these are very high-speed headers that don't really become effective until the engine is running above 7,000 rpm.

Long-track oval cars are still running headers between 1¾- and 2-inch diameter, even though they are pulling amazing horsepower levels. They need the broader torque capabilities inherent in a smaller-tube header. It's plain fact that just about every bracket small-block will be perfectly happy with 1¾-inch headers. While some of the really nasty ones may derive some benefit from 1⅞-inch pipes, a 2-inch header is out of the question unless you're making over 650 hp and running over 8,000 rpm—so don't kid yourself. Stick with what works!

Header Disadvantages

Whatever your application, there are a number of disadvantages related to tube headers that you should consider before making your selection. There are also some tuning procedures that will make or break your installation, so don't ignore them. The major problems with tube headers are not so much disadvantages as they are things you may wish to consider. They are, of course, noisier, but not much if the exhaust system is designed properly. Many people feel that they run hotter, and in fact they radiate heat from a greater surface area, but on the other hand what could be hotter than a cast-iron manifold two hours after you shut off the motor. With headers you can grab the pipes in less than an hour. The chief problem with headers is usually leakage, breakage, rust, or a combination of the three. These are all problems that can be controlled with a little maintenance and making sure you shop for the best quality when you put down cash for your new pipes. In most cases, a header that has a thicker port flange will last longer and leak less. Some makes offer thick-wall pipe for improved noise and corrosion resistance, and paramount in any

To avoid problems, check the flange straightness and mounting surfaces before purchasing a header. A warped flange can be corrected, but can also cause problems later if it is too badly warped. Even after 50 years of header production, it is still possible to buy a header with bolt holes that don't line up.

street header selection is the ease of installation and access to spark plugs.

Other Considerations

When you install your headers, you should at least paint them with a high-temperature paint. Many headers are already painted when they come out of the box, but don't let their shiny new appearance fool you. It is usually plain lacquer and it will burn right off as soon as you start the engine. Modern headers are available with special coatings that resist almost everything. They have a ceramic coating that makes them nearly bulletproof and they look great. The best thing about these coatings is that they don't wear off, burn off, or substantially discolor with use. If you have ever had a set of chromed headers you know how disappointing it is to see them blue once they get hot. After an experience like that, you'll appreciate the versatility of these coatings. Most of the major header manufacturers offer

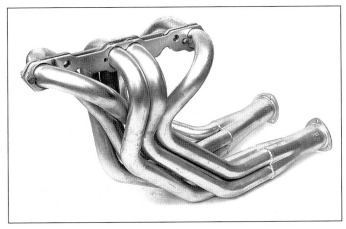

Convenience headers are widely available and they are a good choice for most basic applications. Good street pieces will have 1½- to 1¾-inch primaries and 2½- to 3-inch collectors, depending on the application. These are good headers to use for maximum economy and performance on the street.

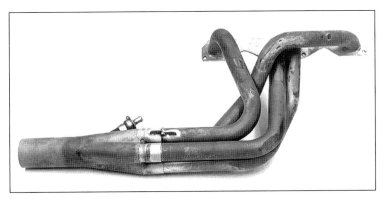

Race headers have an entirely different focus—these are hard working, equal-length, large-diameter tubes. Installation can be difficult, because they are made with fairly straight tubes to minimize restriction. The average small-block racers will start with 1¾-inch primaries and a 3-inch collector for applications up to about 500 to 550 hp. Above that, a 1⅞-inch primary and 3½-inch collectors are probably necessary. Larger headers are also available, but usually aren't required except in the case of extreme engine speed or very large displacement.

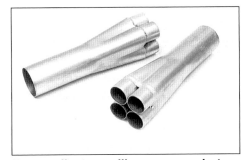

Race collectors will vary somewhat, but as a rule of thumb, they will be shorter and larger in diameter for high-RPM applications, but longer and smaller in diameter for heavier cars with engines operating at lower RPM. Most bracket-racing engines use a 3-inch collector, but some very powerful engines cans take advantage of a 3½-inch collector.

coated headers out of the box, and you can have your own headers coated by Hooker, HPC (High-performance Coatings), and Jet Hot. This adds to the expense, but it is more than worth it. In fact, many enthusiasts have begun coating their entire exhaust systems.

One of the biggest complaints about headers is that they don't seem to work after they are installed on an engine. This is often because the installer did nothing to retune the engine to complement the headers. Headers may require a jetting change (slightly richer) and the improved scavenging often requires a little less total timing, due to better combustion efficiency. It's helpful to install a new set of spark plugs with the headers and run them for a few days before checking their color. You can't really tell much from plug color on a street engine, since there are too many variables, but they will give a general indication of the engine's fuel mixture. If your old plugs were burning a medium tan color, the engine was probably running at close to the optimum air/fuel ratio. The header installation may lean the mixture enough to turn the plugs almost white.

The Complete System

A fully integrated exhaust system continues beyond the header or manifold collector. It doesn't matter whether you're running cast iron factory manifolds or tube headers, performance will be improved if you keep back pressure in the exhaust system to a minimum. The very least you should do is equip the car with a dual exhaust system—but there is a right way and a wrong way to go about it. There are specific points to consider when constructing a truly effective dual exhaust system. The first thing you need is larger-than-stock exhaust pipes that are routed with a minimum of restrictive bends. Two-inch pipe is considered a good size, but if your engine is really healthy and you want to achieve maximum performance, you should use 2¼- or 2½-inch pipes. This is especially true if you are running a large-displacement engine like the 400-ci.

There are also a couple types of bends to choose from. Common dual-exhaust systems made at local shops are often press bent, while performance pipes are available with mandrel bends. Press-bent pipes shrink in size at the bends, but higher-flowing

Use antiseize compound on all exhaust system bolts, especially when attaching to aluminum heads. It will prevent sticking and damaged threads.

Adjustable headers offer a real bonus to a racer savvy enough to take advantage of them. Adding primary tube length has an effect similar to using a smaller primary tube or a longer collector. This can lend a measurable boost to low-end torque and help get a sluggish car off the line more quickly.

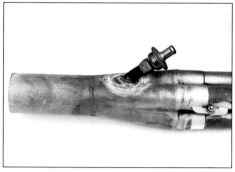

Time-honored crankcase evacuation system tubes should be installed at about 45 degrees to the direction of gas flow. This allows the exiting exhaust gas to pull a slight vacuum on the crankcase and helps to purge vapors and reduce pressure under the rings. This improves ring seal and keeps oil out of the combustion chamber.

Exhaust System Prep Checklist

1. Visually inspect headers for signs of damage, including warped flanges, cracking through bolt holes, poor welds, or obvious leaks. Also inspect for smashed or dented pipes and cracks in areas of high stress and heat.
2. Check the head flange against the cylinder bead to make certain the bolt patterns are placed correctly for your heads.
3. Check the fit of the collector reducers and gaskets.
4. Repair minor leaks with TIG or gas welding rod.
5. File the mounting flange beads to determine thin spots. Fill with weld and refile if required.
6. Cut notches into the end holes in the gaskets to make installation easier.
7. Elongate mismatched bolt holes, if necessary.
8. Installing headers can be a frustrating experience. If the headers have never been installed in the chassis, perform a trial fit to determine tight spots, misalignment, etc.
9. After prefitting, thoroughly clean headers prior to final Installation. If a professional, long-lasting installation is desired, have headers glass beaded or sand blasted, and then paint them with high-temperature header paint. Apply several thin coats. Or even better, have them ceramic coated for a near bulletproof finish.
10. During final installation, take your time and try not to damage the tubes or scratch the paint (or chip the ceramic coating): Wrap the tubes with rags or heavy plastic trash bags to protect them.
11. After headers have been used (heated) several times, retighten bolts and check them periodically.

mandrel-bent pipes have a consistent diameter throughout, even during tricky over-the-axle bends.

You'll want to augment the large-diameter exhaust pipes with good free flowing mufflers. If you really want the truth, this excludes side-pipe mufflers and glass packs. They simply are not an effective alternative to a well-designed muffler. The variety of available mufflers is considerable, but in reality there are a couple of commonly available units that really work, so why look for anything else? Most of the available "turbo" type mufflers, like DynoMax Super Turbos, will work. Turbo mufflers are similar to production mufflers but they offer freer flowing insides with larger passages. Chambered Flowmaster and straight-through Magnaflow and DynoMax Ultraflow mufflers have also become enormously popular in recent years. The different types of mufflers have unique sounds, so listen around before you choose.

If you want a quiet system, add some full-length tailpipes behind the mufflers. If you have built an effec-

Header fasteners include standard header bolts as supplied in most header sets. These measure ⅜ x 1 inch with a ⁷⁄₁₆-inch hex head. In tight spaces, special header studs or Allen-head bolts are often necessary.

Some late-model headers come equipped with oxygen sensor bungs installed. If yours don't have them, consider having some installed so you can monitor air/fuel ratio with an aftermarket oxygen sensor.

Most headers are now coated, but low-buck headers should be cleaned or sandblasted and painted with a high-quality temperature resistant paint such as VHT. For best results, always apply several light coats rather than one or two heavy coats.

Adding headers and a performance exhaust system will always improve performance, but it can alter the signals at the carburetor and require rejetting to establish maximum performance. When headers are installed on a stock engine that is already jetted lean, performance may suffer and the engine may even misfire until rejetting optimizes the air/fuel ratio.

tive system, tailpipes of the same diameter will not hurt performance, but they will definitely help keep the car quieter. It's important that you use a crossover pipe between the two sides of the dual exhaust system. This helps reduce pressure peaks, improves performance, and makes the exhaust note quieter. The tube should be the same size as the exhaust pipes or, if space permits, it can be even larger for more effective dampening. The location is not critical, but you should strive to keep it within at least 18 inches of the collector or at least ahead of the mufflers (it serves no purpose after the mufflers, where system pressure is much lower). If you're having a custom exhaust system fabricated, ask the fabricator to use a thicker gauge tubing, as opposed to standard exhaust tubing. Tubing is available in several different wall thicknesses and you'll appreciate the difference once you hear it.

GEN II SMALL-BLOCKS: LT1 AND LT4

GM's Gen II small-block arrived in 1992 and was used in production vehicles through 1997. It was a revision and upgrade of the Gen I engine, but it isn't to be confused with later Gen III (LS1, LS6, LS2, LS7) engines that are an entirely different animal. There are two primary versions of the Gen II small-block, the LT1 and the LT4. Both second-generation engines retain the 5.7-liter or 350-ci displacement. The Gen II LT1 is not the same engine as the original LT1 1970 1/2 Camaro Z/28 engine, even though it shares the same engine code and general architecture. A smaller-displacement relation, the L99, is a 4.3-liter or 265-ci Gen II used in the 1994–1996 Caprice. It's similar in all respects except for displacement and performance. LT4 engines were used only in 1996 Corvettes and a small number of special-edition Camaros. Most Gen II engines you might be dealing with are going to be LT1s as used in the Camaro, Corvette, Impala SS, Buick Roadmaster, and Firebird.

Gen II revisions were evolutionary, as they still relate to basic small-block Chevy architecture, where the later LS1 is an entirely new engine. These revisions included a mechanically driven water pump and front-mounted distributor, reverse flow cooling, a new intake manifold bolt pattern, and other features aimed at increasing performance, durability, and less glamorous improvements such as oil pan and valve cover sealing.

LT1/LT4 Features and Differences

LT1/LT4, or Gen II engines use reverse-flow cooling, which requires a specific head gasket. They use an external coolant transfer line from the head to vent air from the cooling system. LT1/LT4 engines use a hydraulic roller camshaft with a stepped front journal and a smaller bolt pattern. They also have a front-mounted Optispark distributor and a beltless aluminum water pump, both of which are driven directly by the camshaft. LT1/LT4 engines drive the oil pump via a stub shaft that bolts into the original distributor hole in the rear of the lifter gallery. The cylinder heads do not have coolant crossover passages to the

The LT1 engine, often referred to as the Gen II small-block, was offered in Corvettes and F-body Camaros and Firebirds. This high-tech revision of the small-block featured reverse-flow cooling, a gear-driven water pump, a front drive distributor, and full electronic engine management for optimum performance.

intake manifold. LT1/LT4 engines all have a one-piece rear main seal, but they retain the conventional oil filter mount and starter and motor mount configuration. The LT4 four is sort of a factory hop-up of the LT1. It features a number of changes and beefed-up parts for greater performance and durability.

LT1 vs. LT4 Features

LT1 compression ratio is 10.5:1 versus 10.8:1 on the LT4. The L99 has a 9.8:1 CR. LT1/LT4 cylinder heads are interchangeable, but intake and exhaust manifolds are not compatible. Both engines have cast crankshafts, but the LT4 fillets are undercut and rolled to provide extra strength. The LT1 uses standard ball-fulcrum rocker arms with a 1.5:1 rocker ratio; the LT4 uses roller rockers with a 1.6:1 rocker ratio. The LT1 uses ⅜-inch rocker arm studs, while the LT4 uses ⁷⁄₁₇-inch studs. Some LT4 rocker studs are 10 mm. The LT4 uses lighter valvesprings with higher pressure and lighter spring retainers. The valvesprings are also made from an oval-shaped wire designed to reduce the possibility of coil bind. LT4 valves are lighter with hollow-stemmed intakes and sodium/ potassium-filled exhaust valves. LT4 cylinder heads have an intake port roof that is 0.100 inch higher than LT1 heads.

Cylinder Blocks

All cylinder blocks are conventional cast iron. These blocks are identified by a casting number at the upper right rear of the block. Casting number 10125327 is used for both two-bolt and four-bolt main blocks. The oil pan must be removed to positively identify a four-bolt block. All LT1/LT4 engine blocks have the block ID numerals 327 cast into the side of the block.

If you find a block with 4.3 cast on the side, it is a 265-ci 4.3-liter block with the smaller 3.74-inch bore and a 3.00-inch stroke. The 4.3-liter block carries casting number 10168588. All LT1/LT4 engines retain the conventional 4.00-inch bore by 3.48-inch stroke, for 350 cubic inches.

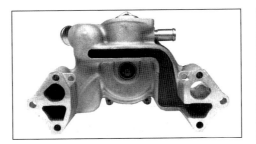

The LT1 and LT4 feature reverse-flow cooling, where cooling water goes to the heads first. This photo shows the LT1-style beltless water pump that is driven off the camshaft. The rounded upper passages match passages on the block that lead directly to the cylinder head. LT1s and LT4s require a dedicated cylinder head gasket because of this reverse-cooling feature.

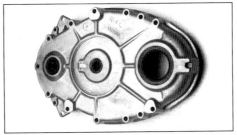

GM used several versions of the front cover. This is an early version, used from 1992 to 1994. Later versions had a much larger center hole for the front-mounted distributor drive. When OBD-II electronics were added in 1996, a mounting boss was added to the bottom of the cover to accept a crank position sensor.

LT1/LT4 blocks are machined to accept a stub shaft with a spiral cut gear to engage the camshaft and drive the oil pump. There is no mechanical fuel pump boss at the front of the block, but the rear transmission-mounting flange is the same as the original small-block and the oil filter and starter flange are still the same. Block preparation for LT1/LT4 engines follows conventional practice as detailed earlier in the block prep chapter. The cylinder castings are slightly

This is the front-mounted distributor that bolts directly to the block and engages the camshaft via a small pilot shaft for centering and a dowel pin that turns the distributor. Earlier versions (1992–1993) featured a splined center hole in the camshaft drive gear (as seen in the photo of the cam gear below). A stub distributor is fitted at the rear to drive the oil pump. If you are converting one of these engines to carburetion, the block will accept a normal distributor at the rear.

The secondary gear teeth on the camshaft gear drive the gear on the water pump drive via the shaft that protrudes through a seal on the timing cover.

longer to promote greater cylinder stability with lightweight castings. There are no tricks here, and standard boring and honing practice is in order.

Crankshafts

Gen II crankshafts are all nodular iron with one-piece rear seals. LT1 cranks have radiused fillets while the LT4 cranks are prepped with rolled and undercut fillets. 1996–1997 versions have a powdered-metal crankshaft-position sensor.

The front of the crank is internally balanced, and this adapter hub is used to install the balancer. It presses onto the crankshaft snout, and there is no crank key.

The damper incorporates the serpentine drive belt grooves. It bolts to the adapter hub and it can only be installed in one position because the mounting holes are asymmetrical.

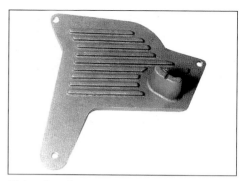

This aluminum cover PN 12367600 is used to plug the hole on the front cover of a 1996 LT4 engine when the stock distributor is removed and a rear-mounted distributor is installed.

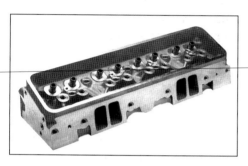

Performance enthusiasts will only be interested in the aluminum LT4 cylinder head, although the iron LT1 head is quite prevalent. Note the wider center bolt spacing for the intake manifold. These heads require dedicated manifolds with matching bolt patterns. Also note that there is no crossover cooling passage. LT4 and LT1 intake passages are different as well, so you must use the correct intake manifold and gasket for your application.

This reluctor ring has four timing teeth and is aligned on the crank via the keyway. The Gen II crank for both the LT1 and LT4 carries casting number 14088526, while the L99 crank carries casting number 10168568. All Gen II cranks are internally balanced. GM part number 12551485 is the high-durability crank with undercut and rolled fillets.

A two-piece damper and hub assembly is used on Gen II engines. The hub adapter is installed on the crank snout with an interference fit. The crank snout key does not engage the hub adapter. It has a notch to clear the adapter. From 1992 to 1995, the key was notched back flush with the crank sprocket, but with the advent of

Gen II Factory Forged Pistons

Part Number	Compression Ratio	Chamber Size	Bore (Oversize)	Pin Type	Notes
10159436	10:1	58 cc	Standard	Pressed	LT-1
10159437	10:1	58 cc	Standard	Pressed	LT-1
10159437	9.6:1	62 cc	Standard	Pressed	LT-1
10159438	10:1	58 cc	0.03 inch	Pressed	LT-1
10159438	9.6:1	62 cc	0.03 inch	Pressed	LT-1
12528828	10.8:1	54.4 cc	Standard	Pressed	LT-4
12528829	10.8:1	54.4 cc	0.005 inch	Pressed	LT-4
12528830	10.8:1	54.4 cc	0.03 inch	Pressed	LT-4
12371059 (kit)	10.1:1	58 cc	Standard	Pressed	8 each
12371059 (kit)	9.6:1	62 cc	Standard	Pressed	8 each
12371060 (kit)	10.1:1	58 cc	0.03 inch	Pressed	8 each
12371060 (kit)	9.6:1	62 cc	0.03 inch	Pressed	8 each

Gen II Factory Piston Rings

Part Number	Type	Size (Overbore)
12528817	low-tension	Standard
12528818	low-tension	0.005 inch
12528819	low-tension	0.03 inch

The LT4 head features D-shaped exhaust ports and smaller 54-cc combustion chambers to increase the compression ratio from 10.5:1 on the LT1 to 10.8:1 on the LT4.

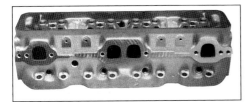

LT1 and LT4 heads feature taller valve cover rails and, of course, center-bolt valve covers.

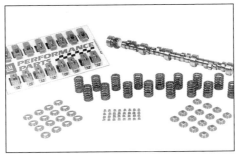

The 350 Hot Cam kit PN 12480002 is a popular off-road upgrade for LT1 engines. The Hot Cam specs are 218/228 degrees of intake/exhaust duration at 0.050-inch lift, 0.492-inch lift with 1.5:1 rockers, or 0.525-inch lift with 1.6:1 rockers. The lobe centerline is 112 degrees.

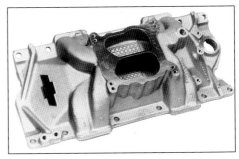

This GM LT4 aluminum 4-barrel intake manifold PN 24502574 is the same and the GM LT1 intake PN 24502592 except that it is configured for 1996 LT4 engines or heads. The intake ports are 0.100-inch higher than the LT1 design. Both manifolds accept standard Holley or spread-bore flange carburetors.

A standard two-port throttle body was incorporated on all LT1 and LT4 engines. These are upgradeable through many aftermarket suppliers.

OBD-II engine management in 1996–1997, the key protrudes farther in order to locate the crankshaft-position sensor reluctor wheel. The hub adapter is secured with a 7⁄16 number 20 bolt and a dedicated flat washer. The combination damper/crank pulley then bolts to the hub assembly with three bolts. All 1993–1995 LT1 engines use crankshaft hub PN 12553250. All LT4 engines and 1996–1997 LT1 engines with OBD II diagnostics use crankshaft hub PN 12550097. The LT1 torsional damper is PN10128489, while all LT4 engines use PN 12551486.

Connecting Rods

Two types of rods were used in Gen II engines. All 1992–1993 LT1s were equipped with traditional forged rods. In 1994, powdered-metal, or PM, rods emerged as the new technology. Some forged rods were still being used, but the PM rods gradually filled the pipeline on LT1 and LT4 engines. Unlike typical PM cracked rods, Gen II rods can be reconditioned, since the parting faces are machined. They are all 5.7-inch center-to-center length with standard 2.100-inch journals. The small end accepts the standard .927-inch, pressed-fit wrist pin.

GM offers the Corvette PM rod PN 10108688 in a kit of eight rods under PN 12495071. They suggest limiting horsepower to 450 with these rods, but we have seen many 500- to 600-hp engines live with these rods. This is particularly true if you limit engine speed to 6,500 rpm.

Pistons

Hypereutectic pistons are standard in all Gen II engines. They have four valve reliefs in a flat deck surface and utilize a standard press-fit 0.927-inch pin, which floats in the pin boss bores. The 0.076-inch thick top compression ring is located 0.233-inch below the deck. The second ring is 0.057 inch thick and the low-tension oil ring thickness measures 0.165 inch. Compression height is 1.089 inch. If you are doing a rebuild, you are probably going with a 0.030-inch overbore. Factory forged pistons are available in this size as shown in the accompanying piston chart.

Plenty of aftermarket pistons are available for Gen II engines, so you aren't limited to factory pistons for performance applications. Remember, if you're building any sort of high-performance engine, your best choice is still a forged piston. If you're going to do anything other than a stock rebuild and mild cruising, you are still at risk with a hypereutectic piston. Forged pistons cost more, but they are pretty much indestructible in most applications. Your best choice in aftermarket pistons is still Speed Pro for both hypereutectic and forged pistons. If you are rebuilding your LT1 or LT4 to factory specs, the Speed Pro hypereutectic piston is a good choice, because it is machined with the factory-engineered barrel on the skirt and it comes with an antiscuff coating.

Camshafts

All Gen II camshafts are steel roller cams. LT1 cams are driven via a link-

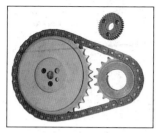

GM's extreme-duty timing chain kit for 1995 and later Gen II LT1 and LT4 engines includes a water pump gear, camshaft sprocket, crank gear, and timing chain for dowel pin driven applications only. It can be used on 1993–1994 engines, but costly upgrades for the camshaft, distributor, and timing covers are required—not a good idea.

belt timing chain with conventional gears, while the LT4 uses a roller-style timing chain. They all have the notched cam nose with three-bolt cam gear mounting on a smaller-diameter bolt pattern than earlier small-block cams. All 1992–1993 LT1 cams have the number 241 on the main cam core just ahead of the first lobe. These cams drive the distributor via the center of the cam gear via splined gears. All 1994 and later versions drive the distributor with a longer cam drive dowel pin that engages the cam gear and the distributor drive. Look for a number 600 or 779 on the front core of these cams. Even later versions used with aluminum cylinder heads have the numbers 242 or 705 on the cam core. The early cam gear with the splined center hole for distributor drive is GM PN 10128349. The 1994 and later gear that accepts the dowel pin engagement is PN 10206039.

Gen II engines no longer need to drive a rear-mounted distributor, but they still use the camshaft rear drive gear to drive the oil pump using a stub drive assembly that bolts into the lifter valley. It engages the cam gear and drives the oil pump. The back side of the camshaft drive gear incorporates a toothed wheel, which drives a small diameter wheel mounted overhead. The small wheel has a small

splined center shaft that drives the water pump.

Oiling System

The oiling system is straightforward small-block Chevy with virtually no changes. The oil galleries above the cam tunnel have standard soft plugs at the front of the block, but GM took a clue from hot rodders and added small .020-inch holes in them. Hot rodders did this to provide additional spray oiling for the timing chain, but GM's intent was to provide an air bleed to prevent lifter noise on startup. If you are building a Gen II engine, you can follow the oiling system guidelines as shown in the chapter on oiling systems.

Water Pump

The Gen II water pump is a reverse flow design driven by a stub shaft. If you throw a belt off, your engine will still cool properly. The reverse cooling water pump is a dedicated design that cannot be replaced with other factory pumps. Aftermarket pump manufacturers now have their own pumps for the Gen II, so you do have some choices.

Intake Manifolds

All Gen II engines are fuel injected, and the manifolds feature a completely unique bolt pattern. The manifolds are multiport injection units with one injector per cylinder. There are no coolant crossover passages in the manifold. These manifolds require care in porting, and in most cases you'll probably want to go with an aftermarket intake if you're planning big power numbers. GM Performance Parts offers aluminum single 4-barrel replacement manifolds for those who wish to use LT1 based engines or cylinder heads with a carbureted application.

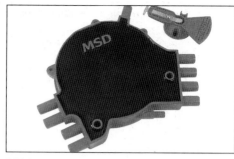

MSD offers a great replacement upgrade distributor for the LT1 or LT4. It delivers higher spark energy and is compatible with all MSD ignition amplifiers.

LT1/LT4 PM connecting rods are available in sets under PN 12495071 or individually under PN 10108688.

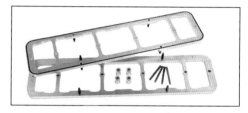

If you want to convert to earlier style valve covers for either functional or aesthetic reasons, these valve cover adapters PN 24502540 will allow you to use the earlier rail mount covers.

Engine Specs and Fasteners

With the advancement of engine design represented in the Gen II engine series come a new set of concerns for engine builders and modifiers. While the standard small-block is relatively insensitive to carelessness in terms of fastener torque and sealing procedures, it also had fewer parts and leaked more freely. Gen II engines have more parts that require proper fastener torque and attention to detail to prevent fuel, oil, and air leaks that will affect engine operation.